Union Jo[illegible]

Aidan Smith has lived in Edinburgh all his life, and is currently Senior Feature Writer of *Scotland on Sunday*. He is the author of one previous book – *Heartfelt: Supping Bovril from the Devil's Cup* – which Irvine Welsh called 'the best book I've ever read about football'. It has been turned into an acclaimed play.

By the same author

Heartfelt: Supping Bovril from the Devil's Cup

AIDAN SMITH

Union Jock

Sleeping with the Auld Enemy

Yellow Jersey Press
LONDON

Published by Yellow Jersey Press 2008

2 4 6 8 10 9 7 5 3 1

First published in Great Britain in 2008 by
Yellow Jersey Press
Random House, 20 Vauxhall Bridge Road,
London SW1V 2SA

www.rbooks.co.uk

Addresses for companies within The Random House Group Limited can be found at:
www.randomhouse.co.uk/offices.htm

The Random House Group Limited Reg. No. 954009
A CIP catalogue record for this book is available from the British Library

ISBN 9780224080156

The Random House Group Limited makes every effort to ensure that the papers used in its books are made from trees that have been legally sourced from well-managed and credibly certified forests. Our paper procurement policy can be found at: www.rbooks.co.uk/environment

Typeset by SX Composing DTP, Rayleigh, Essex
Printed and bound in Great Britain by
CPi Mackays, Chatham ME5 8TD

For Lucy

Maggie Thatcher! Butcher Cumberland! Rachael Heyhoe-Flint!

It's 31 December, the most Scottish of nights. Along with penicillin, tarmacadam, the TV I'm watching, hollow-pipe drainage, deep-fried confectionery, the Ku Klux Klan, the Bank of *England* and – let's not forget – the *pre*-World Cup victory parade, Scotland can lay claim to having invented Hogmanay.

On the Mr Sheened surface, this looks like any other Hogmanay. My mother may not be around, but I've dusted the flat in her memory, in case of first-footers. My father may not be around, but I've bolted the door in his honour, in case of first-footers.

But it's not any other Hogmanay. On this night of nights, when you don't want to be alone but very often are, a woman has agreed to share my sofa, my bouncing-bomb consistency black bun (the local fruitcake) and my enjoyment of *Only An Excuse*, the Auld Year's Night television staple in Scotland – pungent football comedy reminding us of why we aren't invited to the 2006 World Cup in Germany and England are.

And – this is the really good bit – Lucy has agreed to share my life as well.

This summer I will utter two phrases that I never thought would pass my lips. The biggie, the one that matters, is 'I do.' The other one is 'Come on, England!'

A book about a Scot trying to support – or, at the very least, follow – England wasn't my idea. My friend David Begg suggested it as the obvious sequel to my previous book, *Heartfelt*, about a Hibs fan (me) cheering on Hearts, the hated rival team in Edinburgh. That wasn't my idea either.

So, having swapped sides once before, this should be easy, yes?

Well, no. *Heartfelt* was supposed to be a journey into terror, the absolute Hearts of darkness. But now my secret can be revealed: I'd rooted for the Jam Tarts once before.

In 1971, Hearts competed in the Texaco Cup, a short-lived inter-British tournament for Sad Sack clubs who didn't qualify for Europe, and when they made it to the final I wanted them to beat Wolves. You see, in 1971 – a big year for Anglo-Scottish relations in our house – there would have been only one thing worse than supporting Hearts: supporting the team from *England*.

I am Scottish. I was born in Edinburgh and still live there. Once I ventured south, stayed for two years, but didn't like it so came back. South Edinburgh just wasn't me. Your roots are your roots.

From my garden, my old secondary school can be reached with a hefty kick of a Mitre Mouldmaster. If I could produce Peter Lorimer – Leeds United and Scotland 'Hotshot' of legend – from behind a bush, in the way that Woody Allen produced Marshall McLuhan from behind a cinema hoarding in *Annie Hall*, just to prove a point, my old primary school would be within range as well.

Here's an example of how Scottish I am . . .

Me, to my brother, in the pub, watching an evening game on TV, as winter really starts to bite: 'Turned your central heating on yet?'

Him: 'No.' (Long pause . . .) 'You?'

Me: 'No.'

Scots are perverse, and the best example of just what big perverts we are is our attitude to the England football team. If Scotland aren't playing England, we do not transfer allegiance to the neighbours with whom we share a language, a currency, and three centuries of togetherness as first-names-on-the-teamsheet constituent parts of the United Kingdom. No. We really, really, really want England to lose.

Scotland vs England is the world's oldest football rivalry, and the greatest. English people don't seem quite as passionate about it, but no matter: the Scots have passion to spare. For Scots, the rivalry defines them.

On the occasions when Scotland manage to defeat the Auld Enemy it's about more than just that ninety minutes. Like the procurator fiscal (prosecuting counsel in England) when a guilty verdict is returned, we ask for previous convictions to be taken into account: centuries of lording it, unfriendly acts with broad-sword and bayonet, and the most heinous of unintentional slights.

Maggie Thatcher and the Duke of Cumberland! Enid Blyton and Jimmy Hill! Jimmy Greaves and Andrew Lloyd Webber! Samuel Johnson and Emlyn Hughes! Kevin Keegan and Frank '*Call My Bluff*' Muir! Stephen Fry and Mick Channon! Virginia Wade and Walter de la Mare! Gerry Francis and Rachael Heyhoe-Flint! *Terry And June*! 'Your boys took a hell of a beating!'

But hang on, this is not only hysterical, it's historical. The Home International Championship ended in 1984 and the last of the annual Scotland-England matches took place five years later (2-0 to England).

It was a fantastic rivalry back in the day but it's over. We Scots have moved on, we've matured. We've got our own Parliament now, and our own cuddly little smoking ban, so we cannot blame England for all our ills.

Football – especially that match – can no longer be central to our lives. The Scottish team have gone into a sharp decline – the tanner ba' talent just isn't coming through any more (though we can still just about manage the odd glorious failure). Our childhood obesity rates are higher than America's and it's computer games that are central to kids' lives now. Lucy is a teacher. Every weekend, she says, the boys in her class are plugged in to their Xboxes instead of kicking a ball about. An eight-year-old revealed the appeal: 'Aye, and the best bit, Miss, was the end: I got raped by zombies.'

England, meanwhile, qualify for (almost) every major tournament and, if you believe the hype, are getting ever closer to winning one. We should be relaxed about this. Or, if we can't be relaxed, then we should just give one of those existentialist loner soulful stares, the sort much favoured by Steve McQueen (wasn't he Scottish?), and light up a cigarette and . . . well, smoking has been outlawed in public places, but you get my drift.

The great rivalry, especially for me, cannot be life or death any more. I'm marrying into the most non-football family on the planet.

My last days as a single man, therefore, will be my last days as a football fan, or at least the kind of fan I used to be: completely bloody obsessed. So maybe it's just as well I am to spend them supp— . . . following *Ingerland*. That way I can forget I'm even watching football, so when it's over I won't miss what I didn't have . . .

They Strut this Earth like Medieval Popes . . .

'Bloody bastardin' shite!'

You never forget the first time. Like the first time my father stretched to his full nineteen feet and plucked my football from a tree. The first time he picked up his four children like we were felt-covered dolls, and held us aloft to set a new Commonwealth all-comers dads' record.

The first time he ignited the gas burner under the fondue pan, probably the only one in our street. The first time he drove me to school in his orange Renault 4, definitely the only foreign car in our street.

The first time I noticed, at prizegiving, that everyone else's dad had a short back and sides, while his hair was long and wavy-grey and 'artistic'. The first time he read a chapter, yanked from the Olivetti, of his children's novel about pirates and whisky and a heroic cabin boy who saves the day (available in regular bedtime instalments). The first time I saw him on TV, hosting his own chat show.

The first time he told me that the peel in marmalade was the toenail clippings of the workers at the jam factory. The first time he told me that the hole in his neck was a sword wound from the war – the Second World War, which was not a big swordfest. The first time he battered me for coming home drunk (and me too paralytic to feel a thing). The first time he read something I'd had published. The first time I realised he was going to die. And I'll never, *ever* forget the first time I heard my father swear.

'Bloody bastardin' shite!'

It was after The Goal That Never Was, after The Goal That Shouldn't Have Counted Because There Were Some People On The Pitch And They Thought It Was All Over, and around the time that Alan Ball slumped to his knees and Bobby Charlton burst into tears and Nobby Stiles danced a daft jig of joy and Bobby Moore stood removed from the hullabaloo, all serene, the boy with the golden hair.

Actually, Moore didn't have golden hair, not that day, because that day was pre-colour TV in our part of Scotland (pre the fabulous revelation that Blue's eyes in *The High Chaparral* were indeed blue, and so was Emma Peel's catsuit in *The Avengers* – not the leather one, her weekend wear – and so was *Top Cat*'s sidekick Benny the Ball). The golden hair came slightly later, after I was replayed The Goal That Wasn't A Goal etc. at the cinema in a newsreel filler before the main feature (*Shalako*, or somesuch horse opera). I must have taken Moore's gilded barnet, along with the orange of the ball, the turquoise of Sir Alf Ramsey's tracksuit, the red of the shirts I assumed were grey – and coloured in the flickering cathode-ray image supplied by Rediffusion that momentous afternoon.

'Bloody bastardin' shite!'

Denis Law lost himself on the golf course rather than watch England win the World Cup but my father didn't have that refuge. He hated the infernal dimpled-pebble game though I'll never forget the first and only time I persuaded him to have a thwack with a four iron: he cleared the entire pitch 'n' putt course, the pond beyond it, almost the Edinburgh Academicals rugby ground as well. I assume he didn't want to watch the final but, with a nine-year-old son to entertain that afternoon, perhaps he felt obliged to educate this latecomer to football in the game's basics.

'Bloody bastardin' shite!'

That was when I realised that England, the country, was a different place. School did not teach me about the long, crabbit and often bloody history between Scotland and England. Well, it may have done but I didn't take in the lessons, or differentiate between that conflict and any other. No, I learned all about the special non-relationship from my father.

Dad loathed the Londoncentric BBC's mispronunciation of Scottish place names. 'It's COCK-bridge-to-Tomintoul-pronounced-TOOL!' he'd roar at the radio at breakfast time, spluttering marmalade-maker's toenails everywhere. This happened at the onset of every winter, the Highlands route ritualistically the first to be closed by snow.

Then he'd scold my mother for reading the *Daily Express*, a 'Tory rag' that in his view did not have Scotland's best interests at heart. (He read the *Scotsman*.) Then he'd revive some grumble from the night before, possibly concerning southern, bourgeois attitudinising in the *Play For Today*. Then . . . one last blast at the radio . . . a hoot of derision at someone of privilege ('Fortesque-Robinson-Smythe!') or a retired colonel from the shires ('Double-Back-Action-Breech-Loading-*Gore*!'). And he'd go to work, get down to the real business of being monumentally indifferent towards England.

Dad wasn't one of those tartan terrorists who blew the queen's head off postboxes and other official ironmongery; his methods were slightly more subtle. He was a journalist, critic, author, photographer, playwright and television producer – yer actual polymath, Renaissance Faither. His work may not have been anti-English as such but it was definitely pro-Scottish; comment on the English was unavoidable and indeed essential. He made programmes about Scottish cultural life because the BBC – the London-run network, at any rate – ignored it. He wrote a book exalting his home city, Edinburgh. He wrote another called *This Is My Country* (of course the country exalted in it was Scotland). He wrote plays about iconic Scots, such as Mary Queen of Scots and John Knox, and also ordinary ones, like the funeral director, the toilet attendant and a soldier by the name of Jock. By himself, the squaddie told the entire history of the Scottish nation in just over two hours, stopping only for essential-to-the-plot fish and chips, purchased by me.

Written in 1971, *Jock* was a great success. Before its final run at the Edinburgh Festival, it had been seen by more people than any other piece of theatre by a living Scottish writer. Many viewed it as nationalistic, a rallying cry for independence. I have often wondered about this. My father isn't around for a chat about the play's politics and, it would follow, his own politics. But even if he was, I probably wouldn't ask. He was of a generation for whom politics were a private affair. Asking a man how he voted was the height of impudence, like quizzing him on whether he had false teeth.

It didn't really matter; it wasn't essential to the plot of my young life that I 'got' *Jock*. I loved every second of the drama, and especially the big speeches packed with honest, decent and true appraisals of our southern cousins: 'The English! My God they ruffle my feathers. They strut this earth like medieval popes.'

As assistant to the assistant stage manager's assistant, I had to bang a bass drum to signify the horse's charge as Robert the Bruce's second in command at Bannockburn – en route to the Holy Land with his king's heart encased in silver – thundered towards the infidels then hurled the casket into a ring of enemy spears and died over it. And to set the scene for the murder of James I of Scotland, I was the royal court minstrel on classical guitar (fifteenth-century lute not available).

Culloden and Flodden, Calvinism and hair shirts, oppression and just being ignored. Treachery and variety theatre, cesspit squalor and the *Sunday Post*, public hangings (and drawings and quarterings) and a basic lack of guts, cometh the hour. My father painted a bloody grim picture of life in Scotland down the centuries. For light relief he turned, as Scots often do, to England for a spot of gentle character assassination: 'They behave as if God had granted them the divine right to be smug. As if a' their eggs had two yolks . . .'

As I reported for duty behind the drum every night and on the matinee afternoons, *Jock* was like a gold-star student's exam crammer or, more accurately in my case, a thicko's primer: it was the history lesson I skived at school. The birth of a nation and its subsequent befuddlement, told in the time it took a football match to unfold, if you added on extra time and the referee's toss of a coin (penalty shoot-outs had not yet been introduced). Mind you, there were occasions when I skived *Jock* too . . .

The makeshift theatre was tucked into the roof above the Playhouse, one of Edinburgh's biggest and grandest cinemas, whose own closing credits were fast approaching. It had decided to go out with a bang, screening some of the most provocative films of the early 1970s, and during the interval of the play, but also at moments when my services weren't required, I would sneak downstairs and watch a few minutes, always the same minutes, of the movies.

Six nights running, I thrilled to the scene in *Klute* when Jane Fonda declares herself 'the greatest fuck in the world'. Even now when I think of James II, which isn't often, for he was the king who banned 'the futeball' in Scotland for more than a century, I can't get out of my head a brazen, bra-misplacing, unknown-but-not-for-long Melanie Griffith driving Gene Hackman to distraction in *Night Moves*. And there is a two-minute sequence of *Last Tango In Paris* (not *that* sequence) which I know better than just about anything, save for great Scotland goals.

(Scotland's goals against England in the 1970s were rarely great. Dalglish dunted one through Ray Clemence's legs in 1976 and Lou Macari's the following year was decidedly un-silky. But both goals were competition winners in the Home International Championship and my father and I willed them over the line. Indeed Macari's involved such a stramash in the six-yard box that Dad puffed up his cheeks and, with cartoon exaggeration, tried to blow the ball into the net, only succeeding in firing his falsers across the room.)

*

My father also wrote songs. One of them, 'Come By The Hills', was even proposed as a new national anthem for Scotland. But its composer would freely admit that he never penned a couple of lines which summed a nation's character as perfectly as:

What d'you do with the bracelet
What d'you do with the bracelet
What d'you do with the bracelet Bobby Moore?

Put it in your handbag
Put it in your handbag
Put it in your handbag Bobby Moore

It seems faintly ludicrous that the wisest man I knew got such a kick out of this juvenile piece of abuse. I can still see him dancing round his armchair to that terrace taunt, bashed out by the Hampden hit factory after the England captain was arrested in Colombia for 'The Great Chain Robbery' – the alleged theft of a £600 emerald and diamond bracelet when the England team were en route to the Mexico World Cup in 1970.

Other wise Scots of the time thought the same way. In Dad's book, *This Is My Country*, an anthology of musings on the Scottish condition, the novelist and screenwriter Gordon Williams confesses: 'The greatest moment of my life was this year [1974] on the rain-soaked terraces of Hampden when the second goal went in and we'd beaten the whiteshirted swines.'

And if we couldn't beat them, we wanted everyone else to beat them. The other lot could have an appalling human rights record, or be impossible to locate on a jumbo-sized map, or be a nowhere kind of place, hicks-in-sticks . . . it didn't matter. We *always* wanted England's opponents to win.

I can mark out my life in international tournaments, and defeats and disasters for the Auld Enemy. And I assumed every Scottish family was like ours, and behaved in the same way.

Of that 1970 World Cup, another screenwriter, *Night Moves*'

Alan Sharp, declares in *This Is My Country*: 'When I was in Mexico I thought England played very well against Brazil, but it would have been impossible for me to identify with them and support them.'

You just couldn't. England was a different country, and still, to these teenage eyes, a faraway country. Our family knew no English people. My father had a good friend called Fred England but, unhelpfully, he wasn't English. From Nos. 1 to 11, my team Hibs were entirely Scottish, and every week they played other all-Scots sides, give or take the odd Scandinavian called Noggin the Nog and the like who'd been lured to Scotland by our sultry temperatures. And I still hadn't crossed the border by the time I was eligible to place a cross on a voting form.

The 1970s were stirring times for Scotland. In the two general elections of 1974, the Scottish National Party stormed Westminster, winning first six then eleven seats. That year's World Cup also produced a double whammy: Scotland qualified, England didn't. Oh how Dad and I laughed.

The SNP campaigned on the slogan 'It's Scotland's oil' after the discovery of so much black gold underneath the North Sea. Scotland was rich; wealthy enough to split from the rest of the United Kingdom and go it alone.

George Rosie, the journalist and author, recalls the optimism of the times: 'Wild schemes were floated for huge petrochemical works, international airports, whole new towns. Fortunes were made and fingers burnt. It was the apocalyptic hour of the Dreamer and the Artful Dodger. But it was also a massive injection of optimism, energy and hard cash the like of which Scotland had never seen before and will probably never see again.'

'When will we see your likes again?' That's a line from 'Flower Of Scotland', the song eventually chosen to be Scotland's modern anthem. It was written by Roy Williamson of The Corries, who were given their TV break by my father. By the time Dad and I started going to Scotland games at Hampden – we're still in those tumultuous 1970s here – the booing of 'God

Save The Queen' was thunderous. My father loved this, almost as much as the chant which invariably followed:

> Bobby Moore, superstar
> Walks like a woman and he wears a bra

(Who was the true bard of the old Mount Florida slopes – up to his Stead & Simpson stack heels in red mud as another dolly bird beer can full of piss is emptied onto the crumbling steps – and where *did* these fabulous chants come from? My father always wanted to find out. Sometimes we'd play a game, scan the faces in the packed crowd and pick out possible candidates for lyricist-in-residence.)

Whatever your political persuasion, if you were a Scot Nat or a Scot Not, there could be no denying that Scotland in the 1970s had a swagger in its step and demanded to be heard. My 1970s – half spent at school, the other half cub-reporting – were about trying to find my voice. As a confused teenager with a head full of the usual obsessions and also a sizable self-obsession, I didn't fully appreciate that my country was undergoing a life change of its own, shedding its plooks and attempting to grow up. Lashing out at everything, the way bumfluffed, bumptious teens do, I probably couldn't wait to leave Scotland. Of course, I've ended up staying.

In their book *Modern British History*, Mark Garnett and Richard Weight write: 'In this period a more distinct Scottish popular culture also emerged, centred on vociferous support for Scotland's football team, while the Bay City Rollers, a tartan-clad pop group, took Britain by storm.'

The Bay City Drongos? The Rollers and their 'Shang-A-Lang' sound were Scotland's national embarrassment. I may have been politically naive, but aged seventeen I knew my pop music. If I was patriotic about pop in the 1970s it was for the Average White Band who, remarkably, sold soul music back to America and topped the US charts.

The swagger was even more pronounced in the theatre. John McGrath's *The Cheviot, The Stag And The Black, Black Oil* was an angry polemic about the exploitation of Scotland, from the eighteenth century Highland Clearances to the battle over the bounty found at the bottom of the North Sea. *The Great Northern Welly Boot Show* was a musical about the threatened closure and subsequent work-in at the Upper Clyde shipyard and starred a promising young comedian called Billy Connolly. Bill Bryden's *Willie Rough* was also shipyard-set, as was, on TV, Peter McDougall's *Just A Boys' Game*, although in that fantastic film the central characters were never in their crane cockpits. They were always bunking off to drink and fight and drink and screw and drink and ponder the state of cross-generational male relationships.

In the faither-laddie relationship of which I was part, I believed in my dad implicitly (apart from the stories about the toenails in the marmalade and that sword wound; I was *haein' ma doots* about them). Everything I knew about the shaky concept of the 'United Kingdom' I learned from him (and everything I knew about local difficulties in the rest of Europe I learned from Katie Boyle in a shimmering gown during voting for *The Eurovision Song Contest*).

When Dad stomped off to his study in 1966, so missing the World Cup presentation, I stomped off to my bedroom. It was only afterwards that I saw Bobby Moore wipe his muddy hands on the velvet drape of the Royal Box before he accepted the trophy from the queen.

And when in later years, in their attempt to repeat that triumph, England failed to score against Polish clown-goalies (Jan Tomaszewski), or conceded goals to Germans who looked old enough to be my grandfather (Uwe Seeler), or expected the hirpling veterans, Kevin Keegan and Trevor Brooking, to save the day while wearing ridiculously skimpy shorts (1982 World Cup), I believed a loud guffaw was the only permissible reaction. I couldn't wait for my voice to drop so it would have even more impact.

And I believed every word of *Jock*. Year after year at the Edinburgh Festival, this one-man tattoo played to sell-out crowds. The rousing finale always got them, with the old soldier unleashing one more verbal volley at his English oppressors:

> We've seen too much and heard too much to be taken in by any of the old queen and country crap. The ba's up on the slates . . .

Then the bagpipes start up. It's 'Scotland The Brave'. Jock snorts:

> They'll have to do more than skirl a tune at us, won't they? We're our own masters now. We've bowed the knee and touched the forelock once too often.

But as the music builds, his shoulders start to twitch – a 'gallus wee swagger' is how my father recommends it in the script. Jock picks up the Saltire and marches out of the theatre. Every summer, Dad predicted this would be the year when the audience would jump to their feet and fall in behind the 'auld bastard', follow him all the way along Princes Street to their destiny, or the pub, whatever was closest.

It never happened. And Scotland never got Home Rule, at least not then. In 1978 Scotland qualified for the Argentina World Cup, England didn't, and Dad and I laughed even louder. But Scotland performed abysmally under the tragically deluded Ally MacLeod. That swagger of ours took a kicking in Córdoba and the following year's referendum on devolution was a vote too far for many Scots.

In my polling station, I stood tall because I was in my old primary school for the first time since I'd left the place. But hunched over the desk in the booth, I felt pathetically small. Voting for the very first time, on anything, I placed my cross in the 'No' box. Too scared by the alternative, I chose that Scotland should remain attached to a country that all through the 1970s I thought I despised.

How did my father vote? What would he think about Scotland finally getting a Parliament? What would he think about the Scottish team qualifying for five World Cups in a row, then looking like they might never reach the finals again? What would he think about the current generation of 'whiteshirted swines', their six-figure salaries and their hairstyles and their super-celebrity, and the upsurge in patriotism – *English* patriotism – they inspire? I don't know because he's not here to ask.

But we will always have 1966. When Dad was alive, the rest of the family knew better than to bring up a year destined to go down in infamy. And today he would not believe the extent to which that triumph is still banged on about.

The English gave Dad what he called 'the dry boak'. None more so than when they provoked this rant, my favourite from *Jock*:

> And in Whitehall and Westminster and all along their corridors of power they treat us as if we were still savages, painted in woad. A subject race of congenital idiots, a nation of Harry Lauders with curly sticks and wee daft dugs and stags at bay and flyin' haggises and tartan dollies and Annie Lauries and hoots mon Jock McKay ye'll be a' richt the nicht if you can houghmagandie backwards.

Jock dates from a time when Scotland, a large chunk of it, felt driven down by England. Some would say Scots are at their best in such situations. A few would contend Scots need these situations simply to function. And now? Whitehall and Westminster no longer deny us a say in our own affairs. But while we have a Parliament, this has not made us more remote from England. Ideologically, and in every way when I was growing up, I used to think England and Scotland were a million miles apart. I cannot say that today.

There are 400,000 English people who now call Scotland home; many of them live in my Edinburgh. The BBC, where my father worked for twenty-five years, is no longer powered by the insistent thrum of plummy accents.

Three decades ago, the only Scots of influence making their living in England seemed to be footballers. Every club had at least one wild-haired, wide-lapelled, desperado-moustached card shark in the dressing room, and if the Sassenachs were familiar with the vernacular which *Trainspotting* author Irvine Welsh would later take into the mainstream, they might have referred to this fellow as 'the Scottish radge'.

These days, the radge plays a different game. Over the last few years, most of the great offices of state have been held by Scots. Tony Blair was born in Edinburgh. More obviously, Gordon Brown is Scottish. There are many others. To the exasperation of the English, this coterie of 'Jocks' controlling the government, the media and much else besides is the 'Scottish Raj'.

With so many English people living in Scotland, the Parliament perfectly understandably talks a lot about its vision of a 'modern, inclusive Scotland'. Any mention of the great rivalry would doubtless be deemed 'reductive'. So maybe it's just as well that Scotland and England no longer play each other at football.

But the word 'reductive' didn't exist in my father's day and neither did the view that the great rivalry was in any way a bad thing. And if you grew up believing that it was the most important thing, you cannot simply switch off. Whether I like it or not, the great rivalry is part of me. It sits in me like a vaguely benign lump.

My father wasn't a New Dad (thank goodness). For Auld Dad and I, football was our currency, the means by which we communicated with each other, and what we talked about most was Scotland and 'the other lot'. And even though he's dead I cannot break the link. I am his self-appointed representative on earth, checking the classified football results for mispronunciations, such as 'Brechin City' being rhymed with 'wretchin''. It is while saddled with this long-standing, possibly incurable condition, then, that I take on the challenge of supporting – come, on get it right: *following* – England at Germany 2006.

2006. Thirty, no, hang on . . . *forty* years of hurt. It is four long decades since that glistening afternoon when England won the World Cup. They love their anniversaries, the English, but so do Scots.

It is thirty-five years since *Jock*. Thirty years since *This Is My Country*, and I'm the same age now as my father was when he wrote that book. It's also ten years since Dad died after hanging on long enough to see England fail to win Euro '96.

And for all that England believed 2006 to be their destiny, that this was when they would once again win football's greatest prize, I'm afraid that in my mind the fortieth anniversary demands a whole different reaction to flags, rattles, street parties, a joyful unbuttoning of decent, proper English reserve and a spontaneous chorus of 'For he's a jolly good fellow' when Bobby Moore, the boy with the golden hair, hoists aloft the golden trophy.

'Bloody bastardin' shite!'

Gordon Brown, Texture like Sun

I could use some help. More than that, I need a Scot – a pre-eminent one, an example to us all – to show me how to 'do' England.

Gordon Brown is a key member of the 'Scottish Raj'. He is Chancellor of the Exchequer but, bored of being assistant manager to the country, wants a shot at the top job. He will get it eventually, but his leadership bid really kicks in at the beginning of this World Cup year with an appeal for team unity. This is United Kingdom FC and Brown, unmistakably Scottish, has a bit to go to win over Middle England, Little Englanders and Ingerlanders and convince them he's prime-minister material. He wants to reclaim the Union Jack from far-right nutters. He wants it planted in gardens up and down this decking-clad septic isle. And he proposes a national holiday, a British Day.

There is much scepticism about his wizard wheeze. In Scotland the SNP insist that Britishness is so last century, if not the two centuries before that, and point to opinion polls showing that Scots feel emphatically more Scottish than British. Down south, the paper of record for Unmerrie Englande, the *Daily Mail*, contends: 'Gordon Brown has a problem – he is Scottish.'

Brown exudes 'Presbyterian rectitude and a kind of northern bleakness,' says Stephen Glover, which is a bit rich, considering Glover is among the most joyless of the *Mail*'s grey-sky thinkers. 'His particular difficulty as a would-be prime minister arises because the Scots are less loved in England than at any time since the mid-eighteenth century.'

Is this true? I don't know because, for me, the process of integration has yet to begin. There's a World Cup warm-up in Liverpool in February and I think I should be there.

How British do I feel? Not very. But in 2006, Scots and our English cousins will want to ponder the question, what with the 300th anniversary of the Union looming.

If Brown is looking for an instinctive Scottish response to his big idea, then it's this: I approve of a national holiday and reckon I deserve it. After all, I'm giving up a year for this cross-border cultural exchange to follow the English team, and it's twelve months I can ill afford.

The life expectancy of the average Scot is 73.8 years, about three years less than the average Englishman. So the English – and Gordon 'Play up, Britain, play up!' Brown – had better appreciate the huge personal sacrifice I'm making here.

Get to Know Your Team

'Actually I quite like a lot of players in the England team right now.'

Just fourteen words, but you hear them a lot. This is New Scotland talking, and if you remember Old Scotland or even Fairly Recent Hairy And Platform-Soled Scotland, they sound odd and slightly disturbing.

Just fourteen words but they're so resourceful. They can be used apologetically. With out-of-the-closet relief. As an expression of wilful contrariness. Or – worst of all – as a badge of trendiness.

You know the type. Likes the 'different', the 'difficult' and the 'dangerous'. First to get into sea bass and drum 'n' bass. Won't watch films with happy endings (only those with split-screen beginnings and Dogma in the middle). Always holidays in recently liberated ex-hellholes. That's it: supporting England is my fortnight in Baghdad.

Let's start with the goalie. Goalkeeping for a long time was never recognised as a footballing skill in Scotland so it's difficult for me to comment with any real authority on Paul Robinson, except to say that many England No. 1s before him had the intimidating physical presence and 'No jeans, no trainers' certitude of a gatekeeper at an Essex bop. Robinson doesn't. He's no Peter Shilton or even a David Seaman. In fact he makes some Ingerlanders nostalgic for David James.

Gary Neville is the 'shop steward' and commands respect for being a one-club man and always trying to think of something interesting to say, post-match, rather than the usual anodyne guff accompanied by much ear-tugging. He is, however, mental.

Steven Gerrard and Jamie Carragher espouse the same solid, dependable Northern values. Gerrard has a fiancée who doesn't look like she stays in watching reruns of television shows about loft conversions on some deathless lifestyle channel. But that no nonsense, brushed-forward hairstyle of his suggests a man not easily swayed by the celebrity side of football and who would still, just, give this answer to English football's leading question: 'I don't want to go to Chelsea, *like*.' Carragher was once persuaded to reveal his biggest extravagance. 'A wallet,' he said after some deliberation. For a Kirby man, even a slim leatherette pouch would be ostentatious, and after much ribbing from his mates, he stopped using it.

Such modesty is rare, though, when your squad includes three definite starters from money-drenched Chelsea. Four if you count Ashley Cole whose bleating about being offered only £55,000 a week by Arsenal almost causes him to crash his Aston Martin. He regains control of the wheel and – phew, that was close – eventually makes it across town to Stamford Bridge, a notorious transfer deal which earns him the nickname 'Cashley Hole'.

I suppose it says something about Frank Lampard, John Terry and Joe Cole that they wear the blue of Chelski and yet the condemnation that comes the way of their club on an almost daily basis – for their lack of humility, heritage and class – just bounces off them.

Lampard is an all-action midfielder who gets an incredible amount of goals by hitting the ball hard and straight and inviting a wicked deflection. There's no science to his game, or much in the way of art, and you sense he could play in reinforced toecaps on gluepot pitches and be just as effective.

Terry is another throwback. He's a Six Million Dollar Man – not in his constantly flaunted market value but his absolute indestructibility. You imagine an ugly gash caused by a slide tackle which started twenty yards back would reveal wires and transistors rather than flesh and bone. A central defender by name, he probably looks at his ball-playing contemporaries with mild disdain. Unlike them you guess he'd be happier with the old skool, unreconstructed label of 'centre half'.

But it's in Cole that the current England line-up most evokes the 1970s team with which I grew up. He's flash as hell and seems to fly in the face of current thinking about the game. Scots call his almost extinct type 'patter-merchants' and, really, no higher praise can be grudgingly given.

Cole's elusiveness is a special thing when football is so overburdened by systems. But it did not come to his aid off the field when he found himself in a compromising position at a house party with the Page Three stunna known to White Van Man (in his white England shirt) as 'Keeley'. When Cole next took the field for Chelsea, he sported a corking black eye, a worth-it wound which only endeared him to White Van Man some more.

It's a myth that all footballers in the 1970s relaxed after a game with the kids while the wife cooked the Sunday roast. Similarly it's a myth that these days the post-match wind-down of choice for every FA-registered player is a good roasting. But there is no question that the modern English player has money, mock-Tudor cribs, pimped wagons, bling, chunks of Dubai real estate and yes, girls, beyond his wildest dreams.

Even footballers of modest ability earn small fortunes. A pre-World Cup survey reveals that the average Premiership salary is £676,000 – a sixty-five per cent increase compared with two years before – and almost a third of top-flight players are on £1 million-plus. That's handy when, like Wayne Rooney, you allegedly rack up gambling debts of £700,000. But after another two years of this kind of wage hike, the big names must now be able to buy a different set of flash wheels for every day of the week.

Some players think they can do anything they want, that

they're above the law. A few are out of control. Meanwhile, the heroes of 1966, who were paid £60 per England international, have to sell their mementos of that great triumph to keep the wolf from the door.

It is against this backdrop that a demanding public and an even more demanding media will judge the men of 2006. These 'spoiled brats' and 'prima donnas' – the words of the Queen, no less – must rise above the sleaze and greed and prove themselves worthy of the amazing hoopla.

Exactly how are they the 'golden generation', anyway? In football the term was first conferred on Luis Figo, Rui Costa and the rest of the Portugal youth team twice crowned world champions at their level. These England players haven't won anything as internationalists; indeed some bear the scars from defeats by Portugal at successive Euro Championships, games lit up by thunderous goals from . . . Luis Figo and Rui Costa. The 'golden generation' is really pushing it. Stealing a superlative, abusing its meaning, cheaply banding it about – that's one sure way this England mob will wind up Scots.

The tearaways of the 1970s that I pretended to hate but secretly loved have been treated kindly by history, or rather nostalgia. Nowadays, despite failing to get England to two World Cups, they're referred to as 'characters'. The current lot have already achieved more by qualifying for Germany but Rio Ferdinand is going to have to score the winner in the final – and with an overhead kick – before I start to think he's anything less than preposterous.

Ah Rio. Apparently the marketing men love him. In their calculations of predicted spin-off drek potential, the Rio brand is as big as the Rio Grande. Alongside his record label, fashion line, video messages for your phone and hair-braiding, Ferdinand is presenting a 'hilarious' ITV show called *Rio's World Cup Wind-Ups* in which he plays practical jokes on his teammates (e.g. six-feet-seven-inch Peter Crouch laughs at a dwarf). This promises to make him as big a 'national treasure' as Jeremy Beadle.

On the back of what, exactly? He's not as good a central defender as he thinks he is, and thinking is very much the problem here. Why can't he concentrate during games? Why can't he treat football like the corn-rowed hair or the beard-sculpting and acknowledge its intricacies and give it the same attention to detail?

Michael Owen? Speedy, unshowbizzy, decent. Well, fairly decent. And after successive Dives of God to get England penalties against Argentina in the previous two World Cups, he's probably hoping for the chance of a unique hat-trick. Rooney? Everybody loves the assassin-faced baby, the ultimate street-footballer. And Scots love Crouch and Owen Hargreaves precisely because England fans don't.

Now . . . have I missed anyone?

'Day-Veeeeeed!'

Ah yes, David Beckham . . .

I didn't forget about him back there. But this is difficult. (*No it's not, you've never liked him.*) OK, what is slightly tricky is proving that I didn't buy the Beckham hype, the Beckham bedspread, the Beckham night light, the Beckham homoerotic picture book – none of it, *ever.*

It's easy to be wise after the event, and the non-event. But I can dig out a yellowing cutting of a newspaper column dated 14 December 2002 in which I revealed my New Year resolutions and top of the list was: 'I must stop being mean about David Beckham.'

For the rest of that piece in the *Scotsman* I proceeded to be very mean about the England captain and the 113,539 viewers – I counted them – who voted him into second place in the BBC Sports Personality Of The Year.

Beckham finished runner-up on the strength of scoring a highly debatable penalty in a group game against Argentina in the 2002 World Cup. The rest of his year was distinctly average. He was part of a Man U team which won nothing. He got an injury ('Oh no, it's the second metatarsal!') He did manage to discover Japan that summer, and also planted a flag in South Korea – or so it seemed from the hysteria that greeted his presence in the Far East where obsessed oriental girls ('Day-veeeeeed!') queued up to lick his toilet bowl. But England went out meekly in the quarter-finals – key Beckham moment: jumping out of a tackle as Brazil scored their equaliser – with the eventual champions' coach Luiz Felipe Scolari rating England as less problematic than Belgium. Beckham did not beat Argentina by himself. Nicky Butt was man of the match. Ellen MacArthur finished behind Beckham in the voting and she sailed round the world single-handed.

The accused in this BBC outrage were nicknamed 'The White City 113,539'. And in my column I continued the rant: 'It's just footballfootballfootball all the way with you lot, isn't it? Except in Beckham's case, it's not just football. It's hair, big ties, nail varnish, diamond earrings, Posh, the kids, more hair ("It's David Back-comb!"), those goal celebrations (rehearsed on the training ground, him on the back of the scorer), hanging tough with Elton John and boyfriend for gay crossover appeal . . . the whole interminable, branded, what's he wearing *now*?, life-as-one-big-photo-op palaver. And you bought the lot, suckers.'

Who else in 2002 was talking about Beckham piggy-backing his way onto the sports pages (sometimes the front)? No one.

Who is doing it in 2006? Here's the *Independent* of 30 October, in an article about how his star is starting to fade: 'The reporter [an unnamed member of the Madrid hack-pack] says the player – even when not scoring – does what he can to associate himself with success. "When a goal is scored he is the first to congratulate the scorer. That will be the picture . . . it's always Becks and the scorer." '

So what happened in 2003? Did I stick to my resolution? No, and it was the same story in 2004 and 2005. I'm not claiming I was the first to murmur dissent, or that I then protested the loudest. But there have been times, honestly, when I've felt like the loneliest person in the world, hollering into a bitter wind – the Henry Fonda character in a remake of *Twelve Angry Men* called *113,539 Deluded Sports Fans.*

Why can you lot not see what I see? That he doesn't run with the ball. That his whole game is based around the ball being stationary. That he plays for free kicks, feigning fouls by hitching up his feet and spreadeagling himself ('Ooo, I'm a starfish!')

That the whole team play for free kicks, to get him into position for another dead-ball situation. That he'd turn football into American football, given half a chance. Or merge it with golf.

If the invention of the wheel was a fairly important one for mankind, then Beckham trying to halt a football's definite, truthful motion is one of the most dire threats that civilisation has faced. He must be stopped. And the ball must be kept moving.

Three years ago, Beckham had two underwhelming World Cups behind him and one underwhelming Euro Championship. He was going to have to get his finger out in Portugal, no doubt about it. So you might have thought BeckhamWorld would have been a bit more restrained in the build-up to Euro 2004. Fat chance. The BBC carried out a state-of-nation survey before the tournament and discovered that thirty-seven per cent of Britons rated Beckham 'more influential than God'.

A couple of weeks before Euro 2004, with the Cross of St George fluttering and expectant England all aquiver, I found myself in the National Portrait Gallery in London viewing a video installation of a sleeping Beckham by the artist Sam Taylor-Wood, who had apparently filmed the great deity dozing in a Madrid hotel room. *Apparently.*

Who sleeps in full make-up and jewellery? Which of us softly brushes his hair from his face while in the Land of Nod, then seductively runs his hand across his best-a-man-can-get chin – then hugs himself?

In the hour-long film Beckham didn't dribble, not once. At Euro 2004 in Portugal, he didn't dribble, not once. And another big tournament, where a big performance was expected of this big player – the biggest there is – ended with him thumping a big penalty over the bar, over the stadium roof, with the ball eventually coming to rest in Spain. (More or less true: the fan who caught it lived in Madrid).

In my hounding of Beckham, friends thought I was mad. But they had bought the Beckham hype, the Beckham sarong, the

Beckham Alice band, the Beckham tattoos, all thirteen of them, including the Hindi dedication to his wife which managed to spell her name 'Vhictoria'. The *Scotsman*'s sports editor, Donald Walker, definitely thought I'd lost it when I found cause to rubbish The Painted Fool's most famous goal from open play. There have not been many of those, of course, but when he scored from seventy yards against Wimbledon in 1996 I questioned what a so-called attacking midfield player was doing in his own half of the field.

OK, that might have been over the top. And I accept that in the 2001 World Cup qualifier against Greece he was brilliant. If you don't count Teddy Sheringham conning the referee into awarding the foul that resulted in his free-kick goal, he turned the match around entirely by himself. Rarely can one player have had such a superhuman impact on a game.

But surely never has a single goal been more rerun than that one. Surely no player has dined out for so long on a solitary performance – the only occasion he has dominated a football match the way he hogs the headlines (Style visionary! Black – *black* – icon! Metrosexual! Natural disaster sympathiser! Holding midfielder! Wait, this is even funnier . . . sweeper! So famous the female contestants in *Big Brother 3*, debating the ongoing situation in the Middle East but also body hair, name their front bottoms after him!)

Looking back over my David Beckham rants, I am slightly embarrassed there have been so many. Sixty-seven mentions in six years when I'm not even a dedicated sports journalist is some going. And the kindest of them was merely sneering. There have also been eighteen mentions for 'Derek Beckham', which was how he was fanfared in America in 2003 on a less than triumphant promotional tour. I wanted everyone to start calling him Derek but my campaign foundered against the sheer might of his PR.

For the past six years I have crouched down in a camouflaged hut stuffed with surveillance gear called BeckhamWatch. My world view has been narrow and warped and, looking back, I accept that I definitely should have got out more. But now I'm getting married so a lot of the old obsessions (football, music, the obsessively, compulsively, disorderly fascination for the world's best-known OCD sufferer) will have to be stored away in the attic. I'm required to hope that Beckham has a great tournament in Germany, to crown his career. Anything to make the madness stop.

Wayne Rooney is here now and he can win games by himself so some of the pressure is off Derek. But he is still the captain and after four – count them – less than glorious performances on football's biggest stages, he must surely want to deliver at this World Cup to at least partially justify the incredible fuss and bother.

If he doesn't, then I suppose he will be able to continue for a while as the world's first virtual footballer: the one who doesn't need the ball to be moving to be involved in the play, who doesn't need to score from a free kick to have the nation reminded of his dead-ball heroics which did for the Greeks, who doesn't need to be the goal scorer to be the prominent face in the celebrations and who doesn't need to do very much – he can just be pretend sleeping – to annoy me.

But eventually there comes a point for all footballers – even ones bigger than God – when there will be no looking forward, only back. At that moment, Beckham will be sat on a porch in America. This is football oblivion, and for him it's a good fit. For a long time he's been a US-style sports star stuck in the wrong country. England, bless it, is the home of the Corinthian spirit and still retains some suspicion of the American way, through which a sportsman can attain the aura of a movie idol. (Scotland rejects it outright. Of course this is easy to do when you're never likely to produce a Derek-sized footballer).

What will Germany bring? Can our hero add to the goal against Wimbledon and the goal against Greece – how modest those opposition look in bald print! – with something more definitive and DVD-deserving?

Or will we end up having to time-capsule *this* for an incredulous future age: photographs of his fifty-seven different hairstyles and 'unique fashion sense', snaps of him as the 'family man' accompanying newspaper stories about how he was a 'role model' for other dads, as if he'd invented the concept of quality time with children, as if he'd founded fatherhood . . . and not forgetting the 'world exclusives' of the (alleged) affairs, with the spa assistant who spraytanned him and the nanny in the gilded Beckham family bubble who then used the tabloid notoriety to launch her own career as a 'celebrity' providing hand relief for pigs.

Only if you were feeling charitable – maybe only if you weren't me – would you insert this addendum: he shared a profession with the heroes of '66, with Stanley Matthews and Tom Finney and Duncan Edwards. In his life he also played football.

First Opal Fruits, Then Marathons . . .

Inspired by the World Cup, Mars are changing the name of their famous chocolate bars. They hope that 'Believe' will inspire England in Germany.

What a selfless act! Though I suppose it's not unconnected to the company's desire for a sizable chunk of the £1.25 billion which the Centre for Economic and Business Research estimate will be pumped into the UK economy as a result of the tournament.

Not Only Clementine but Clementina, Too

Lucy and I met in the modern way, that is: down the health club, in a fitness class called Bodypump.

We chatted about this and that, about whether during the squats exercise, the instructor would, as usual, sing into his hands-free mike a lyric of his own design to Kool and the Gang's 'Celebration': 'There's something goin' on . . . *in the legs*.' And I must have let a full minute pass – long for me, better watch out, I'm slipping – before I asked the inevitable question.

'So you're English?'

'No, Scottish,' came the slightly miffed reply.

Idiot. What did I have to say that for? She must have thought I had a hang-up about English people. (She didn't think this. I was just being paranoid about how much I'm perceived as being paranoid about the English.) She *sounds* English. Or English-*type*. Well brought up, that's for sure, but then everybody sounds well brought up next to me and my keelie kind. And before long I will be getting her to talk, not dirty, but with perfectly rounded vowels.

'Go on, say it.'

'No.'

'Go on, please. I won't ask again.'

'OK, but this is the last time: "Carlos *Santana* wore a *bandana* but he never played Auchterarder and come to think of it neither did *Bananarama*, or the Bonzo Dog *Doo-Dah* Band or Pink Floyd at the time of *Ummagumma*, or the Mighty *Wah*! *or* any of the leading practitioners of . . . *ska*." '

When I say 'ska', with my head jammed down hard between my shoulders, it is spat out quickly and sounds threatening, like 'scar', or ugly, like 'scab'. Lucy actually pronounces the word as if there is a final 'r', but she stretches it, rather like she's putting it through a session of *pilates* ('Say it, say it!'), and makes it languid, lyrical – far more beautiful than this music has ever been.

But she doesn't buy that compliment, and nor should she. It's ridiculous that I'm still making fun of accents – no, just the English accent or the English-*type* accent – at my age. My only defence is that I'm my father's son.

Auchter-*ah-dah* in Perthshire, where Santana and the rest never performed live, was nonetheless the teeming metropolis to which Lucy's family relocated from the deep south of England. 'I cried all the way to Birmingham. I'm the oldest, I was being wrenched away from Sussex and all my friends, and I didn't like the sound of Scotland one little bit,' she says. But now she's the only one of four kids to have put down roots here. The dreichness of Scotland seeped so deep into her mother's bones that when it came time for her parents to retire, they shot right past England and didn't stop until they reached south-west France.

Lucy's private school taught her lots of things we didn't get at Broughton High. There were prizes for deportment and grooming. Lucy herself won the Swinton Cup, awarded to the girl who'd shown the most 'courtesy and consideration'. She played lacrosse and tennis – neither of them especially big in Scotland – and before hockey games the team would psyche themselves up with a song set to the theme of the BBC's *Match Of The Day*:

> We're followers of Jesus
> He's captain of our team
> We do our training with our teachers
> Perfection is our dream . . .

You might wonder if Lucy's Scottish education wasn't in fact rather anglicised. You could say with absolute certainty that mine was Scottish. We got football, football and more football. Apart from when the sports field was too muddy and we were hustled indoors for Scottish country dancing. At the time I hated it but now, at a wedding where there are English present, I look on smugly at their clodhopping attempts to join in.

'Oh I *love* Scottish country dancing,' said Lucy, on our second date, thwarting my attempts to assert Scottish superiority. She first learned the moves in Sussex, in a garage, which made the Gay Gordons seem top secret and highly dangerous. And her Perthshire alma mater refined them to a degree that leaves me standing. Lucy knows more dances than me, and can dance all of them better. 'I'll teach you,' she said, cutting me to the quick.

In *This Is My Country* my father – describing the class-based restrictions of his young life – wrote: 'Other people went to parties, had holidays, travelled in trains, knew the next episode of *Flash Gordon*, saw tries scored at Murrayfield, were Episcopalians, answered the telephone, knew what steak tasted like, and said "fuck" as if it was spelt with a "ph".'

When I read this to Lucy she says: 'Well, that's me, isn't it? Apart from the *Flash Gordon* bit.'

They say opposites attract, which is just as well, because Lucy knows girls called Flavia and Finola, Banna and Zannah. Then there's Ginny, who once worked for Trinny (of T and Susannah). She knows not only a Clementine but a Clementina, too. And let's not forget Cleodie and Jacobina and Aviva and Octavia and Thomasina. Or the fact that her best friend Joanna's granny lives in a castle where the Queen Mum used to stop off for tea on trips to the Highlands.

I, on the other hand, have a mate called Rab.

To clear her student debt, Lucy worked in big houses. She can usually flick through a copy of *Hello!* and spot a former employer whose incredibly precocious children's bottoms she used to wipe. Watching television, she will recognise a leaking, draughty mansion where she once cooked forty pheasant for dinner that's now being rented out to ITV for a 'two-part psychological thriller'. And when I think I'm being funny, bestowing on Celtic's Dutch striker Jan Vennegoor of Hesselink the nickname 'The Countess of Wemyss', she can silence me by saying: 'Actually, I know the countess.'

Making fun of the way people speak. It's not big and it's not clever. 'You would *never* win the Swinton Cup,' says Lucy. And she's right. Scotland muck up, yet again.

England: An Abuser's Guide

Ridiculously, I am quoted in *This Is My Country*. The index positions me between Shankly, Bill and Stevenson, Robert Louis. And my eight-year-old's reasoning goes like this: 'I've just got the one grumble about Scotland – why are places so far apart?'

When you're eight, everywhere else is a moon mission and then some. And beyond strung-out Scotland, and the 'are we there yet?' ennui of caravanette holidays – the 'I spy something beginning with S . . . slag heap!' documentation of the landscape – the distances between us and other football nations were completely unbridgeable. Brazil's football was on another planet – in every sense. World Cups, like Christmas, seemed to take forever to come round. I wasn't a deprived child, apart from in one crucial area.

The Scottish First Division simply wasn't enough. You loved your Scottish team, in my case Hibs, you loved them more than anything, but beyond the fortnightly home games – away matches being too skinhead-scary – access to a supremely modest league was limited.

This was how limited . . .

Every Saturday there was one BBC Scotland teatime results show, staffed by dour reporters in TV test-card patterned sports jackets. You could tell they had raced from their matches to local studios to file on the hoof and you'd think that would lend some zip and zing to their despatches – but not Alastair Dewar. 'Our man in Edinburgh', the most lemon-sucking lugubrious of the bunch, the most Bergmanesque, could find even 4-4 draws tedious.

Dundee-based Fraser Elder fancied himself as a comedian or a heroic chronicler – Ernie Wise or Ernie Hemingway, he couldn't decide which. The Aberdeen correspondent whose name I have forgotten let out a girlish yelp and jumped out of his seat when a bulb popped in a studio light and smashed on the floor. When it was Peter Thomson's turn, I waited for my father's ritual groan: 'Pissed again.' I wanted Thomson to better a blooper of legend – 'And we'll find out on Saturday when Celtic play *Scotland* at *Murrayfield*' – and when he didn't, I started to wonder if Dad, not for the first time or the last, had made it up.

That's not a spectacular gaffe, is it? But it kind of proves my point about Scottish football. The raw meat of the game served up by the local TV stations amounted to scrag-ends. Measly action, and measly incidental comedy, too. We had to get our kicks where we could.

After the results had come in there was a long wait while we endured some so-called golden age Saturday night television (*Doctor In The House, Dee Time, Look – Mike Yarwood!*) before the first of the wonky, wooden-tripoded highlights shows. BBC Scotland's *Sportscene* was presented by Archie Macpherson, and there was a second programme on Sunday afternoons, just after *Randall And Hopkirk (Deceased)* and *All Our Yesterdays*: STV's *Scotsport*, fronted by Arthur Montford.

As with the Beatles and the Stones, or more relevantly for me, David Bowie and Roxy Music, you were either an Archie man or an Arthur man. Archie was tall enough to be able to dispense with a commentary-box gantry, his Weetabix weave adding extra inches. His approach to the game was intellectual – lofty in every sense. This wasn't just football, it was history in the making. These games, these throw-ins, were matters of state importance. Could Archie, like Richard Dimbleby, find the words to suit the occasion? Yes he could, and his favourite word was 'woof!'

Arthur was avuncular, with the demeanour of an ever-dependable hardware-store manager. His approach to the game was more subjective than Archie's. In fact, when he shrieked 'Watch your back!' at Gordon McQueen while the Scotland centre half dithered during a World Cup qualifier, the fans-with-typewriters jibe directed at the Scottish fitba meeja by their English counterparts seemed beyond dispute. His favourite word was 'stramash'.

I was an Archie boy *and* an Arthur boy and still it wasn't enough. So I watched *Football Focus* on *Grandstand* which even though it was presented by a Scot, Sam Leitch, contained only a token, tacked-on snippet of the Scottish scene. I scoured the pages of *Charles Buchan's Football Monthly* for a cursory, condescending paragraph about Celtic and Rangers. Both the programme and the magazine were English-produced, and English football dominated both. But when you're desperate to be 'lost to football', any football will do. Inevitably, like water torture, like the drip-drip-drip through a rusty hole in a stand roof, the Sassenach version worked its strange allure. Indoctrination was inevitable, whether I liked it or not.

On *Sportscene* Dad and I watched English action in the same sort of bite-sized chunks English shows offered of Scotland. But even that was enough to confirm that English football was more tantalising: killing play by footballers with groovier haircuts against a backdrop of bigger crowds. Watching Scottish football, I'd never seen as exuberant a goal as that scored by Manchester United against Spurs: a Denis Law shimmy in the left-back position finished by Bobby Charlton running into view for a whoomphing skelp (cue commentator Kenneth Wolstenholme: 'That's a goal fit to win the league, the cup and even the Grand National!') Or as innovative as Ernie Hunt's volley for Coventry City against Everton from Willie Carr's donkey-flick free kick. Or as daft as the keeper's kick from which Alex Stepney scored for Man U against Spurs in the FA Charity Shield, the ball bouncing over Pat Jennings on the parched pitch. Or a goal that inspired a delirious celebration like the parka-swarm in the mud acclaiming Ronnie Radford for little Hereford against Newcastle United in the FA Cup. And I'd certainly never seen anything as thrilling and chilling as the . . . not total football, the *totalitarian* football of Leeds United who forced Southampton to undergo a ball-reaquaintance course after a 7-0 annihilation.

Scots had significant parts in many of these vignettes. Bill Shankly, the Liverpool manager, reckoned that every good team needed two Scots in it (though he added that 'if you've got three that's asking for trouble'). And was there ever a shot harder hit, on the drop – a ball which plummeted from the sky like a skua on the hunt for lunch, straight onto a right boot packed with dynamite – than the great Peter Lorimer's against Manchester City? (Note: some have 'greatness' thrust upon them. Others like Lorimer and Roxy Music's drummer, 'the great Paul Thompson', © *New Musical Express*, just are.) Scottish involvement was not a prerequisite; I was loving this supplementary football, this *English football.*

That is, when I was allowed to see it. The Scottish Football Association ruled with an iron fist in those days and severely limited the number of live games a Scot could watch on TV. There could be no coverage which might possibly lure even one fan away from attending a fixture and the confirmation-click of the turnstiles, even a meaningless, end of season, two-men-and-a-dog affair involving Glenbuck Cherrypickers, and I mean no disrespect to the splendidly named amateur Ayrshire team of the legendary Shanks.

In the late 1960s and early 1970s, music was psychedelic and clothes and 'gear' were hallucinogenically hued. But don't try telling a football-obsessed Scot that it was a time of wild hedonism. Don't try telling me there was even the occasional good time. When Dad listed the commandments of John Knox and his Presbyterian party-poopers in *Jock*, he could just as easily have been talking about General Secretary Willie Allan and the SF Bloody A:

> They dressed the nation in hodden grey . . . no more singing and dancing, fast days instead of feast days. No ornament. No joy.

Such smacked-arse-no-supper treatment of a nation of football nuts has made us the psychologically flawed people we are today. For in the years when there was no World Cup, our paltry helping of live matches could consist of just the European Cup Final (only if a British team was involved, of course) and the Home International between Scotland and England – the diabolical whiteshirts. This made clashes with the Auld Enemy even more significant, even more warlike, if that was possible, and it wasn't.

Generally I reckoned I had a pretty clear idea of what being English meant. It meant the superior sneer of the man in the Schweppes commercials. It meant Henry McGee, snivelling stooge for Benny Hill. It meant Derek Nimmo, the stammering parson in *All Gas And Gaiters*. It meant John Alderton, the stuttering teacher in *Please Sir!* It meant John Le Mesurier, the stumbling sergeant in *Dad's Army*. It meant Terry-Thomas and Jimmy Edwards and Ian Carmichael. It meant henpecked husbands in a zillion suburban sitcoms.

It meant St Custard's, alma mater of the heroically dim Molesworth (a boarding school, not my sort of educational establishment, sounded terrible, but nevertheless I was intrigued and even envious of some of its rituals and privileges, most especially the football pitch *in situ*, goal nets included). It meant St Trinian's, the girl's equivalent, also drawn by Ronald Searle, and actually inspired by a school in Edinburgh. It meant Lord Snooty, pipsqueak peer of the *Beano*. It meant Lord Charles, the monocled, sozzled aristo worked from the back by ventriloquist Ray Alan (catchphrase: 'Silly arse!') It meant *Face The Music*, the telly quiz for classical music buffs hosted by Joseph Cooper, he of the 'silent piano', and featuring Joyce Grenfell, she of the St Trinian's films (everything links up) and a more thunderingly precious affair you could not imagine.

It meant Zachary Smith, the conniving coward in *Lost In Space*, played by Jonathan Harris, Bronx-born, but who watched hundreds of English films to help him devise the right accent for a career in effete, plummy villains. It meant George Sanders, like Harris of Russian descent, who similarly realised early on that a haughty English tone could take you far in Hollywood.

It meant the chinless wonders of Osbert Lancaster's cartoons, their inheritances dwindling, flicking cigarette holders at great, yawning fireplaces and grumbling about the onset of permissiveness in the Penguin book given me by my father . . . along with the volume featuring the cartoons of Norman Thelwell and its generously arsed gymkhana Jillys and Jemimas.

It meant 'Mr Showjumping', Raymond Brooks-Ward, shrieking 'It's gorn! It's gorn!' when a fence toppled at the Horse Of The Year Show. (This was one of Dad's greatest impersonations, especially after the inclusion of Brooks-Ward's own jump technique. The commentator was interviewing Lucinda Prior-Palmer when the microphone sparked, causing him to leap like a lord and set a new record for the Puissance Wall).

It meant singing the 'Ascot Gavotte' from *My Fair Lady* in 'bool in mooth' accents at the demand of my primary-school teacher: 'Every duke and earl and pee-*ah* is hee-*ah*.' It meant men in cravats. It meant men in spats and bowler hats. It meant men in 'Threadgold Thoroughgrip Garterettes', subject of a daft spoof ad in Spike Milligan's *The World of Beachcomber*.

It meant the rich, obnoxious buffoons in the documentary *The Fishing Party*, members of Margaret Thatcher's New Right constituency who became the unwitting stars of her least favourite TV show, for bragging about money, privilege, their families having been in England 'for ever', and how the primary function of a wife was 'driving one home drunk from parties'.

And of course it meant Monty Python's Upper-Class Twit Of The Year Show. I know the names of the contestants like classic football team line-ups: Vivian Smith-Smythe-Smith, ('has an O level in chemo-hygiene'), Simon Zinc-Trumpet Harris ('married to a very attractive table lamp'), Nigel Incubator-Jones ('best friend is a tree'), Gervaise Brook-Hampster ('used as a wastepaper basket by his father'). Disciplines included: Kicking A Beggar, Insulting The Waiter and Taking The Bra Off The Debutantes.

The Englishman's function was to be laughed at, loudly, with my father leading the chortling. But this was never a universal truth . . .

David Coleman was English and still he commanded absolute and total respect. He did not slight Scotland like other English football 'experts'. (Father, again: 'It's not For-*FAR* Athletic! Wrong bloody syllable!'). During Scotland-England internationals we desperately wanted to be patronised by him so we could feel black-affronted; it never happened. Coleman was more than fair. 'A quality goal from a quality player,' was how he described Archie Gemmill's delirious dribble leading to maybe the greatest Scotland goal ever, against Holland in the 1978 World Cup.

Coleman was magisterial at the viddyprinter on *Grandstand*, and it was through the Saturday teatime results service that I learned the names of English cities and towns. This has left me, rather like the health-club lunk who has concentrated exclusively on his biceps, with an overdeveloped knowledge of English football trivia and an underdeveloped appreciation of anything else about the country.

His star quality was sufficient for his name to go straight into the programme titles. With *Sportsnight With Coleman* – the equivalent of Tom Cruise getting his name above his films – he bestrode sports coverage like a colossus; he opened his legs and showed his class. Then there were his football commentaries. Archie Macpherson and Arthur Montford could make Scottish football sound deathless even when the games were exciting. Coleman could make English football sound thrilling even when it was merely so-so.

He screamed his way through games. Later, *Spitting Image* had him scream so much his head exploded. I thought that was cruel. It suggested he was deranged, that spontaneous combustion was inevitable and unstoppable, when in fact the hysteria was always measured, with the self-destruct button kept in reserve for a game's most crucial moments, such as . . .

'CLARKE! 1-0!' That was Alan 'Sniffer' Clarke of Leeds United, a skinny, languid, apparently disinterested but utterly deadly striker scoring the winner in the 1972 FA Cup Final against Arsenal. It was a header, but from way out, easily the farthest-travelled headed goal in all of football.

Coleman gave us few reasons to wave a Saltire in his face though I remember him presiding over a *Sportsnight* contest which these days would be called *Commentator Idol*; Ian St John was a contender so of course we rooted for our man.

Quiz Ball, Top Of The Form, Criss-Cross Quiz, It's A Knockout . . . we cheered for the Scots in every telly competition because we couldn't get enough of the great rivalry. Same with *Miss Great Britain* (go on, Dad: 'There he is, Mr Reverse Bloody Order, look at the wee squirt, he only comes up to their bosoms – Eric Bloody Morley'). Same with *Ask The Family*. In my recollection, the English children on this show were always swots with severely parted hair, the Scots were always little horrors that only mothers could love, but they were our kids, and indeed our head lice.

English boys saw almost as little live football as I did in the strictly rationed late 1960s and early 1970s but they did get their FA Cup Final. I resented that hugely.

Then, on one miraculous May afternoon, after the usual opt-out and a deathless 'And now for viewers in Scotland . . .' announcement which usually meant a screening of *Genevieve* with Kenneth More or somesuch frightfully-awfully English movie, pulverising in its politeness, we were allowed to see extra time direct from Wembley.

It was 1971 and Arsenal were bidding for the league and cup

double against Liverpool. I remember my father speculating that a revolutionary-minded technician at Beeb Scotland's HQ in Glasgow, infused with the spirit of 'Stop 'Nam' and 'Ban The Bomb', had deliberately pulled the wrong lever – the one marked: 'DANGER: EXCITING LIVE FOOTBALL. MUST NOT, REPEAT NOT, BE TRANSMITTED TO MANKY SCOTTISH HOMES AND CAVES' – to feed the climax into our living room. 'He's now smoking his last cigarette,' quipped Dad, before mimicking the sound of a firing squad.

What exotica! Football as it happened, goals as they were scored, long hair as it billowed and bounced. The normal hostilities with England were suspended during that half-hour, which seemed to last until the middle of the following week. Did England have anything else going for it apart from showpiece games, lustrous locks which would almost certainly be checked, post-match, in the rear-view mirrors of Jensen Interceptors – and of course the climactic surges of David Coleman's commentaries? Oh yes it did . . .

Top Ten Most Fanciable Englishwomen (in reverse order, à la Eric Bloody Morley):

10. The blondest, most uniform-flouting, most aware-of-her-body-and-its-effect-on-men St Trinian's girl.

9. Julie Christie. More my father's type, and I include her here in his honour, for *Shampoo* and her shocking dinner-table request at the political rally.

8. Sally, the 'Tuesday girl' of the eponymous hero of *Skinhead*, Richard Allen's bootboy penny dreadful, for the scene where he calls round while her mum is shopping in Ilford, with its bargains and greater variety . . . and she unzips his flies *right there* on the doorstep and he says 'Can't you bleedin' wait?' and she says 'No, Joe . . . feel me!'

7. Susan Stranks. Oh how we yearned for the *Magpie* Action Woman to make a follow-up visit to that trampoline centre. (An obvious pick, but I don't want you getting the idea I've thought about this list *too hard*.)

6. Fiona Fullerton. Later went global as a Bond girl but to the discerning, permanently on heat, bumpy-bus-journeys-do-it teen – the sophisticate in the tented trousers – her performances as the randiest of the nurses in *Angels* were superior. Once married to Simon MacCorkindale, the posh English actor, who then moved on to No. 1, the bastard.

5. Carol Cleveland. Monty Python crumpet ('Nudge nudge, wink wink!') – American, but played English in a trade deal with George Sanders and Jonathan Harris.

4. Penny Spencer. Sharon Eversleigh in *Please Sir!* Movie fans of the 1940s had their sweater girls. We had Shazza, modelling one of C&A's skinny-ribbed wool-mix polo necks so fulsomely that you wonder how the company ever ended up failing and being forced to shut down.

3. Gabrielle Drake. A drama centred round a road haulage firm was always going to need some serious distraction. As a direct consequence of *The Brothers*, all British truckers are rampantly heterosexual. All their American counterparts wear dresses.

2. Madeline Smith. Fall girl in *The Two Ronnies*, the butt (though most often cleavage) of so many of their gags, selflessly submitting to fiendish corsetry and circulation-imperilling bustiers to portray the dumber brunette in period playlets. Ronnie Corbett only came up to her chest which probably explains why he never complained about the lot of the stunted Scot.

1. Susan George. Apparently the first Englishwoman I had the hots for was the bandleader, Ivy Benson. I was only three years old. Ignorant of the *Straw Dogs* controversy, I didn't see one of George's films until 1975's *Mandingo* and even then the fleapit caught fire causing mass evacuation before the scene where she beds her big black slave. This obsession was stimulated and entirely sustained by regular come-hither snaps in jersey-dress and wet-look boots in the *Daily Express*' William Hickey column, also a safe house for Nos. 2, 3 and 6 as well as Judy Geeson, Debbie Watling, Susan Penhaligon and Vivien Neaves, all of whom narrowly failed to make this list.

In Scotland we were still obsessing about the great rivalry – 24/365, in fact. There could be 364 days until the next Scotland-England match but we would fill them somehow. Any Scottish achievement in the weird world beyond football was us getting one up on the English. I was on permanent alert for tenuous connections, mentions in despatches, fame by association. Nothing was too small, it all counted. And no slight by the English was too small either.

But there was no doubt that English football, even when there wasn't a single Scot on the field, was irresistible. I loved it when the flair players – hair players – strutted their stuff, but I also loved the casual, *Clockwork Orange*-style violence, the neck-high tackles, and the comic-thug nicknames: 'Chopper', 'Bites Yer Legs', 'Steals Yer Sweets'. I was going to have to get myself an English football team.

Arsenal. It had to be The Arse, especially after that Charlie George winner in '71, that 'Shag me now!' goal celebration, that long, poker straight, *girl's* hair fanned out on the grass. Yes, they were my team.

Except: the first replica strip I owned, after making my mother run around town to find it, an epic quest rivalling the one she'd undertaken a few years before for the edition of *The Beatles Monthly* containing the lyrics to 'She Loves You' (why?

Because the song used such big words?), was Manchester United.

In 1968 Man U, managed by Matt Busby, equalled the feat of Celtic the year before and won the European Cup. They boasted a tremendous triumvirate: Denis Law, the Scot (I grabbed onto the cuffs of my strip, just like him); Bobby Charlton, the Englishman, but a true gent; and George Best, the Irishman, fancied by Mum, who had his own TV show, a skills school at which I was a real swot, dodging the power cuts during the miners' strikes by getting myself invited for tea at friends' houses to ensure I never missed any of it. Yes, in 1968 it was Man U all the way for me.

Except: the first Subbuteo team I owned was the all white of Leeds Utd. I think that via Arsenal I must have swapped from Man U to Leeds, a defection unthinkable if it involved the real, true feelings of a real, true Englishman. Man U were starting to decline, Leeds were an emerging force. They had more Scots than Man U, including our captain, Billy Bremner. And I loved that clean, classy, single-tone livery.

Almost as much as I loved the clean, classy, single-tone livery of Liverpool and their Scottish quota of Kenny Dalglish, Graeme Souness and Alan Hansen. But midway through my Liverpool years I had a fling with Nottingham Forest who, if their brilliant manager Brian Clough was so inclined, could field a team containing five Scots, surely an English First Division record: John McGovern, John Robertson, Kenny Burns, John O'Hare, Frankie Gray.

I was loyal to no one, and to every English team with a Scot in it. In our house, viddyprinter updates on these player-pioneers' progress down south was greeted with no less excitement than telegraph-drum bulletins about dark continent explorers. 'Hark!' my father would cry. 'Some football results from the savagelands!'

Dad did not have an English team so for once I could not be influenced by him. Choosing one of my own was possibly the first statement I made about myself, all by myself. But by flitting between clubs I was behaving like *a girl.* Picking one over another using the non-rigorous criteria of what constituted a 'nice strip' was laying yourself open to the most damning verdict a father could give of a son during the macho 1970s: 'Big jessie!'

How else was I to choose? I had no affinity with these teams. I'd never been to England. As a family we never holidayed there. Every summer without fail we crammed into our Renault 4 and headed up Scotland's east coast to find the fishing village with the most Presbyterian views of the North Sea, and there we stayed.

Friends went to 'the Lakes' or 'the Dales' or other English places which sounded familiar and welcoming but were completely alien to me. We behaved like the Broons, the model Scottish family as featured in the *Sunday Post*, and didn't stray beyond our but 'n' ben.

When I did finally venture south, it was to the Lake District for my first lads' holiday. Keith Taylor, Dave Whittle and I fell out all the time. We drank ginger beer in the Red Lion pub in Kendal and – you thought only girls did this? – persuaded ourselves we were intoxicated. We collected pictures of the glorious Susan George from the gossip columns and decorated our tent with them. Today we talk of this holiday in the manner of 'Hail, the conquering heroes!' and conveniently forget that the planned two-week trip only lasted four days before we turned the Morris 1100 towards home after falling out for the final time, barely speaking all the way back up the road. (I know, I know . . . you're thinking: how many times can *Express* 'man about town' Hickey contrive a gratuitous mention plus sultry snap of Susan George in just four days? Answer: a lot.)

I can't really blame England for that holiday going wrong. Or blame it for me returning from an interview for a job as a weekly newspaper sports reporter in High Wycombe with my tail between my legs – when it was fear of leaving home that caused me to muck up the opportunity.

Or for me devising my own punk rock heritage trail for my first visit to London, marvelling at the number of Aberdeen Angus Steakhouses but failing to locate the Rough Trade seven-inch single empire and getting mugged. Or for me missing the bus home from my first, and only, Knebworth rock festival. (Although the girl whose sleeping bag I was trying, and failing, to worm inside by pretending that I too had read, and *ohmigod* adored, all of Sylvia Plath's oeuvre was indeed English.)

My first encounters with England were completely unremarkable. Not England's fault but the explorer's; he'd been timid and dim-witted. At a border checkpoint, I might have felt obliged to declare the baggage of history, but it would have been only half understood.

I *thought* I hated England but in moments of clarity and also maturity, I could just about work out that the portrayals of Englishness which made me laugh were caricatures. And I eventually realised that most English people weren't actually like Vivian Smith-Smythe-Smith and the rest of the Upper-Class Twits.

As the 1970s turned into the 1980s Margaret Thatcher came along and undid all the good work of Susan George. Thatcher's Tories became the ruling party in Britain but she was 'no friend of Scotland'. I spent that decade as a news reporter covering the fallout from her government's hard-line policies: picket-line battles during the miners' strike at the Bilston Glen and Monktonhall collieries in Midlothian, the sit-in at the closure-threatened Henry Robb shipyard in Leith, anti-nuclear demos at Torness in East Lothian, poll tax protests everywhere, and the boycott by black African nations of the 1986 Commonwealth Games in Edinburgh.

Scots didn't want – didn't vote – for any of this. The Tories were obliterated at the polls north of the border. And in the 1980s, Scotland and England seemed so remote from each other. I had just started to get acquainted with England; now it was a foreign land. *Daddy, why are places so far apart?*

These days I'm in England every other week, mainly in London interviewing showbiz types, and on the days I travel by train the flatness of the final stretch can still unnerve me. Only when I see Arsenal's Highbury, or now the Emirates Stadium, do I start to relax. As they say, you never forget your *second* time, your *second* English team.

So what do I think of England now? I have not grown out of all of the petty, playground-formed prejudices. From the age of eight in the dread year of 1966, my life has been one long Scotland-England confrontation played out through football and everything else as well. I still snigger when I hear an accent my father would greet with 'Top hole, Cyril!' And I still split my sides when an Englishman declares that his team are going to win the World Cup. So I have much work to do if I'm going to join the whiteshirts and *believe* (© Mars Inc.)

Right now, it annoys me that the Scottish actor David Tennant plays *Doctor Who* with an English accent. Why can't the Time Lord be Scottish? After all, Tennant's home town of Paisley is hardly unfamiliar with alien life forms. I know what my father would say: 'Another bloody BBC conspiracy.' I also know this complaint will seem petty. But it's not easy being Scottish.

The great rivalry continues . . . Peter Nicol, the Scottish squash player, decides for the furtherance of his career to play for England (and supports the whiteshirts at the World Cup – boo!) Jeremy Paxman, the *Newsnight* interrogator and Hammer of the Scottish Raj, cries on screen when he discovers he had a Glaswegian granny (hurray!) Superchef Gordon Ramsay refers to David Beckham & Co. as 'we' (boo!) Gail Porter, the Edinburgh-born lads' mag pin-up, flashes her magnificent bare arse on the walls of the Houses of Parliament (hurray!)

I have a peephole perspective on the world but would say in my defence that I'm simply a product of my generation. Forty years ago, if you loved football and Scotland vs England was one of the few certainties, then you invested it with tremendous importance. A boy of today with such easy access to so much football is spoilt for choice. But I wonder if the senses aren't dulled by the European Champions League. Maybe, because of that competition's stirring anthem of union, the long lines of handshakes by top players who encounter each other so frequently, the games lose their edge. For me there was Scotland and, because we needed someone to play, there was England. That was it. And because the clashes took so long to come round, they were monumental.

For a long time, all I did was take from England. I took football and put nothing back. I stole a vague affection for a team. Only sometimes, on the morning after, would it still be there. I infiltrated the trading of match programmes, redirecting some of them over the border. I swapped a doubler of 'West Bromwich Albion' in my Esso Club Badges collection for a complete-the-set 'Derby County'. Mind you, all of that was nothing compared with England's pillaging of Scotland years before and . . . woops, there I go again.

Maybe as I try to speed along the process of assimilation I should remember those moments in my youth when England was a force of good.

I should remember David Coleman – being Colemanised is a lot more pleasurable than being colonised. And of course I should remember a hazy summer's afternoon, deep in the heart of England . . . the warm grass, the sultry air, that long, poker-straight *girl's* hair fanned out, and panting intimations to 'Shag me now!'

Not Charlie George – Susan George.

'Any Old Icon, Any Old Icon, Any Any Any Old Icon . . .'

OK I admit my English reference points are not definitive. They're personal, a bit perverse, football-oriented, stuck in 1970s Tellyland. But lists by their nature are subjective. Who can claim they know the absolute quintessence of Englishness?

The government do, at the start of World Cup year. Twelve English icons are nominated by the Department for Culture, Media and Sport. In no particular order, they are: the Spitfire, London's Routemaster bus, the Angel of the North, the SS *Empire Windrush* – the boat which brought 500 immigrants from the Caribbean in 1948 – William Blake's 'Jerusalem', Hans Holbein's portrait of Henry VIII, the FA Cup, Stonehenge, the King James Bible, *Alice in Wonderland*, Punch and Judy and a nice cup of tea.

These are English choices, not British ones – the DCMS having decided that Scotland, Wales and Northern Ireland already possess enough national identity of their own, and that England need a leg-up.

The historian David Starkey criticises the list for being 'quaint and banal'. It does seem safe, as if the English are embarrassed by their national history and don't want to offend anyone. The DCMS point out the list is merely a starter pack to get the public to cast their votes on a website called Icons Online.

Right away, suggestions come in from the opinion formers. Michael Gove writes in *The Times*: 'As for the Spitfire, it's a wonderfully politically incorrect choice, but I'd go further in risking European wrath by celebrating the Lancaster bomber.'

Gove is taking the icons issue seriously; Stuart Jeffries of the *Guardian* less so. His 'definitive' picks include Richard and Judy ('A bit rubbish and that's why English people love them'), Slade's 'Merry Christmas Everybody' (the English know the words to that one better than they do 'Jerusalem'), the Princess Diana memorial fountain in Hyde Park (completed over-budget, quickly filled with bathing dogs and dirty nappies, now fenced off to stop it being used as a public urinal) and – maintaining the military theme – the SA80 rifle, the one which jams repeatedly in hot and sandy conditions, where our boys often fight these days.

It must be tough being English and being so confused about your national identity. I thank God every day that I'm Scottish and know exactly who I am.

You see, my icon is a pirate copy of *Braveheart*, bought from a fake-handbag stall in Bangkok, the 'true story' of the 'ultimate Scotch hero' but actually bunk, starring an Australian who thinks he's American, shot on the heathery hillsides of . . . Ireland.

For a number of years after the film's release, it was *the* calling card for a Scot abroad. Ferrymen on Elba, Armenian taxi drivers in New York and passport control at Stansted Airport all greeted me the same way: 'Ah, *Braveheart*!' If your English was limited, you only needed these words to acknowledge a Scot. Sometimes they were accompanied by the thrust of an imaginary dagger.

I hate *Braveheart*, the 'warrior nation' baloney it inspires, the buttons it presses so easily for cheap, patriotic stirrings. And yet . . . the first time I saw the film was in London's Leicester Square. I ran out of the cinema looking for a face-painter to daub me in as close a shade as he could find for the fearsome woad. But *Braveheart* was released in 1995. Surely, post-Parliament, Scots don't need to rely on its (hairy) knee-jerk appeal . . .

In February of this World Cup year, Scotland play England at rugby and – this doesn't happen very often in the oval-ball code either – we win. Before the game, in an attempt to get the debentured home support in the mood – reserved seats, reserved expressions to match – there is a pageant from some of Mel MacGibson's extras, complete with Saltires, flaming torches and burst-sofa hairpieces.

While welcoming the victory, Hugh MacDonald in the *Herald* notes: 'The Murrayfield experience can be very strange . . . It is not for those who hold hopes for an inclusive, modern Scotland. I thought the Edinburgh wind was sending a chill up my back until I realised it was merely a cringe induced by the cast of *Braveheart* leaping about before kick-off.'

But if we cringe, the English whinge. This is Martin Johnson in the *Telegraph*: 'There is something slightly immature about using a rugby match to air centuries-old grievances . . . It is hard on the face of it to see how the Scots can get so fired up by singing that terrible dirge 'Flower Of Scotland' . . . The Welsh, the Irish and the French also have grievances against the English [but] the Scots are the only ones to have an anthem entirely devoted to them.'

It's exactly this reaction – from an Englishman – that makes me want to acclaim *Braveheart* as a cinematic masterpiece. You see, it's that rare thing: an epic of subtlety and restraint, a tale torn from the pages of history books and told without bombast or sentimentality, in the great traditions of Hollywood *vérité*.

Setting the *Record* Straight

The first time my father told me about it, the fabled newspaper headline went like this: 'DUNDEE MAN DROWNS AT SEA: 1,500 ALSO DIE AS *TITANIC* HITS ICEBERG.'

Later I heard about alternatives, 'ABERDEENSHIRE MAN . . .' and 'BROUGHTY FERRY MAN . . .' The fact there are so many versions of the headline suggests it is probably apocryphal. But to my mind the rivalry also hints at a perverse pride in the most parochial pronouncement in the history of the print press. We don't deny it ever appeared. We keep mentioning it. We're not embarrassed by it. We want it to be true. Yet another claim to fame, or infamy.

The *Daily Record* does not think of itself as parochial. For years it has been the paper of the working man – and required reading for the country's leaders. For years it has been the best-selling title in Scotland. But during the World Cup summer, after a long and bitter circulation war with the Scottish *Sun* culminating in claim and counterclaim over which paper was the true voice of Scotland, it is finally caught and overtaken by its rival.

In another life, I worked for the *Record*. The paper is based in Glasgow, which is as far in the mind from Edinburgh as England is from Scotland. As a sensitive middle-class lad from the east coast I wasn't really cut out for the rough and tumble of the tabloid scene down by the banks of the River Clyde. In Glasgow, they serve fish and chips with vinegar, not brown sauce as in Edinburgh, and, even more disorientating, the sausages are square-shaped.

But I like to think I learned a few things during my four years there. When the disabled work-experience lad deserts his post and the cry goes up from the newsdesk, 'Where's the bloody raspberry ripple?', you are certainly toughened up.

I was employed by the features department, which demanded of its staff exclusive interviews with big Scottish stars, every day. The really big ones, such as Billy Connolly and Robbie Coltrane, didn't speak to the paper and Bobby Carlyle joined that exclusive club after a hack 'doorstepped' his wedding. When the reporter was later roughed up, and the culprits claimed to be friends of Carlyle, the *Record*'s editor was appalled. He decided to 'defend' his reporter in the tabloid way – with a highly scientific test of public sympathy. A cardboard cut-out was lugged onto the streets of Glasgow and bus-stop queues were asked: 'Do you want to punch our Rick?' Unfortunately quite a few ordinary and presumably law-abiding people did.

If you couldn't find a Scottish star then you 'put a kilt' on one. This involved locating some obscure Caledonian ancestry. At movie publicity junkets at London's Dorchester Hotel I squirmed when I heard Scottish tabloid reporters ask of distinguished Hollywood actresses: 'Have you ever tasted haggis?' But it quickly became apparent that if I was going to keep my job, beggars for bylines couldn't be choosers.

I wasn't exactly the top dog on the showbiz beat at the *Record*; mangy mutts like me had to scrabble around in Soapland for our stories. Apparently, when on stage, Phil Lynott of Thin Lizzy used to casually enquire: 'Any girls here tonight got some Irish in them?' Then, in response to the squeals, he'd say: 'Any of you want a little more?' This was the approach suggested to me when I was to interview the *Neighbours* actress Kimberley Davies. I resisted, but managed to put a kilt on the 'telly turn-on' by forcing out of her the confession that, yes, somewhere along the line, she had Scottish antecedence. Another scoop for Smith. Another victory for Scotland.

Slowly – ploddingly slowly – I got the hang of working for a paper that branded itself 'Scotland's Champion'. I understood that one of its guiding principles was making Scots feel good about themselves. And of course one of the ways to make Scots feel better about living among the heart disease world champs, in the top lung cancer hotspot, next to so many victims of cirrhosis of the liver, was to try to undermine England's supremacy on the sports field.

Kimberley Davies' kilt was metaphorical; I never actually got to dress her in one. But I did put one on Will Carling. Highland dress was hired on expenses, and a room booked at London's Claridge's Hotel, so we could get amazing shots of the England rugby captain – 'Bumface' to the *Record*'s readership – reclaiming his 'Scottish roots'. The stunt was an attempt to throw the England camp into chaos the day before the annual clash with Scotland. It didn't work; England won.

The *Record* is really a football paper, though, so I wrote stories about great advances in camera definition proving to our complete satisfaction – yes, finally, at last – that The Goal That Wasn't A Goal should indeed have been disallowed.

Before he died I got Kenneth Wolstenholme to admit that while his name, voice and anxiety about pitch invaders may have forever made him synonymous with 1966, his place in commentator immortality was slightly tarnished by the assertion at another final whistle: 'They'll be dancing in the streets of Raith tonight.' Raith, as every Scot knows, isn't a place; the Rovers of Fife play in Kirkcaldy.

But my Watergate – my Bob Woodward moment (we share the same birthday) – concerned Jimmy Hill. The man Scots love to hate was to be the subject of an exploding cigar gag for the BBC's Comic Relief. Alan Hansen was on the same spoof panel of pundits; thanks to his involvement the story could be written up as long-overdue revenge for Hill refusing to recognise Scotland as a football superpower. By faintly devious means I managed to get hold of a still picture of the great moment.

Result: still the only front-page splash of my national newspaper career.

These 'exclusives' at English expense kept me in a job. Of course they were first in the pile the following day for fish-and-chip wrapping (hold the vinegar). But I wasn't writing them against my will. I enjoyed perpetuating half-truths and pumping up myths. And those four years must have had some bearing on my prevailing view of Scotland, and England.

'DUNDEE MAN DROWNS AT SEA' is a classic Scottish headline. 'SCOT CHEERS ON ENGLAND' is just bonkers.

How it Stacks up for Sven

England are going to Germany with a lame-duck coach. In January, just five months before the World Cup, Sven-Goran Eriksson falls for the oldest journalistic wheeze in the book – the fake-sheikh sting – and his greed, dishonour and sleekitness are laid bare over pages one to seven of the *News Of The World*.

Following the revelations – 'Sven's Dirty Deals: £15m To Quit England And He Will Tap Up Becks' – the Football Association announce he will leave the post after Germany. Sacking him is not an option. He earns so much that the compensation would cripple the game's governing body.

So Eriksson's rock 'n' roll reign – much more Guns N' Roses than anyone expected of a gnomic Swede in elevated shoes – will come to an end. He began in spectacular fashion: the 5-1 demolition of Germany in 2001 was England's first win on their great rivals' turf for forty years. Now it's forty years since Serene Bobby and You-Know-What. What are his chances of overcoming the hoodoo, of slaying the dragon? In the previous two tournaments, England were last-eight wimp-outs. In both quarter-finals they led. Both times they were reeled in and snagged up in crafty meshing. Luiz Felipe Scolari – 'Big Phil' – coach of first Brazil then Portugal, even looks like a big-game fisherman.

When the big matches came round, England under Eriksson didn't have it. At key moments the players looked to the coach for ideas and the coach peered through his funny specs at his raised shoes. He lacked passion. He lacked courage. So there remains a serious doubt about his ability to motivate and inspire.

Oh, for some of the risk-taking that has characterised every other aspect of his England tenure. The business with the sheikh, obviously, when he criticised his players and plotted for his next job. Consorting with Manchester United and Chelsea before that. Also, the commercial opportunism. While pledging his commitment to delivering England the main prize, he finds time for a number of endorsements including *The Sven-Goran Eriksson Classical Collection*, a CD of Svennis-approved mood music.

More risky still was the affair with Ulrika Jonsson. And the affair with Faria Alam, the FA secretary (who also had an affair with FA chief executive Mark Palios). He had played away – spectacularly – and that might have done for him. Instead his fiery Italian girlfriend, Nancy Dell'Olio, chucked some plates around and poured herself into a red-spangled catsuit to stand by her man. Then Eriksson's salary was more than doubled to £4.5 million, forty-five times that of the prime minister. Overpaid, oversexed and (still, very) over here.

Lame duck or Toilet Duck? Eriksson's domestic fastidiousness was revealed in Alam's kiss 'n' tell ('I Had Palios On One Side Eyeing Me Up And Sven On The Other Feeling My Leg') when she described how, before having sex, he insisted on loading the dishwasher.

In the TV splurge of World Cup programming, there's a Channel 4 film called *Sven: The Coach, The Cash . . . And His Lovers*. Director Alison Jackson cleverly mimics CCTV and telephoto intrusion to capture the 'private moments' of the rich and famous with the help of actors. Here she snatches 'Sven' manning the dishwasher, the ludicrous stud in his Y-fronts and socks. We see him grope 'Ulrika' at the fridge while she covers her countryman with yoghurt and – Swedish treat – herring. Then, after the real Faria remembers her 'very giving lover', we see his lookalike giving it to her body double on the same FA conference table round which the blazered bufties of the governing body were first persuaded by a Scot – former chief executive Adam Crozier – to hire him as coach.

What do I feel, as a Scot, about Sven and the way England treat him? The natural inclination is to laugh, to wonder if the appointment was all a fiendish Scottish plot. But, getting involved in the English cause, as I'm obliged to do, I'm beginning to have some sympathy for the man.

He's disliked and distrusted for a large part because he's foreign. The affairs, especially the one involving Ulrika-ka, the top pin-up from the mid-1990s when football first got sexy, may have improved his credibility on the terraces, but the rest of England seems appalled by the dalliances. They want their England manager to behave like a saint and talk like Greavesie. As Giles Smith puts it in *The Times*: 'Sven has always been judged . . . by people who appear to confuse the status of England coach with that of the Pope and hold him to standards of personal and professional conduct that would be risible anywhere beyond the highest of public positions.'

It was ever thus. Graham Taylor was likened to a turnip, Glenn Hoddle to the loony prophet David Icke, Kevin Keegan to the crap comic Bobby Ball. Early on, Eriksson remarked of his predecessors: 'They were more or less killed, all of them.'

Do England really want to win this World Cup? You'd think not, judging by some of Eriksson's press. 'England muck up' seems to be a much better story than 'England triumph'. You wonder if other nations find the glory in despair like this, and are quite as fond of self-flagellation. Simon Barnes, also in *The Times*, says not. 'The combination of an out-of-control tabloid press and a readership that thrills to the destruction of the head coach is something no other country can offer,' he writes.

An amateur psychologist might speculate on the English attitude to the national football team being not dissimilar to the English attitude to sex. There's this tremendous obsession with it but, at the end of the day (Brian), they don't actually like it very much.

All Points South

I'm on a train, on my way to my very first England match. Father, forgive me.

David Beckham and the boys are limbering up for the World Cup against the faded aristocrats of Uruguay. The friendly is at Anfield because the new Wembley isn't ready. I'm not ready. Not for Ingerland.

The Scotland I've left behind is covered in snow. The Scotland team I've left behind are frozen out of the World Cup. Scotland do play tonight, but only in a support role. They are fodder for Switzerland – also A-listers in Germany. *Switzerland?* What did they give us? As Orson Welles remarked in *The Third Man*: 'The cuckoo clock.' Oh, and the Toblerone. Toblerone vs the telephone (to say nothing of other Scottish inventions such as the suspender, capitalism and Bovril)? In terms of contribution to the greater good, it's no contest.

There is one immediate and crucial difference between Scotland games and England games. For a Scotland match, I could be minding my own business, across the other side of the country, without a care in the world (or the World Cup). A couple of hours before kick-off I'll be jumped from behind, bundled into the back of a van smelly with desperate sweat and rotting fish, marched up to the Hampden turnstiles with cold steel pressed against my neck, then ordered to wave my arms around for the entire ninety minutes to make the paltry crowd look bigger. England friendlies, on the other hand, tend to sell out without recourse to the fireworks display, the dancing-girl sideshow or indeed the press gang.

I didn't realise this until I logged on to TheFA.com website to try and buy a ticket. I imagined that for a wintry night in February, there wouldn't be a problem getting hold of one. I presumed that the nation – England – would still be in thrall to club football and ITV's *Dancing On Ice*.

Previously on this programme, former England goalie David 'Safe Hands' Seaman dropped his skating partner. Some of us were willing him to top this and fling her into the carpentry box (flashback to some ancient enactment of the Olympics, and a sign-off from skate supremo Alan Weeks heard only by my father and therefore very possibly a lie: '. . . And now over to Harry *Commentator* in the *carpentry* box.')

The game is sold out. This is such an alien concept for a Scot. But hang on, that means the game is sold out for Sven-Goran Eriksson, even after the fake-sheikh sting, despite the Toilet Duck image. Sold out for David Beckham, despite the David Beckham image. And sold out, too, for Gary Neville and Rio Ferdinand, back at Anfield so soon after the Liverpool-Manchester United FA Cup tie where enmity between the two sides plumbed new depths, with Liverpool fans trying to overturn the ambulance ferrying United's badly injured Alan Smith to hospital.

Sold out? Surely in England there's still a north-south divide. I'd read how the Liverpool international Roger Hunt, a hero of 1966, used to get booed by London fans who accused him of taking Jimmy Greaves' place in the team. ('They forgot it was Geoff [Hurst], because he scored the hat-trick,' recalled Ray Wilson, the left back. 'It was embarrassing. Roger stopped playing for England, told Alf [Ramsey] he'd had enough.')

Surely England fans put club loyalty before any other. I mean, who actually supports the national team? At the 1966 World Cup Final – my first game of any kind, watched on TV, and of all the matches in which a Scot had to be blooded – the crowd was lots of men in short back and sides and collars and ties and you would never have believed that the 1960s were just about to swing.

In the 1970s, when England didn't qualify for World Cups and Scotland did, and Scottish fans stormed Wembley every other year, the answer was: 'Nobody.'

In the 1980s, it was the hooligans, from the Euro Championships of 1980, when you could barely see the action on the pitch for the Turin *polizia*'s tear gas and water cannon, all the way back to Italia '90, when the team, by then football's pariahs, were dumped in Sicily in the hope the thugs could be better controlled on an island. They weren't.

But since Euro '96, so we're told, it's been anyone and everyone. Ordinary, decent fans could cram into a crumbling Wembley and sing 'Football's Coming Home', a song with minor chord changes of a cheap potency and a major message:

> We invented the game, just like we used to rule the world. The Empire has gone – dashed bad luck – and with it our faith that in football, the English way, is the best way. Those fiendish Hungarians put an end to that in 1953. But in 1966 we fixed it so we could win the World Cup. Here we are hosting another major tournament. 1966, 1996. Dig that crazy symmetry. Maybe, if we play all our games at Wembley again, we can win again. And when it's England we all rally round the flag, don't we? Well, don't we . . . ?

I was *haein' ma doots* about this. On Radio 1 this morning, Chris Moyles was slagging off England supporters for not being patriotic enough. Maybe, this once and only once, he has a point. Take the example of Roger Nouveau Football Fan.

Roger was the character in the 1990s BBC comedy series *The Fast Show* who mocked football's new, improved sexiness. Within the space of a thirty-second sketch, he could swap clubs three times. For the joke to be funny, Roger had to be rooted in reality. The inference was that the new breed of 'supporter' regarded football as a fashion statement and had no real empathy with the game. In short, that the sport's cool rating was a sham.

In wee countries with big dreams it is possible for fans to come together as one. In Scotland forty years ago, and for a good while afterwards, the football public seemed to do this. If you couldn't be at Hampden in person you were certainly there in spirit. My dad's friend, the screenwriter Alan Sharp, who went on to script the Hollywood version of *Rob Roy*, always wore a dark blue strip under his jumper – this was pre-replica shirts – just in case an SOS was tannoyed across the terraces: 'Can anyone in tonight play centre forward?'

But for the last few years it's been a popular sideshow to the football to taunt fans of our two biggest clubs, Celtic and Rangers, over their lack of commitment to the national side. The Old Firm don't care about Scotland. They think their cause is greater. Their players develop 'groin strains' on the eve of internationals, only to miraculously heal in time for the next ritual slaughter of Inverness Caley Thistle or St Mirren. The best indigenous talent at provincial clubs is bought and mostly ruined by the Old Firm. Celtic and Rangers no longer want to play in Scotland, believing the English Premiership is gagging for them. Their bigoted fans sing songs about Ireland instead of Scotland. Nowadays the average Tartan Army foot soldier will support East Fife or Queen of the South. And so Scotland has become a little bit more anglicised.

In England, I can't imagine fans of the biggest Premiership clubs – Man U, Chelsea and Arsenal – all walking out their front doors to join the big, friendly, joyous throng at the top of their streets, all marching in Lowryesque fashion to the game. Tonight, I might meet boys from the Mersey en route to Anfield, but I do not expect to complete the set as described in Elvis Costello's 'Oliver's Army' and encounter boys from the Thames and the Tyne as well. It won't be one nation under a groove, one size fits all. I don't believe the hype about this England team, never mind the even crazier symmetry of 1966 and 2006. I don't think I'm alone in that.

My train passes through Carlisle. Carlisle United used to have a player called Ray Train. I know this because when you grew up in the 1970s like I did, the kipper-tied omnipresence of Jimmy Hill and Brian Moore meant you had no option *but* to know about English football, even in the outer reaches, the frontier towns, the one-season-in-the-top-flight wonders.

What else do I know? That Reading used to have a player called Terry Bell. In first year at my secondary school everyone chose an obscure English side to support from afar, and Reading were mine (making them my eighth or ninth English team). I also know that Orient's match programmes are the size of pub beer mats, or they were when I bought a fusty 'starter bundle' wrapped in newspaper from Steve Earle, the mail-order king. And I know that every Saturday the town of Torquay is in a tumult, or it was when my father and I used to convene on the G Plan for the classified football results. 'Don't tell me,' he would groan, 'Torquay United's game is a late kick-off *again*. Just what *do* they get up to down there?' We speculated about the reasons for the commotion. 'Burst ball,' I would suggest, because to my young mind I couldn't imagine anything worse. Dad's diversions would of course be more inventive, and often quite gruesome: 'Runaway bull on pitch . . . bull gores Torquay chairman's wife, charges off with her bonnet . . . ref takes out gun and shoots bull, it blocks Torquay's goal with Bradford Park Avenue on the attack, they demand a penalty – pandemonium!'

The next time Torquay kicked off late we'd play the game again and I'd repeat Dad's scenario from before and he'd smile and say 'Well done, son!' and let me win. This became a running gag between us, updated in birthday and Christmas cards. In later years I was pretty pleased with 'A stage of *Death Race 2000*?' but Dad maintained a high standard to the end of his life: 'A busy market? A stamp fair on market day? The fair being officially opened by "The Major" from Torquay-based comedy classic *Fawlty Towers*?' Hours of endless fun.

As is passing through English towns on the train, listening to the announcements for connecting services, and thinking about what the place names mean to you. Inevitably it's all football-related. For instance, Preston – 26-0, English scoring record, though still some way short of Arbroath's world-best 36-0. Burnley – one-time football aesthetes; now better known as a BNP heartland. Huddersfield – team of Frank Worthington, Elvis impersonator, Northern playboy and occasional footballer, whose brief entry into management wasn't a complete failure, with one of his Tranmere Rovers players declaring: 'At least we all learned how to trap the ball on the back of our necks.' Wigan – home of Northern Soul, the music cult with the football tribe following.

In Wigan today the platforms are empty but it's not hard to imagine them teeming with, well, platforms – a mass of stack heels, high-waisted Oxford bags, tank tops, classic sports holdalls, the fist logo everywhere.

Finally I arrive at Manchester Piccadilly Station. I've got to interview Jason Donovan before I can head over to Liverpool for the game, so I take the free bus service to the Apollo Theatre where the fallen Aussie pop idol is touring in a musical.

In the city centre the shops are full of Easter merchandise and I think of how my father used to dismiss a religious celebration I assumed had universal significance: 'Ach, it's an *English* festival.' (He said this about Christmas, too.) But I like Manchester. It's been the scene of memorable days on the show-biz beat. I saw an edition of *Stars In Their Eyes* filmed here. I watched backstage at Granada TV as camp scenehands of a certain age, nostalgic for the days when all television was taffeta-trimmed and *ba-ba-ba-ba*, pulled the special-effects lever during a rendition of the big song of the day, Celine Dion's 'My Heart

Will Go On'. And when dry ice enveloped the stage, I heard one of them squeal, without the merest hint of irony: 'Roger, it's *just* like the Atlantic!'

A fog shrouds the city today. On the bus journey, people talk to each other in a way that never happens in London or, it must be said, Edinburgh. And the chat from the local celebs has always been good – or at least it has always seemed so at the time.

Badly Drawn Boy got me drunk in Chorlton. Mark E. Smith of The Fall got me drunk in Prestwich. The comedian Peter Kay gave me a guided tour of his native Bolton: the branch of Boots where his future wife worked, the nightclub where, as a bouncer, he refused *Coronation Street*'s Des Walker admission because he was wearing white jeans, and finally his bedroom at his mum's house with the box of tissues handily placed by the bed and the videos piled right up to the ceiling. 'Don't show them in your photograph,' he cautioned me, 'or I'll get me *Genesis: Invisible Touch* nicked.' And the poet Simon Armitage, technically a Yorkshireman but with his heart very much in Manchester – and United – helpfully defined my nationality for me: 'Being Scottish – it's a cause, isn't it?'

All four are English – Northern English. A four-man defence of my favourite dramatists would be of the same stock: the Alans Bleasdale and Bennett, Ian La Frenais and his sidekick – and, all right, adopted Northerner – Dick Clement. From Bleasdale in Liverpool they would spread out across the Pennines, keeping a high line all the way to Newcastle.

There are doubtless some fine writers in the south but many, like Rio Ferdinand, who later this year will launch himself onto the literary scene as the author of *Rio: My Story*, lack self-scrutiny. A Man U player but London-born, Ferdinand doesn't appreciate the difference between talking a good game and playing one, between fannying around with the ball and just hoofing it, and between compulsory drugs testing and shopping for bedlinen.

Even Eriksson, for whom he seems one of the Great Uncriticisables, felt the need to call him 'lazy' while being duped by the fake sheikh. Within the golden generation the coach has created an even more exclusive club – let's call them the 'platinum ponces' – and Ferdinand seemed to have all the necessary accreditation. Maybe, though, Eriksson is getting tough.

On the short train journey to Liverpool after my interview, I'm thinking of all I've learned about the Northern perspective and how it might inform my attempt at an English accent while I haggle with a ticket tout. But just as I arrive at Lime Street Station I get a call from my paper's sports desk that a press-box seat has become available. Aha! This England team are not so must-see, after all! The clamour to be at their *third-last* fixture before Germany is actually quite resistible.

Liverpool is a city with a pulse powered by football's ebb and flow; no Liverpudlian is allowed to be vague or non-committal about its rival clubs. I didn't have Ken Dodd down as a football fan before interviewing him. But, to help secure us a table in a crowded restaurant, Doddy introduced me as 'a direct descendant of the great Bill Shankly himself, God rest his soul.' Football is the currency here.

Like Manchester and Glasgow, but not London or my Edinburgh, Liverpool is full of comedians. I get in a taxi to find myself sharing it with a small boy and a three-legged dog. 'He doesn't bite like,' says the driver. (Come on, I'm thinking, make with the punchline.) 'But the lad's got rabies and hasn't eaten for a week. Now, where to, mate?'

'Anfield.'

'Ah,' he says recognising the accent, 'the home of football. Well I won't call you "Jock" on account of the fact Crazy Horse used it *derogatoredly*, like. But you lot gave us Shanks and we love ya for that.'

Crazy Horse of course was Emlyn Hughes, ex-Liverpool

captain, midfield rampager and wind-up merchant supreme. Of all the England players of his era, he seemed to revel the most in victories over Scotland. If he'd only made the one reference to 'Jocks' in his entire career that would have been sufficient for us to demonise him, installing him as an Ugly Sister alongside Jimmy Hill in the pantomime warm-up for the great rivalry.

In the Everton district, as half a dozen England fans pose for photos waving Union Jacks beneath the sign for the New Derry Social Club, the cabbie asks me about the day job. '*Scotchland On Sunday*? Is that the paper full of these letters from desperate women . . . the ones who've run out of knitting wool?'

'No, that's the *Sunday Post*.'

He asks about my book which he presumes will be a slim volume, much like the *Swiss Book Of Naval Victories* and – ha ha – the *Everton Book Of European Cup Wins*. Finally, he drops me within sight of the famous old ground. As I shut the cab door, the boy, who sat in bemused silence throughout the journey, is asking his dad why 'that one spoke funny, like'. With no Scots in the Liverpool team now, the Scottish accent must be alien to his generation.

Like small, squat defenders marking a tall striker at a corner kick, the red-brick houses around Anfield hunker up hard and tight to the ground. The roads are dark and some have exotic names. At the end of Vienna Street a middle-aged woman – caked-on make-up, tower of blonde hair, *nightgown* – is standing in her doorway telling a policeman that, no luv, she's not working tonight. As a prozzie? I think of Wayne Rooney and wonder how he'll play.

A souvenir stall flogs the just-launched 'Spirit of '66' red England shirt for £29.99. That's cheap for a strip; it must be a copy, with gold numbering which soon peels off. It does, though, bear the gold star above the crest – an elitist touch (Uruguay, who have won twice as many World Cups as England, will modestly take the field starless). This huckster is selling Ingerland by the pound: bucket hats cost £8.99, teddy bear mascots £12.99 and David Beckham towels, a bargain at £14.99.

The pub across the road, the Albert, promises a 'hearty welcome'. I could do with a drink to steel myself for the game and so step inside. It's rammed. Lots of shaved heads. A square-shaped Ingerlander in a Burberry baseball cap stands on a table to lead the community singing:

No surrender
No surrender
No surrender to the IRA

On second thoughts maybe I'll just get to the game nice and early, like all the saddos with their travel rugs.

I head round to the players' entrance where a large crowd has gathered. The fans are like pop tribes in their clamour, surging forward when a bus pulls up. This one is carrying the Uruguayan team. ('Boo!') Then a sleek car arrives – it's Nancy Dell'Olio, Eriksson's girlfriend.

One of Our Cilla's Mucky Kids: 'Nancy, I love ya!'

Nancy: 'Thank you!'

Mucky Kid: 'Show us yer rat, then!'

Rat? That's what I think the lad said. He's gone in a flash before I can check. Like a rat up a drainpipe. It could have been 'rack', the Saturday name for a woman's embonpoint, which is more universal, but I prefer to think the boy has a pudenda agenda, complete with exclusively Scouse terminology.

I am only a few yards from the media entrance at Anfield but the sheer mass of England-style humanity is blocking the door. The stewards tell the hacks they must approach from another direction involving a trudge round the houses. As I don't know where I'm going, I follow Brian Woolnough from the *Daily Star*. Woolnough takes charge of Sky Sport's *Sunday Supplement* even though it's supposed to be Jimmy Hill's show. Filing the shortest bulletins of all the journos, he's not prone to faffing. He's incredibly tall and difficult to lose. For all these reasons I reckon he's my best hope of finding my way.

A couple of young reporters I don't recognise tag along as well, including one who's phoning in copy on the hoof, re Frank Lampard's fitness. 'The 27-year-old has had a scan . . . hoping to be fit for Chelsea's date with destiny in the Nou Camp . . . no, Nou *Camp. Camp*. As in . . . as in . . . *Colin and friggin' Justin*.'

'*Who?* Bloody hell, they're the mincers who do that home makeover show, the *Jock poofs*.'

Finally, at long last, as the tunnel legend has it, 'This Is Anfield'. A silver-haired commissionaire ushers us into one of the media rooms. These rooms didn't exist before; they've been hollowed out of the bowels of football grounds to accommodate the sport's incredible success, and its incredible conceit. They're always low-ceilinged affairs, and fit to bursting with hacks eager to grill Eriksson under TV lights which bounce off his rimless specs and cause his large forehead to gleam with sweat. But right now, while the coach briefs his players, the journos make do with meat on sticks as part of the complimentary pre-match buffet and engage in transfer-rumour chit-chat.

I scan the room for my favourite hack-packer . . . the one on the cases of Eriksson and Beckham most often . . . there he is: James Lawton of the *Independent*, gratifyingly less coiffured than in his byline pic. One of Rod Stewart's old grey raincoats won't let him down.

'Lawto' apart, most of the hacks look prosperous; following the progress of this England team clearly has its compensations. The footwear of choice – apart from the man from the *Guardian* who sports trendy trainers – is an expensive loafer, suede and low-slung, of the type you just couldn't wear in Scotland in February.

Paul Wilson of the *Observer* and Martin Samuel of *The Times* are others on whom I can depend for the dashed-off damning piece. Some of these guys are incredibly hard on the team, the manager, the FA, often all three in a single sentence. They can be searingly lukewarm about England, ferocious in the manner they deliver the unconvinced shrug. Normally I love this stuff, but now I must try and be more positive about England, to look for the good in this team and not blame them for the sins of their fathers. Sorry to my father for that.

It's almost kick-off and England's sneering chroniclers soft-shoe shuffle their way up to the press box. I'm in front of Terry Butcher and behind Graham Taylor: a former England hero and a less than illustrious ex-England manager. Alan Smith, another player-turned-pundit, asks me a question. It's a voice familiar from TV but, in person, the Midlands accent is so thick that I cannot understand what he's saying until he points at the shiny document in my hand.

'The *prew*-gramme. Where did *yew* get it?'

I've met all the giants of showbiz, oh yes: Frank Carson, Dannii Minogue (three times) and the always-out-of-shot 'feed' for Dick Emery's catchphrase: 'Oo, you are awful . . . but I like you!' Now, finally, at last, I've met my first England footballer.

My seat is in a spillover area of the press box. On my left is the man from Uruguay's *El Observador*; the desk to my right is empty. It's reserved for *Shoot!* who dismayingly haven't turned up. Once upon a time, *Shoot!* and in particular the player Q&As (Car: Ford Capri; favourite food: steak and chips; likes: winning; dislikes: losing) was my dream job.

The Kop looks smaller than on TV. It doesn't sway or sing the Beatles songbook any more, but it's still a great football vantage point, so: respect. It has witnessed many electric nights, even one or two involving Scots: Graeme Souness skin grafts, Kenny Dalglish arse swivels, Joe Jordan's handball which, crazily, gloriously, earned a World Cup-qualifying penalty for Scotland. But tonight the Kop is packed for England and in good voice:

England till I die
I'm England till I die
I know I am I'm sure I am
I'm England till I die

It's bitterly cold but many fans are in their strips. There are so many whiteshirts that I suddenly feel very Scottish and very small, like Ronnie Corbett when his view is completely dominated by No. 2 English Pin-Up Madeline Smith's milky cleavage.

The balconies between the upper and lower levels of the stands are ideal for draping banners. The flag of choice at England games now is the Cross of St George. On the horizontal bar of every flag, the names of towns and teams are proclaimed in white. Tonight's roll call includes places I've never heard of (Flitwick, Halesworth, Leigh-on-Sea). There are places with comedy names which my father persuaded me he had made up until I heard Les Dawson cracking jokes about them (Scunthorpe, Cleethorpes, Giggleswick). And there are teams that have become part of football's 'disappeared' (Blackpool, Stoke City, Luton Town). But there is no representation from Chelsea or any of the other big knobs.

Que sera, sera
Whatever will be, will be
We're going to Ger-man-ee
Que sera, sera

Indeed 'we' are. And for that these fans are extremely grateful. Eriksson walks round the perimeter of the pitch before kick-off and is cheered; the fans in the front rows are even eager to touch his hem.

I expected the musical director of *The Sven-Goran Eriksson Classical Collection* (RRP £14.99) to get a cooler reception, given this is the first international since his encounter with the joke-shop sheikh. But it seems everyone here is happy to forget about that, and about the disappointments of the previous two tournaments. They appear to have bought the hype, the dream and the £14.99 David Beckham towel as well. They *believe* (© Mars Inc.)

Beckham is standing in the centre circle now, hands on the shoulders of a mascot, and . . . this is quite a moment for me, to find myself in the presence of the man after all this time, and all that jeering from my sofa.

He's masterful at these official duties: the pennant exchange, the meet 'n' greet, the smiles for the cameras. He must love the line-ups for the dignitaries because the other twenty-one players are static, just the way he likes them. How he must wish that the games themselves were like this, though Eriksson is confident the world will see 'the best' of his captain in Germany.

Tonight's big cheeses are – drum roll – 'the Football Association'. Hang on: the game's governing body in England presenting the team to themselves? Isn't that a bit self-regarding? But then you look at the giant banner covering the entire centre circle: 'TheFA.com'. Then you look at the balcony: the flags have been removed, presumably under stewards' orders, and the hoardings now read 'TheFA.com' right round the stadium. This, according to the irritating Americanism, is 'Team England'.

The latest enactment of the people's game (ha ha) begins and Steven Gerrard is first to show. He's taller than he looks on TV, and with Gigantor strides, covers the distance between the halfway line and the Uruguayan penalty box in a nanosecond. He just eats up the turf.

The play is fast, much faster than I'm used to in the Scottish Premier League. My friend David Whittle had told me about trips to watch Arsenal with his son – having failed miserably to interest the lad in the 'family team' Hearts – and how the pace of the matches took the breath away. I doubted this; probably I didn't want to believe it.

When you've watched football played a certain way, the

Scottish way, for the best part of four decades, you are not exactly gagging to see with your own eyes an English version this effortless, this super-slick. So for a few moments I'm probably a bit stunned. I don't like what I'm watching but it is undeniably impressive.

It doesn't last.

Rio Ferdinand genuinely believes himself to be one of the flair players, But when the star of *Rio's World Cup Wind-Ups* takes time out from his hectic schedule to attempt an outrageous 180-degree pivot on the run well inside the Uruguayan half, he emerges on the other side without the ball. His opponent looks at him as if to say, with apologies to noted 1980s philosophers Duran Duran: 'Your name is Rio and your head is full of sand.'

Then Uruguay show Ferdinand how it's done, scoring with a biffing drive from twenty-five yards. Suddenly England are toiling and Wayne Rooney is hurling himself into tackles he has only a thirty-seventy chance of winning.

Rooney gives the impression he used to work in a circus, a stunted strongman as wide as he is tall who was discovered by Eriksson tipping over trucks. The England team is a kind of circus anyway, so the tenacious troll quickly fitted in. Eriksson – Sven-Goran Barnum, the ringleader – gives the other acts time off when Rooney is in the mood. They stand back to watch him chase hopeless causes and breenge into opposition players. The Croxteth force of football nature is fearless, but right at this moment, aimless as well.

Where's the captain? Beckham, the heir to Serene Bobby, is on my side of the field in the first half so I feel privileged to witness this inglorious cameo at close quarters: a corner from the fabled right foot fails to beat the first man . . . the ball comes back to him but again his cross hits the defender. Beckham gives chase. Pretty boy – ugly runner. He sticks out a bandy leg and hacks the man down. This happens directly in front of me. I see him scowl at the ref, sneer at his yellow card as if to say: 'Do you know who I am?' Something derisory half forms in my mouth, then I remember where I am. The press box is supposed to be impartial. The man from *El Observador* smiles at me as if to say: 'Fool, this is the way football is. Beckham is God, thirty-seven per cent of the English public think so, ITV produces ninety-minute hagiographies about him, that once-great paper of record, the London *Times*, sucks up to him something terrible, and his posterful face could sell you an *eight*-bladed razor. In the commercials your facial hair may be magnified so it looks like the spikes which impaled horses in ancient combat, but King David will ride straight over them. Resistance is futile.'

In the second half Beckham gets to fire in a few free kicks. At the moment the ball is struck, flashbulbs go off all round Anfield, but surely only in the manner of tourists dully pointing at what everyone else is pointing at. He's like *The Mousetrap*, an English icon, still going strong but no one can remember why.

These days the people come to watch more in hope than expectation. If we keep the circus analogy going, Beckham is down to his very last trick: 'Roll up, roll up! Gasp At The Incredible Free-Kick Man!' The ageing illusionist's powers are waning. He's not the only one who can do this stunt now (dead ball, whipped, get it up and down); in fact, he never was. He's struggling to keep up with players with a better strike rate who also do that crazy dribbling thing and is reduced to performing from memory. The crowd ooh and aah like in the old days but something about their response has changed. I'm reminded of that Harry Houdini biopic with Tony Curtis bidding for immortality while manacled, upside down, in the water chamber. It seems to be death or glory with Beckham now, and the punters will cheerfully take death.

Or is that just me?

It *is* just me. The England faithful are on their feet to acclaim a late comeback as if it's their divine right, as if this really is to be their year. The equaliser is scored by Peter Crouch, subject of much scepticism. The beanpole striker is another carnival act, a freak-show escapee and the most inappropriately named footballer since Kilmarnock's less than fortress-like defender, Danny Invincibile. I mean, when does the six-feet-seven-inch Peter ever *crouch*? His billing is: 'Be Astonished And Amazed By Giraffe Man!'

And Joe Cole hits the winner. In Circus England, the big top with so many marquee names, he's the cute one in charge of the dodgem rides who has the local girls fantasising about being groped up the back of the shooting range, his rough, oily hands all over them. In the movie version Cole would be played by David Essex with an earring and a red-spotted neckerchief. Does this metaphor have any more life in it – can I keep those plates spinning? 'Oh what a circus,' sang Essex once, 'oh what a show.'

This was only a moderate show by Circus England. Friendlies are fraudulent affairs: they're not real games. And, stuck in the press box, I couldn't meet real fans.

I came to Anfield to scoff and some of the big fancy-dan names were obligingly unimpressive. That's probably as good a start to my England tour of duty as I could have hoped for.

And here's a funny thing. Confronted by the whiteshirts like this, up-close and in 3-D, the FA beaks drooling at their awesome box-office power and the swooning fan-love enveloping the stadium like a £14.99 David Beckham towel, I feel more attached to the Scotland team than I have been for some time.

Now I want to say sorry. Sorry for not supporting Scotland with more fervour. Sorry for the times I laughed when they mucked up. And sorry for that desperate afternoon in 2002 when on a godforsaken hillside, a place where it seemed that only death happened, my country found themselves two goals down to the joke footballers of the Faroe Islands and I was urging them on to their worst defeat in history, one that would have plunged the nation into darkness, so I could experience what a hundred years' sleep, *Brigadoon*-style, felt like. Sorry, Scotland, sorry.

But it's already too late for apologies. I'm going to Ger-man-ee, *que sera, sera* – with the whiteshirts.

Weller for Men

Now I'm dreaming about England footballers. The other night, it was Keith Weller in the FA Cup, in the deep midwinter – in white ballet tights. Leicester City were away to Ice Station Zebra – the tie no one wanted. In perishing conditions, the mercury had frozen. The man from the *Leicester Mercury* had frozen, entombed in a giant Glacier Mint while phoning in his match report. But *still* Weller continued to glide across the skating-rink surface, the (orange) ball Araldite-d to his right boot as he triple-salchowed past big, skittering defenders.

Worse than these dreams, when I wake to look at my wife-to-be, her head on the pillow, her hair arranged in an elaborate combover – it's a style from a time when rugs really had to be tied down, because winters were winters, not the wimpish, nanny-state kind we have now, and pitches were pitches and if they weren't rock hard, the mud was flying everywhere – when I look at Lucy I *still* can't get England footballers out of my head.

I think I'm marrying Ralph Coates.

Devils in Skirts

I'm Scottish, I'm getting married, so what do I wear? Ah, but it's not as simple as that. You see, I hate the kilt . . .

OK, hate's a bit strong but I can't stand the plastic Scots, professional Scots and porridge-packet poseurs who swing it with such smugness.

Much of the time it's being swung to get one up on the English with their zero national identity, their provisional membership of the international football community (not yet the full licences) and their two-left-feetedness on the dance floor at mixed marriages.

What's not to like about any of that? I know, I should like it all. But, rejecting a highly promising position, that's very Scottish. It was Hugh McIlvanney, the doyen of football writers, who first coined the phrase 'snatching defeat from the jaws of victory'. That's what Scots do.

I've worn the kilt only a handful of times. Not owning one, I've always hired mine from the Edinburgh Royal Mile whigmaleerie emporia which sell a highly romanticised version of my country to the Dwights, Skips and Bart Hockum IIIs visiting 'Skatland' in search of their ancestry.

The sensation of climbing into a skirt wasn't strange or silly, it just wasn't especially memorable. I did not feel like one of the 'devils in skirts' or 'ladies from hell' that were supposed to have terrified the kaiser during the First World War. What was I expecting? To feel heroically Scottish? I don't know.

For those weddings where I was a guest, the selection was

limited and I couldn't find my own tartan – this despite Smith being the most popular name in Scotland. So I queued up with other lads to be fitted with one of the half-dozen available patterns. Some of these poor saps, I thought to myself, were grooms. (Prepare to meet thy groom!) In neighbouring changing booths, 'macs' manqué were being fitted too. We may not have loved the tartan, the boys and me, but we didn't like non-Scots trying it on. The kilt was ours to be ferociously ambivalent about.

Invariably the kilts borrowed for such occasions were knackered and didn't hang right, and because I didn't know whose hurdies these kilts had caressed before I came along, and whose neat-lager sweat they had soaked up during an eightsome reel, I kept my pants on. So I wasn't a 'true Scotsman'? Big deal. I hate that phrase.

The rig-out was always completed by worn-shiny jacket, moth-eaten sporran, bobbly socks and the kind of shoes lacing up the calves that reminded me of another line from *Jock*: 'Wee explosions of custard and mince . . . candy floss at throat and wrist . . . and *chamois leather dancing pumps*.' Dad always laughed when presented with this vision of a decidedly camp ghost-of-Hogmanay-past, reminiscent of the type of prancing fool with fixed grin forever paired with, and totally dominated by, a stout, unsmiling dragon on an Andy Stewart goggle-box heucherama such as *The White Heather Club*, which in World Cup year will be voted one of the twenty worst-ever TV programmes. I can hear Dad laughing still.

Sometimes, when the Scotland-England football rivalry was at its pettiest and also its most life or death, when the Home International Championship was the proper climax to a football season, I was vaguely endeared towards the kilt simply because it was an expression of self the English lacked. And at times when the Sassenachs almost found an expression, such as in 1977 when they draped Union Jacks from the upstairs rooms of their red-bricked crescents and threw street parties to celebrate the queen's Silver Jubilee, the Scottish hordes spoiled things by steaming into London, transforming Wembley into a clan gathering and going extensively mental after a 2-1 win that meant we were, when the title still meant something, champions of Britain. That June afternoon I was patriotic about all things Scottish: crap Scottish weather, crap Scottish food, crap Scottish television (my father's programmes excepted; they were brilliant), the crap caber-tossing movie *Geordie* – everything.

Music-wise, 1977 was the apotheosis of punk, and I was proud that a Scotsman, Jamie Reid, the punk movement's artist-in-resentment, had been responsible for sticking an iconic safety pin through HRH's hooter. But the Tartan Army who plonked Saltires and Lions Rampant in the sacred Wembulee turf were making a bolder statement of punkery. As 70,000 hairy Scotsmen rampaged across the home of English football, the kilt had never looked lovelier.

Three decades ago, Scottish football fans wore the kilt unselfconsciously, with whatever else came to hand. Eventually, an entire uniform was assembled: kilt, white towelling sports socks which had gone grey, many of them purchased 'erra three-pairs-for-a-pound' from the vendors in Glasgow's Argyle Street who only sold hosiery and gas lighters . . . and Adidas Sambas.

This was before trainers became omnipresent. They gave the impression that Scots, not the Joe Jordans but the merely mortal, were always playing football and were ready for a kickabout at any time. Which indeed, back then, they were.

It was a classic look. Or at least it seems so now. But it wasn't contrived. Then, from over yonder glen, the 'galoots' appeared . . .

In the 1970s and 1980s, Scotland had a fine team and loyal fans whose only ostentation was their absurd World Cup dreaming. A short while later the side went into decline, and their failures became something to celebrate.

In Timbys. Rugged boots and chunky socks gave the impression the average Scottish fan had stomped across mountain ranges, engaging in the odd bit of vicious hand-to-hand with murderous tribes, simply to get to the match. The glengarry cap suggested fully paid-up membership of an actual army.

Gregory Burke is the most talked about young playwright in Scotland. In World Cup year, his play Black Watch, a tribute to Scottish military tradition, is the smash hit of the Edinburgh Festival. During his research, he was urged by an uncle who remembered it to read Jock. He ended up doing his own thing – brilliantly.

Black Watch is hugely stirring. But is it the work of a true patriot? Burke has a problem with one very distinct expression of Scottishness: 'I have a real beef with the Tartan Army. It's got all those elements of Scotland that grate on me. It's sanctimonious and very pleased with itself.

'They all think they're Ewan McGregor or Alan Cumming. They're all: "We're the wonderful, glorious Tartan Army and everyone loves us." Really, guys?

'I lived in Dunfermline in the 1980s which means you don't wear [football] colours. Some of my mates were in France for the 1998 World Cup and they got hassle from the Tartan Army who thought they were casuals. My mates were like: "Why would we want to dress like choobs? We wouldn't go out like that in Dunfermline High Street and we're certainly not going to do it on the Champs-Elysées."

'But I suppose I have a very complex relationship with the national teams, Scotland and England. I haven't been to a Scotland game since 1986; it's not me at all. I had a forces childhood and grew up in Gibraltar so used to support England. When I moved to Dunfermline at the age of sixteen I had an English accent.

'I really liked English football in the 1980s when no one else did and it was scarred by hooliganism and crowds were really small. I lived in London for a bit and ended up supporting

Millwall. They were crap but they were real. And as much as football was reviled at that time, a culture did come out of it, for instance the fanzines.

'But in Germany I really want this England team to do as badly as possible. I don't like the players, their money, their ridiculous lifestyles. Football has lost all contact with reality. Basically in this World Cup I want to see millionaires greetin'.'

Braveheart's Mel MacGibson can take some of the rap for the emergence of so many 'warrior nation' poltroons. And how I wish that Russ Abbot had been hung, drawn and quartered, rather than William Wallace.

It was Abbot who created the character C. U. Jimmy, a tedious caricature of a Scot with hair the colour of Irn-Bru under a tam-o'-shanter the size of a manhole cover – deflecting attention from the complete lack of a brain. In the 1980s Abbot was one of the unfunniest men on television. But so little attention was paid to Scotland that even a joke against them – in ITV prime-time as well – was better than being ignored. The look quickly spread to the terraces.

I don't know what is worse: a Scot in a C. U. Jimmy bunnet-and-barnet combo singing 'We're so shite it's unbelievable!', or a Scot with an orangey tan, gym-honed pecs and a smirk which says 'Me? An ambassador for my country? Why thank you . . .' Prat or poser, he is, I will concede, not wholly of his own making: blame must be attached to – who else? – England. When English hooliganism was at its worst, the Scots saw an advantage in good behaviour. The Scots were just as wild in the 1970s but in the following decade they rebranded themselves 'the best-behaved supporters in the world'.

This gave the Scots a rare feeling of superiority over the English and they revelled in it. When England fans disrupted another tournament with their fighting and pub furniture-hurling, the Scots tut-tutted, sympathised with the besieged locals, puffed out their chests some more, planted another

Saltire in the moral high ground . . . and checked the news reports to make sure no one had described the thugs as 'British'.

So let's recap: I squirm at my fellow Scot for being too modest in his aspirations. I squirm when he's too cocky. I squirm when he glories in his team's mediocrity. Whatever he does, he cannot win with me.

I squirm when he presents a dour face. I squirm when he flaunts a sunbed complexion. The English may have no national image, but the Scots can have too much of one. Put a bloody kilt on the Scot as well and he's completely insufferable.

Squirm is the wrong word. It should be cringe. The 'Scottish cringe' is an actual medical condition which has baffled doctors for centuries. Why do Scots – when the country claims it invented rock 'n' roll – put themselves down so much? *Precisely because it claims it invented rock 'n' roll.* This actually happens in World Cup year, a boast quickly rubbished.

Ah, but when a seventeenth-century book written by an Aberdeen grammar school teacher, newly translated, describes a bunch of Scotsmen 'passing' a football – unheard of in 1633 – and this seems to confirm that Scotland *invented the sport*, more than 200 years before the FA was formed, then understandably, *obviously*, that's different. And, as of right now, football joins our long list of gifts to the world.

But there really is no logic to being Scottish for I also squirm when the Scot glories in 1967. This was the year Scotland beat England to become 'unofficial world champions'. I admit to having a blind spot about this 3-2 win on account of missing the game though some pressing business with a girl called Elizabeth Allan (pressing, of my hand in hers, was all we did). But Scots can hardly complain about the English banging on about 1966 when we do the same about a far lesser triumph.

Scotland was obliged to take a dim view of the 1977 pitch invaders. But recently that act of vandalism has been topped by a gang of tartan terrors who carry out their terrible deeds with the blessing of the highest of offices, the Scottish Parliament.

Tartan Week is an attempt to promote Scotland in America and, it follows, the whole wide world. Every spring a planeload of politicians and D-list celebs descend on New York and don kilts for a gruelling week of junketing and partying that makes zero impact on the Big Apple. Back in Scotland, Tartan Week has taken little time to establish itself as a national embarrassment. 'An orgy of self-indulgent, pseudo-Scottishness,' writes the political commentator Brian Wilson in *Scotland On Sunday*.

The event's nadir came in 2004 when Jack McConnell, Scotland's first minister – our prime minister – took to the Manhattan streets in a pinstriped black kilt which he combined with a nancyish ghillie shirt. The desired aim was doubtless to marry old and new Scotlands, the dependable and traditional with the sleek, modern version. But even Sean Connery would struggle to carry off that look. Like *The Office*'s David Brent, McConnell sports a hairstyle which hasn't changed since 1987. He has the figure of a man who, like Brent, eats lunch in his car. He looks like a spivvy salesman.

When pictures of his fashion fuddery were relayed across the Atlantic it's no exaggeration to say that a little part of Scotland died. As 'cringesome' moments go it was right down there with Scotland goalie Stewart Kennedy trying to garrotte himself on his crossbar during England's 5-1 Wembley mauling in 1975. Right down there with Alan Hansen and Willie Miller tackling each other for the ball against Russia and sealing Scotland's fate in the 1982 World Cup, which was itself a moment of Scottish comedy double-act buffoonery to rival anything by the Krankies. And the worst of it was, McConnell's kilt was way too short.

I had the misfortune to be in New York during Tartan Week 2004. My trip had certainly not been planned round the affair. I stumbled across a pipe-band parade as you would members of your own family engaged in something shocking and sleazy. The Irish get swanky Fifth Avenue for their big march on St Patrick's Day. Scotland were relegated to seedy Sixth Avenue and a more sorry, flea-bitten, wheezing assemblage representing your country you've never seen.

In the evening my friends and I gatecrashed a Tartan Week party in Manhattan's East Village, reasoning that we were Scots and had a right to be there. Within minutes, we were wondering how we could apply for political asylum. The bar was full of Rod Stewart lookalikes, all big hair and brocaded jackets. Jockery was unbound. But the main offenders weren't Yanks with overcooked Scottish connections; they were real Scots making real idiots of themselves.

When *Peter Pan* creator J. M. Barrie declared there was no greater sight than a Scotsman 'on the make', he could not have envisaged this bunch of chancers and chanty-wrastlers. Brian Wilson again: 'I cannot imagine any other country believing that the image it wants to present in the twenty-first century is of tubby politicians in national costume. Anywhere else would try to conceal them. The only good news is that the rest of the world, including the USA, is not remotely interested.'

So, *anyway* . . . what to wear to my wedding? The marriage is in France, in high summer, which for some would suggest a linen suit, but never for a Scot – that's too Mediterranean. While you're gallivanting around in such a garment, your house would surely be raided, your budgie kidnapped. Morning suit is too English. Ah, but there will be lots of English people at the wedding. The kilt it is, then.

And this is how a Scotsman's mind works. He hates the kilt but secretly likes the fact it is admired the world over. In the end, mildly desperate, he turns to it.

Of course, there's also the Auld Alliance, the 'special relationship' that's supposed to exist between Scotland and France. On my French wedding day I should probably look Scottish. I know that whatever happened in the past the Auld Alliance these days is a one-way affair. Scots talk it up, the French just shrug, the way Americans do when Oor Jack steps gaily. I know the Auld Alliance is exactly the kind of tartan-draped tenuousness I dislike about my country, but I believe in it all the same. The kilt it has to be.

Out of sheer Scottish – we're world champs at this, if nothing else – *perversity*, I first try Pride of Scotland in Princes Street. This is a recent innovation, a bucket shop for tartanalia. *Everything must go.* Step inside and you'd think Scotland, the whole country, was closing down. Half-price bagpipes are piled up like seal cubs after a bloody cull. A floor-to-ceiling window display of shortbread blots out the sun that's trying to crest Edinburgh Castle. There are tartan-fringed comedy breasts, and tartan-fringed comedy arses. 'The Story of Scotland' is told in entirety on a tea towel. And while hideous electrified reels are blasted to the max, Scots-Hindu girls in tartan saris and Scots-Chinese ones in mini kilts rush around serving the 'macs'.

Other countries must have their equivalent of this taradiddle but I don't imagine it's worse than this. (When I tried to write 'taradiddle' there my computer failed to recognise the word and changed it to 'straddle'. Kind of proves my point. The Scots can take balderdash, baloney and tosh onto a lower plain, one that is all their own.)

Lucy is with me in Pride of Scotland. 'You like this place?' she asks. What she means is: do you approve of such a tawdry representation of your fair land?

'No, I hate it, and if Dad was still alive, he would surely firebomb it.'

She can tell I'm half-hearted about this expedition; certainly not *Bravehearted.*

'Come on,' she says, 'I'll take you to the shop where my father got his kilt.'

'What, your father has a kilt?'

'And my brothers.'

Of course this spurs me on. Of course, competitiveness, a latent sense of ownership of the plaid and some more of that old-time *perversity* send me straight to Macphersons in the West

End. Right away you can sense that this is where proper kilt business happens. There's stern purpose written on the faces of the staff, all of them mature enough to predate the fads for zany checks, leather kilts or other 'hip' manifestations that the likes of Robbie Williams orders made to measure when he's in town. On the counter a clip folder stuffed with photographs – *How Not To Wear The Kilt* – features Richard Branson sporting his back to front, pleats showing, and the inevitable, dreaded McConnell. Half an hour later I have been fitted for an Ancient Smith. I text my brother, who suffered in all those hire booths with me, to inform him of this epic event but my phone won't let me write 'kilt' predictively. I tell you, it's all an English conspiracy . . .

The day I get the message that my kilt is ready Calum Kennedy dies. If anyone summed up 'Scotchland' as my father saw it and loathed it, then Kennedy, a singer you would euphemistically describe as 'traditional' – wandering the lonely glens, serenading sheep – was that man. Even my mother entered the debate when his name cropped up. 'That awful heedrum hodrum,' she would say of Kennedy's music. Still, he's dead now and in his life he gave pleasure to some. I just hope today that I don't summon up his spectre.

I return to Macphersons anticipating a merely functional transaction. I hand over the balance of the £450 and get a clump of green and blue cloth with red and yellow stripes in return. I barely give it a second glance, but in the changing booth something strange and wonderful happens . . .

> The kilt is a corruption of the Highlanders' original feilidh-Mor, the big blanket or plaid . . .

This is the start of the great set piece in *Jock* when our hero picks up a bundle of drab-coloured cloth ('Made of wool, roughly dyed . . . six yards long and two yards wide') and arranges it on the floor. Looking back, there wasn't much stagecraft involved in his transformation from hunched military-museum curator into fearless kilted brave, but at the time it seemed completely thrilling.

> There's only one way to get into the kilt – and the secret baffled the Sassenachs for centuries.

I shift and shoogle in front of the mirror . . .

> Arrange the pleats and adjust the height from a kneeling position so that it almost touches the floor.

And since this is *my* kilt rather than just another hire job, I have to accept that on this hugely notable day I have never looked *more Scottish* in my life.

There have been other great moments in my couture history. First Levi Sta-Prest. First Doc Marten boots. First Ben Sherman shirt. But I didn't actually covet a kilt, so my reaction to owning one has surprised me.

And I've just remembered this . . . my father had a kilt and I'm pretty sure it was an Ancient Smith. I used to sneak into his bedroom and marvel at its roughness and its heft. But I never saw him wear it.

Obviously we've been talking here about more than just a swathe of tartan. It wasn't just those borrowed kilts that previously were so ill-fitting. I didn't feel comfortable with certain aspects of Scottishness and indeed still *hae ma doots*. But at the end of this weirdly magical day, as my made to measure, exclusive-to-me kilt hangs on the wardrobe door, it's the last thing I see before I drift off to sleep, dreaming about perfectly performed reels with tens all the way for artistic expression. The following morning I wake up and start admiring it all over again.

How do I feel, just gazing at it, never mind wearing it, never mind being about to marry Lucy in it, flicking her Coatesy combover in it and hearing her say 'I do'?

Absolutely bloody fantastic.

Wembulee, Wembulee . . .

Every Scot who has ever travelled abroad with the national football team has a story or ten to tell.

Legend has it that in the name of dark-blue dreaming a submarine was chartered to the Argentina World Cup. I know of three men who took part in that disastrous campaign and returned with South American brides. The ultimate prize, you might think, but a 'souvenir' of Wembley – and England was definitely deemed 'abroad' in those days – was greater.

David Gray is a policeman in Gretna, the funny little wedding town on the Scottish side of the border with England. These days he's an upstanding member of the community, but in the year before the 1978 World Cup, with Scotland fancying they could win the trophy and England staring non-qualification in the face for the second tournament running, he was a fully paid-up member of the Twin Towers invasion force.

'My dad was a miner in Kirkconnel, Dumfries and Galloway, and the miners' welfare ran a Wembley Club,' recalls David when we meet during Gretna's fairy-tale charge to the 2006 Scottish Cup Final. 'We each paid in a couple of quid a week which was a lot of money in those days. The tricky part was getting tickets and by that I mean the English allocation. Luckily I had an auntie who lived in Mansfield.

'We did London in a fair bit of style, staying at West End hotels. I went down about four or five times and in 1977 I got on the pitch. The result was momentous so I wanted a trophy. I ripped up a clump of turf as big as a dinner plate. Technically that was vandalism. And theft. Maybe that should have prevented me becoming a policeman, but there you go. I put the turf in a poly bag and kept it moist overnight in the hotel bath. Then I went back up the road and presented it to my dad.'

Gretna didn't used to figure on the football map. For a couple of seasons, a millionaire's patronage transforms them into the Chelsea of Scotland, the difference being that other fans like Gretna. The town has had to get used to the laws and lunacies of football rivalry like everywhere else. Its geographical location means that in any of its pubs you can bump into Scots, Cumbrians, some of indeterminate origin, those who adhere to the belief that in football ''owt can happen' and the inevitable Celtic and Rangers supremacists.

David says that during Euro 2004 a Cross of St George flown from a local Sheffield Wednesday fan's window was set on fire. Under new legislation which makes him laugh, he had to investigate what was deemed a 'racially motivated attack'.

He is not making light of the incident, but when he was growing up in 1970s Scotland, his exposure to football tribalism came early – 'Every day in the school playground, games of nineteen-a-side were "Proddies versus Papes"' (Protestants vs Catholics in Wild West of Scotland-speak) – and was a constant after that.

So what does he think now of his part in the 1977 turf war? 'I could tell you it was small revenge for what the English did to us at Culloden but that wouldn't be true. I did it for a laugh, and because everyone else was doing it.' And the grass trophy, does it still have pride of place? 'No, Dad died and we had the garden paved over.'

Isn't that typically Scottish? You land a fabulous trophy, then you rubbish it.

Bob Russell is one of my oldest friends. He's an accountant now, which for him is very long trousers. One of those annoying types who was brilliant at all sports in his youth, he was also a natural at attracting calamity. Nothing in Bob's teenage years was incident-free, including his Wembley misadventure of 1973. Down the years we had fallen out of touch but I manage to track him down to deepest Fife, to invite him to my wedding but also to get his memories of that trip:

'I was sixteen with no ticket and no money for travel – but full of hope,' he recalls. 'The first lift I hitched on the A1 was an ice-cream van. I'm in the back, being thrown round the serving area, knocking over sweet jars – Soor Plooms, Cola Cubes, Parma Violets – when the electrics start to spark. Pretty soon there's smoke everywhere and the driver's shouting at me to put out the flames. I think I used American Cream Soda. The van gave up the ghost in Worksop.

'The next lift was a motorbike with me sitting pillion with no helmet, weighed down by a big rucksack. Still, I managed to knock off another hundred miles. Next, this OAP wanted to show me how fast his Reliant Robin could go.

'Not fast enough. I missed the match. We lost 1-0, which was sufficient reason for a party. At 3 a.m. I got arrested. The police told me: "You're dressed in black and you look suspicious." I was taken to the station and made to strip naked and stand in a cell until morning. What a great trip that was!'

I've known John Fraser for even longer than Bob. He quit Scotland and its glorious failures twenty years ago, and is now a playwright in Sydney. He went on two sojourns to Wembley, the first in 1986:

'The golden era of Scotland vs England had been and gone. In those days of rising thuggishness, the FA desperately wanted the game stopped – but simultaneously wanted it played because it was top box office. Solution? Schedule it midweek to foil the Jocks. Typical FA logic. Margaret Thatcher being in her pomp, few in Scotland had bosses to fool and jobs to skive.

'My girlfriend of the time was a Shetlander. One night I came back to the flat in Edinburgh to find thirteen male friends of hers sleeping there. A football team from Lerwick were Wembley-bound so I decided to join them.

'We hired a minibus from Thrifty. This being the 1980s, hire companies weren't too keen on football excursions so one of the lads – kilt, and in the place where the sporran should be, a frying pan with a plastic sausage and two eggs – had to convince them we were going nowhere near Wembley.

'Transport secured, we scooped up another member of our party while he was en route to the university library and with a laugh and a wave we were on our way (historical note: the Scotland-supporting kidnappee was a Rangers fan. That's how long ago this was).

'The van rolled gently south for the rest of the day and drink was taken. The radio blared out "Rock Me Amadeus" and other 1980s atrocities. It took twenty-eight minutes for six Happy Eater staff to rustle up toast in a deserted service station. We mocked silly English place names like Dry Doddington and Long Bennington. And as darkness fell we came to rest outside a pub deep in Thatcher Country. The guv'na was one of those English types who called everyone "squire". I explained the need for accommodation, omitting the words "Scottish" and "football". We shook on a deal and he asked if the highly dedicated, international standard sports team I'd just described might care for a light refreshment. "Fifteen pints of lager and fifteen double whiskies please."

'The night turned into a sort of whisky-and-darts Olympics with Shetland claiming all the gold medals. All the guys with white socks fired into the local talent while the rest . . . actually, this being the 1980s, everyone wore white. The game? I have no recollection but apparently Scotland lost 2-1.

'Two years later I was living in London, deep behind enemy lines and Andy Roxburgh [the schoolteacher-turned-national coach] had begun his chloroformic reign. It wasn't just my life that had changed. Scottish supremacy on the terraces was being seriously challenged. English nutters had finally emerged to pose questions of the invaders, and not just the notorious wide-ohs from Chelsea and Millwall either. Most seemed to come from places that don't really exist, like Port Vale.

'Thankfully the Scottish lot hadn't yet undergone their makeover. It would be a few years before their numbers were swelled by paunchy Central Belt accountants intent on singing "Doh, A Deer" ad nauseam. Most of our songs concerned Jimmy Hill; the rest speculated on which of the England players were 'poofs'. That was all of them apart from Bryan Robson, who was allegedly suffering from an SDT. That's right, a standard dialling tone.

'But when we assembled at the traditional meeting place at Trafalgar Square the pubs would quickly fill with silent, smartly dressed English yoof – casuals. Soon there were running battles with English gangs picking off Scots outside Underground stations and the fighting continued all the way out to Wembley.

'Unfortunately I remember this game – a shocker – though Roxburgh was doubtless proud of the lack of passion from the boys in dark blue. The fighting, on the terraces at least, was continuous.

'We met some Geordies who were supporting "Scotland and Peter Beardsley". Their man went on to score the only goal of the game. How did they react? I've often wondered. Perhaps they leapt in the air, simultaneously punching themselves in the face.

'We were beat, and worse was to follow. The next day, still tartan-clad, still pished, we got a ball and roamed Finsbury Park intent on revenge. The only English lads who would play us were all about eight years old. We managed to pull one back when the score got to 0-6.

'That year was the end of something for Scotland. And, for England, the beginning of something. In those marauding casuals, I do believe we were glimpsing the green shoots of recovery for glorious English pride.'

So there you go: sex, travel, history, political awareness, guerrilla gardening, beer, an understanding of the benefits of saving money, the odd bit of football – this was Wembulee for the Scots. I pity the future generations denied its important life lessons.

'Metatarsal . . .'

I can't remember where I was when I heard the news about Wayne Rooney's injury, nowhere remarkable anyway. Not like a friend, a fellow journalist and Scot, who shall remain nameless:

'I was in a sex shop in Soho, er, researching a story. You know how in these places everyone avoids eye contact and pretends they're the only one there, though if that really was the case they'd be completely freaked out? Well, that day was different. That day when the shop radio announced they were going live to the hospital, we all turned round – turned round from the XXX movie shelves and the dildo stands and the fetishwear section and faced into the middle of the store. That *never* happens. So loyalty-card customers tell me, anyway.

'*Metatarsal.* The injury that didn't exist until David Beckham suffered it, before the last World Cup. But this is Wayne Rooney, England's great hope, the *only* hope. All those training sessions and tactic talks seem to boil down to one strategy: "Give the ball to Wazza." I know I'm Scottish but players like Rooney transcend football rivalry. So there I am in the sex emporium and as the grim bulletin sinks in I'm looking at the other customers and they're all clutching their purchases – the guy with the Strap-On Hollow Extension ("No erection required . . ."), the guy with the Automatic Stroker ("This incredible mustabator [*sic*] . . ."), the guy with the Virtual Veronica – and I'm thinking: "This is special, no one is being furtive or guarding their own personal space and no one feels dirty. Yes, we're sad and defeated but this is *community*. And we're all sharing a moment and filing it in the memory banks so we can cherish it, just like we did when we heard that Rod Hull had died."

'"Bummer," I say.

'"Too right," says my new friend, standing next to me and staring emptily at his own movie selection – *Midlands Shaggers 2*.'

'I Think We Will Win the World Cup'

The traditional climax to the English domestic season is the FA Cup Final.

'Abide With Me', managers in their best suits leading out the teams, captains presenting the players, the cabbage-patch pitch, Charlie 'Shag me now!' George, Bob Stokoe's trilby, Bill Shankly's hand-jive, Tommy Docherty with the trophy lid on his head, Mick Jones with his arm in a sling, a sacrifice made during the cross to set up . . . 'CLARKE! 1-0!' So many memories . . . A pity this very English affair now takes place in *Wales.*

But as soon as club football is done and dusted, Sven-Goran Eriksson joins his players in talking up their desire, their hunger, their *destiny.*

In the draw for the group stages DestinyEngland, ranked ninth in the world, have got lucky. They will start against Paraguay, rated thirtieth and there simply to make up the South American quota. Next it's Trinidad and Tobago (fifty-first), the smallest nation ever to compete in the finals and only in Germany to party. The final match is against Sweden (fourteenth), traditionally tricky opponents, but by then qualification should be assured.

14 May, and in 'The Big Interview' in the *Sunday Times,* David Beckham is in confident mood. What, even though Wayne Rooney is a serious injury doubt? And surely the inclusion in the squad of Arsenal's Theo Walcott is just a desperate gamble when the seventeen-year-old is untried in the

Champions League, unused even in the Premiership and unseen by the national coach?

'Theo will be a player that no one at the World Cup has seen or heard much about,' argues Beckham. 'He could be special for us.'

In the coverage of the Cup Final – Steven Gerrard inspires Liverpool to victory over West Ham – one eye is already firmly fixed on Germany. 'Gerrard the man for the summer,' runs the headline in the *Independent on Sunday*.

The following day, England fly out to their training camp in Portugal and regular *Times* columnist Gary Neville writes: 'We have the quality to end forty years of hurt.'

At the Vale de Lobo complex in the Algarve, Rio Ferdinand echoes Neville's boast. And Eriksson claims: 'I think we will win the World Cup.'

Remembering that Sir Alf Ramsey made the same prediction in 1966, the *Observer* describes the coach's statement of intent as 'eight words that could turn out to be history repeating'.

Eriksson is ultra-cautious by nature. On this day everyone was anticipating some typical Eriksson-ese: 'I think we will *do* a very good World Cup.' But in his bold assertion, and the rapid elevation of Walcott, he's gone from Volvo assembly line to sauna sex party. Actually, come to think of it, in Eriksson's case that's not much of a jump at all.

'Cole ready to peak' . . . 'Lampard determined to shine' . . . 'This time there will be no excuses, vows Neville' . . . 'Super-fit Owen thrills Eriksson' . . . 'Walcott is ready and Rooney will be, says coach' . . . 'Sol: I'm happier, I'm more alive' . . . 'Lampard: Now is the time'. These are all headlines from the last few days before the final warm-up matches. They come from English broadsheets, who like to think they're above the tabloid frenzy for reams of unchallenged direct quotes from players.

After beating Hungary 3-1 and Jamaica 6-0, the latter game featuring a hat-trick for Peter Crouch, and a daft robo-dance celebration (all of which the *Observer* decides merits the headline 'Wayne who?') Beckham gives his last 'formal' interviews before the squad leaves for Germany and confirms his own fitness is 'exceptional'. Come on then, David, are England going to win? 'This is the best, the strongest and the most confident England team I've ever played in,' he says. 'This is the best chance we've had.'

5 June, and the headline on the front page of the *Daily Telegraph*'s sports section reads: '15.30 today: Flight BA 9200C Luton to Karlsruhe'. Not that the most sober and reserved paper in the country *believes* (© Mars Inc.) the day is momentous or anything.

And once the players have settled into their hotel in Baden-Baden, the bravado-bravado continues. Two days before England's opening match, the *Guardian* reports: 'Lampard wears weight of expectation lightly.' And Ferdinand – go on Rio, my son – warns: 'This time we fear no one.'

England are pretty confident, aren't they? In 1978, the last World Cup for which Scotland qualified and England didn't, a farewell lap of honour for Ally MacLeod's team was staged at Hampden Park. After the calamitous performance and early exit from Argentina, the open-top bus procession was condemned as stupid and more than a touch arrogant.

What do these England players do? Oh, nothing much, just swing down to David and Victoria Beckham's Hertfordshire mansion with 500 of the rich and famous, eat Gordon Ramsay's food, dance to James Brown's music, and thrill to a charity auction at which Ashley Cole throws £75,000 at one of Beckham's old watches. A private party? Not likely. 'Full Length & Fabulous' is broadcast on prime-time ITV.

So let's hear Eriksson again: '*I think we will win the World Cup.*'

'Such a Lovely Place, Such a Lovely Place'

The England team check into the Schlosshotel Buhlerhohe in Baden-Baden and – anticipating a long and successful stay – ask the girl at the hotel desk to hold their booking until 9 July, the date of the World Cup Final.

This is a pretty swish place. The view from their mountain-top in the Black Forest must, according to the *Guardian,* make David Beckham and the players feel 'like lords of all creation'.

There's certainly great glamour in this team. Sportswear commercials, modelling contracts, grooming endorsements. The most glamorous thing I ever saw Bobby Moore do, in a piece of black-and-white footage still shown as a reminder of a simpler age, was swing down to his local and buy the missus a Babycham before his regular game of darts with Martin Peters. This lot are in a whole different realm.

Instead of *Shoot!* questionnaires, they turn up in newspaper showbiz gossip columns, men's magazine fashion spreads and page after page of *Hello!*, where the players are asked, with that magazine's spotlight-and-thumbscrews rigour: 'Tell us about your fantastic lifestyle.' All of them are instantly recognisable, even to a Scot. And this Scot is forced to admit that there's a guy who plays left back for us, and has done for a while, whose name I struggle to remember (sorry, Graham Alexander).

At the Buhlerhohe, during World Cup down-time, the England superstars could flick back through the hotel's register and find the names of Nelson Mandela, Bill Clinton and Kofi

Annan. But none of the statesmen had a supersize mattress ordered for them like Peter Crouch.

The entire squad have their pictures on the doors of their rooms. This would be useful if you were coming back pissed every night, but we're talking world-famous athletes at the peak of their powers – DestinyEngland.

Still, those mink-lined corridors can look very samey and, after a while, super-luxury can get tedious. To try and ensure Baden-Baden isn't any more stressful than it absolutely needs to be, the wives and girlfriends have been brought along for the duration. Meet the Wags.

England are the only team in serious contention for football's greatest prize to have their players' partners virtually in residence. But Sven-Goran Eriksson dismisses worries that their presence will be a distraction.

Last one into the Buhlerhohe gets Hitler's old room.

'Football Isn't About Politics . . .'

The eighteenth Mundial is almost here, excitement is mounting and even Scotland is getting in the mood . . .

Believe, say Mars. 'Believe – Ma Arse' retorts Edinburgh graphic designer Sandy Robb who slaps his slogan on a T-shirt to flog to Scots who, like him, are fed up being told they should be supporting England.

The official England song is released, but Embrace's 'World At Your Feet' is earnest and turgid and won't inspire in the manner of a rapping John Barnes (1990), Mick Mills in his cosy Admiral pullover (1982) or, best of all, the blazered-up 1970 squad promising to win the cup for 'the folks backs home'.

So the Scottish edition of the *Sun* launches a competition to find an alternative, and advertising company boss Richard Melvin, also from Edinburgh, wins with 'Come On Jason Scotland', dedicated to the St Johnstone striker hoping to shoot Trinidad and Tobago to glory against England.

Then the *Daily Record* compiles an all-time worst England XI (there are places for Peter Crouch and Owen Hargreaves) and creates a board game called Drivel Or Quits to counteract the effects of all the English hosannah-ing from the commentators and pundits (our own Alan Hansen included). The Scottish *Daily Mirror* chips in with a story about German fans rushing to buy the Archie Gemmill 'diamond' strip from 1978 – recently voted one of the three coolest football shirts of all time – to wind up the England masses.

The *Scotsman* reports on the BBC's controversial choice of

Handel's 'See The Conquering Hero Comes' as their World Cup theme – the music celebrates the massacre of Bonnie Prince Charlie's Jacobites by the Duke of Cumberland-led government forces at Culloden in 1746. This sparks a row over exactly how many Scots fought alongside 'Butcher' Cumberland, with historians pointing out that there were Englishmen in the Jacobite ranks.

But, no one wants to whip up anti-English feeling. As quickly as the c-word is mentioned – Culloden – it is softened. Ted Cowan, professor of Scottish history at Glasgow University, points out that Cumberland's bloody triumph was hijacked by London but it was never a battle of nations.

There could be a few reasons for this non-aggressive stance. That Scots now acknowledge, in a UK sense, England's football omnipotence (unthinkable). That Scots have reached a level of maturity regarding their relationship with the Auld Enemy (unlikely). That more English live in Scotland these days, that more Scots actively follow English teams than in the past, especially kids, and that newspapers will harm their own sales if they go for the jugular as in days of old (definitely).

A BBC poll claims two out of three Scots want England to win the World Cup. The findings are greeted with some scepticism but the Scottish *Sun*'s ultra-patriotic Bill Leckie throws in his tam-o'-shanter with Sven's men.

'We're us, they're them,' writes Leckie. 'We're cats and dogs, chalk and cheese, Joe Pasquale and funny.' The English can be 'arrogant and insular' and they've done 'piles of rotten stuff' to Scotland down the years. But, convincing himself that he's doing a far, far better thing by supporting England, he concludes: 'You grow up and you move on . . . we'll never be a stand-alone nation until we stop being so insecure.'

Then the real fun begins . . .

Gordon Brown opens up the World Cup wallchart free with his newspaper of choice, studies the teams and their prospects, and declares: 'That's it, I'm supporting England.'

Jack McConnell, Scotland's first minister – a Labour man like Brown – opens up his giveaway ninety-six-page World Cup guidebook and announces: 'It's Trinidad and Tobago for me.'

In a dig at Brown, McConnell admits that as Scotland's premier there is pressure on him to say he's backing England. 'But football is not about politics so I will not be,' he asserts.

Now football *is* about politics. Brown *has* to support England. He wants to be Britain's prime minister one day but among the English there is distrust of his Scottishness. There is also a backlash against devolution, a grumble that Scotland is doing better out of the settlement than England because English taxpayers are 'subsidising' their northern cousins. With an extra £1,406 public spending per head, the Scottish Parliament can provide free health care for the elderly and scrap university tuition fees.

So, like the footballer newly signed from a rival team, an anxious Brown spouts some patronising nonsense in the hope of endearing himself to a suspicious support. He doesn't come out with the standard line: 'I never knew this was such a big club.' It's actually much worse.

'Remember that Gazza goal against Scotland at Euro '96? Lobs the ball over *their* carthorse centre half, forget his name, hits it on the volley – whap! Dentist's chair celebration – glug, glug! Football's coming home! Scotland's going home! Get it right up you, Jock gits!' I'm paraphrasing, of course, but Brown does go as far as nominating the devastating Paul Gascoigne strike as one of his magic moments.

Why couldn't he just have parroted the old Harold Wilson line about how England always win the World Cup under Labour? Does he really think Middle England will swallow that Gazza guff? Among the sceptics are his former press officer Charlie Whelan, who reveals that after Scotland's defeat by the Auld Enemy in a Euro Championship play-off three years later, the chancellor 'sulked for weeks'.

Brown, of course, speaks from Westminster. McConnell is the

head of the Scottish Parliament which opened for business in 1999. It has limited powers – Billy Connolly calls it the 'wee pretendy Parliament' – and as with the cream of Scottish football talent in the 1960s and 1970s, all the best Scottish politicians have been lured to England.

Holyrood wants to be noticed. It's jagged and modern and Spanish in design. Fortunately the site used to house an old brewery so is undeniably Scottish. But this is no deferential annexe to Westminster. It looks nothing like the Houses of Parliament; it doesn't want to sound the same either. Let's pay a visit . . .

The 'Parly' is located at the bottom of the Royal Mile. This ancient thoroughfare – which dates back to medieval times – is historic enough to qualify for two Starbucks. Fortunately, there is some acknowledgement of the pre-Starbucks world on the café walls. Unfortunately the pictures hark back to a time when this part of Edinburgh was an 'idependant burgh' (*sic*).

Further on, there's more teuchery and heuchery . . . and then Bene's, a chip shop declaring: 'We sell deep-fried Mars bars'. This is a main tourist route, so it should be assumed that the – what's the opposite of delicacies . . . depthcharge-icacies? – are offered up with lashings of irony. I almost miss the sign in the window, though – the 'Mars' bit throws me. Come on, get with the programme: it should be 'deep-fried *Believe* bars'.

Finally, the old, dour, cheap, hackneyed and joke manifestations of Scotland disappear. There's a swathe of green where the royal corgis piddle when the queen is in town, then, at last, the business address of 'the best small country in the world'.

This is a phrase often spouted by Jack McConnell who, like the Parliament, has yet to impress. His backing for Trinidad and Tobago would, at any other time, have me hailing him as a great statesman, but I must remember who I'm supposed to be supporting.

McConnell is obviously trying to find favour with unreconstructed Scots who espouse the underdog spirit rather than those such as Brown who believe in the bulldog kind. The Perthshire branch of the Tartan Army are quick to approve. 'The whole point of football is rivalry and England are our greatest rivals,' says their spokesman John Kaylor. Even David Beckham says he understands McConnell's position and acknowledges the first minister's 'patriotism'.

Like Brown, though, McConnell is playing a slightly desperate political game. His analysts report that Scots do not believe he stands up for Scotland as much as the SNP leader, Alex Salmond.

McConnell's Labour administration has been warned to expect a serious challenge from the Nats at the 2007 Holyrood elections. His spin doctors urge him: 'Wrap yourself in the Saltire.' They believe the most passionate pro-Scotland gesture he can make right now is to cheer for 'ABE – Anyone But England'. (A fat lot of good it does him, come polling day.)

Oh, and there's another reason McConnell is not backing Brown, backing England: he doesn't like him.

The Scottish football community state their preferences. National team manager Walter Smith declares his backing for Italy out of admiration for their coach, Marcello Lippi, but adds: 'I don't think anyone who is Scottish can turn around and say they are supporters of England.' Scottish celebrities, some whose last invitation to take part in a vox pop concerned the introduction of decimalisation, add their tuppenceworth.

While McConnell causes radio debates in England to spontaneously combust, Gordon Brown is melting the phone-lines of shock jocks in Scotland. The story starts out as a silly-season affair. But very quickly it seems only right and proper that the front pages should be dominated by a debate which strikes at the heart of nationhood, for Scotland *and* England.

Magnus Linklater – pre-eminent talking heid and a former editor of the *Scotsman* – rates Brown's acclamation of the Gazza goal 'as controversial a statement as has ever been issued by a Scottish politician'.

Who are we and how do *they* impact on our national identity? For Scots this is the eternal – infernal – question. England's attitude to Scotland, for long enough, 299 years to be precise, has been: 'They don't like us, we don't care.' But now the English are asking the question of themselves, and of Scotland. Our non-support of England never bothered them before. It does now.

I wish my father were around. He would not be surprised to discover that football, and England, are still defining who we Scots are. And he would love to be joining in the stooshie.

After all, this is the man who gave me a shockingly early introduction to the power of swear words. And on the fortieth anniversary of 1966 and all that, he would argue there is no bloody way Scots should have to fall in behind England and cheer for a bunch of show ponies whose rider demands for Germany include forty-eight cans of hair mousse.

The 'luxorexics' – excessive self-pamperers – led by David Beckham would enrage Dad, of that there's no doubt, but he would be more concerned about the Scots who are perfectly happy to support England. These are not people, he would contend, on whom we can depend to keep the passion of football alive. If we stop feeling the intense rivalry which is at the heart of the game, then we stop caring about it.

Holyrood notwithstanding, my father would claim that Scotland has lost enough of its own identity already without us having to 'bow the knee and touch the forelock' in deference to England and notions of political correctness.

And his alter ego Jock would surely agree. As the football row rages, the Royal Scots, Britain's oldest regiment, are disbanded. In Dad's play, Jock declared: 'To have an army led by a piper is like going into a cup final two goals up.' Now Scotland don't have a football team worth the name, *or* an army.

As England basks in a heatwave, Jack Straw, the Leader of the House of Commons, urges Scottish MPs to support the English team and expresses the hope that the World Cup will inspire 'real ecumenical feeling' between the different nations of the UK. Fat chance.

Back in the frozen north the chittering classes get involved and the *Herald*'s Ian Bell informs the England team they will have to win the blasted cup without him. Supporting England, he writes, would feel 'dishonest, like a show of excessive politeness towards someone you barely know. You intend no disrespect; certainly no harm . . . but when you attempt to embrace a cause that cannot be your own, by any possible definition, you are faking it.'

That's a very polite, reasoned argument, but Bell has plenty of grumbles with the English recruitment tactics. 'Some of us are just weary – an old complaint – of being conscripted to causes not our own by TV commentators with a tendency to forget Scotland's existence. Some of us, try as we might, don't feel particularly British, and fail to understand why a proxy vote for England is somehow compulsory. Some of us see British/English as a device for political ends we reject. Some of us just dislike being lectured on our imagined civic duties.'

You could be cynical about political intentions. You could argue, with some justification, that there is only one thing worse than a baby-kissing politician and that's one who kisses a football badge. Football, in World Cup year, in DestinyEngland year, has become a political football.

But what a fine time to be a Scotsman! Downtrodden or plain old disregarded for centuries, suddenly he's the man most wanted.

He's roamed the planet for centuries with what these days is universally described as an 'attitude problem'. Scotland patented crabbitness, oh yes it did. Now, to paraphrase David Bowie in 'Space Oddity': 'The papers want to know whose hair shirt he wears.'

At last, English people, and those in the world beyond, are anxious to discover what he thinks! About football! More crucially, about England! We're at the epicentre of everything and when we scuff our tackety boots, tectonic plates shift! We are almost vaguely significant!

In the *Scotsman*, Robert McNeil savours the delicious dilemma and cannot help prolonging it: 'I've long believed Scotland should declare all-out war on England. However, I believe it churlish not to support them at football. Accordingly I will not be supporting them at football.'

On 27 May, less than two months after the opinion poll claiming two thirds of Scots are supporting England, seventy-eight per cent in a Scottish *Sun* survey say they won't, after all, be cheering for the Auld Enemy.

Then on 3 June, six days before the World Cup kicks off, the Commission for Racial Equality steps in. They warn public figures of the need to ensure the tournament is a 'force for integration' and urge fans against using it as an excuse for racism.

Already they've had complaints. Sports-shop bosses reporting big sales of Trinidad and Tobago strips out of 'pure hatred' for England have caused offence, as has the demand for 'ABE' T-shirts.

Says the Commission's Ali Jarvis: 'We've been monitoring exchanges in the media and noticed an anti-English tone. In one newspaper, someone wrote on Monday they were not supporting England. By Wednesday someone else was saying that all English people should leave Scotland as they're a scourge on the land.'

Maybe I'll be better off taking my chances with the Barmy Army.

Taxi for Smith

'Yer daein' *whit?*'

My taxi driver can't believe it. And even though it is 4.45 on a Thursday morning, even though the roads are dead, the transport planning cock-ups are not inconveniencing him, the radio is not crackling with news that will rile him . . . even though the skies are clear, another scorcher is forecast, in a few hours' time he'll be on the golf course, a few days after that in his timeshare, and before he knows it he'll be finished with cabbing for good, he feels the need to rant.

'Naw, naw. Ye cannae dae that. Ye cannae.'

The tirade involves the usual suspects: Jimmy Hill, Maggie Thatcher, 'Butcher' Cumberland, the three-pronged forward line in the all-time terror XI. It lists the big defeats: Culloden, Ravenscraig and the oilfields of the North Sea. It details the creeping anglicisation of everyday Scottish life (Carling beer, gazumping, rogue bank holidays). And any minute now, I'm thinking, my cabbie is going to make me walk to the airport.

'Ye see that?' He points to the 'Scotland Forever' pennant hanging from his rear-view mirror. 'Ye see that?' He points to the little, domed, clear plastic snowstorm evocation of Edinburgh Castle on his dashboard. Then he shows me the tattoo on his arm: 'Remember Bannockburn'.

This is a proud, proud Scot who can probably see the good in every single one of his countrymen: Frank Haffey, the desperate goalkeeper who let in nine at Wembley in 1961, the chronic verseman William McGonagall, all those pop groups (Travis,

Deacon Blue, Garbage, the Blue Nile, Del Amitri, etc.) who sing about the rain, shamed daytime telly satyromaniac John Leslie . . . even the journalist responsible for 'The Honest Truth' in the *Sunday Post*, a column where revelations such as the recent discovery that the earth is not flat does its best to keep Scotland small and hunched and grateful. I have managed to cause this man deep offence before I've even got past the end of my road.

'How the flamin' fuck can ye support *England*?'

He's right, of course. How can I?

'Hey England! Don't be Antisocial Behaviour!'

Passport – check. Phrasebooks (German *and* English) – check. Suntan lotion – check. *Jock* – check. *This Is My Country* – check. Spare pants – check. John Bull Repair Kit – check. *Schadenfreude* (justifiable, Germany is its home; extra-explainable since we're talking England) – check. Cyanide – check. OK, my World Cup can begin.

England's opening match is against Paraguay in Frankfurt. According to the German-born member of the office's IT team kitting me out with a laptop, this is the least attractive of the tournament's host cities. 'Just a black hole,' she says. But I don't care. This is my first-ever trip to Germany and I don't know why it's taken me so long to get its stamp on my passport.

I carry with me at all times two iconic German images. One is Helmut Schoen, the wily fox in charge of the West German team at the 1970 World Cup in Mexico (note: all international managers, when they've been around for a bit, are referred to as wily foxes). In the picture I have in my head it's the England-West Germany quarter-final in Leon and Schoen is in the dugout, his arm round Jurgen Grabowski, and he's pointing down the right touchline and telling the blond winger exactly how he wants him to terrorise the England defence, fire howitzer crosses at their goalkeeper Peter Bonetti – the stand-in nicknamed 'Tiddles'. In my memory I can see Schoen clearly but Grabowski is indistinct, so I have him played by *Cabaret!*-era Michael York. Nevertheless his late, dramatic entry was 'the best substitution in the history of association football', according to my father (note: when Dad wanted to hammer home an important point about football, about either Scotland's moral superiority or how England expects but rarely gets, he always used the word 'association').

The other top Teutonic image is the cover of the Roxy Music LP *Country Life.* Roxy's artwork always featured a woman wearing few clothes; *Country Life*, released in 1974, had two, and both Eveline Grunwald and Constanze Karoli were German.

In response to a question popular at my secondary school, 'When did you first (*fnar, fnar*) come across Roxy Music's *Country Life* album?', I was sixteen, a key stage in a young man's development. I had lots of questions about life. I had lots of questions about the cover. The women seemed to be trapped in headlights, a long way from the autobahn. What had they been doing in the forest? How did a sixteen-year-old lad from Edinburgh gain membership to their secret sex club? What had happened to Constanze's bra? What was Eveline doing with the index finger of her left hand?

The sleeve was, I admit, easy to love. All the more so when, with a more mature eye (but not *that* mature), I got the joke behind the design. Bryan Ferry was sending up the magazine *Country Life*, an English institution. At the time the mag featured lots of active, apple-cheeked gels. None, however, were quite as outdoorsy as Eveline and Constanze.

While I had an early understanding, thanks to my father, of why the England football team were there to be generally mocked and occasionally despised, I had no short-trousered appreciation of England, the country and its history. Germany probably influenced me first.

'*Achtung!*' '*Gott in Himmel!*' '*Nein Kammerad!*' These were my first German phrases. Although the lunch-break game of choice at primary school, before football became the passion of life, was 'Japs and Commandos', the involvement of the Japanese was an anomaly: Germany were *the* great foe in my playground. I pass the playground most days, I pass it today on the way to the airport, and it's amazing to think of how much venomous fun could be packed into such a tight, tarmacked spot.

Blame DC Thomson for my first German obsession. The comics world turned slowly and the Dundee-based funhouse were in charge of ratcheting the big, grinding wheel. I was a Child of the Space Race. The Russians should have been the sinister but ultimately slow-witted enemy which the heroic Brits always vanquished in the final cartoon box. But DC Thomson were suspicious of new fads such as the hula hoop, boil-in-the-bag rice and Communist superpowers with a serious rocket capability. So in the mid-1960s in our playground, as directed by DC Thomson's excellent publications, the *Victor*, the *Hornet* and the *Hotspur*, we were still smoking out Germans behind the bike shed a full twenty years after the Second World War had ended.

My second German obsession came a decade later. A relative latecomer to beat music, I had to be quick and daring if I was going to amass a decent-sized LP collection, one that was appropriate to my age, hair length and muso pretensions. I devoured the *New Musical Express*, *Melody Maker* and *Sounds* and didn't differentiate between Chicory Tip and the Mahavishnu Orchestra; it was all eminently worthy of investigation. But disposable income was limited and I had to rely on budget albums to earn me my common-room cred.

On the racks of the local record shop, Faust's *The Faust Tapes* and Amon Duul II's *Live In London* entranced me with their weirdness and their cheapness. 'Those are Krautrock,' explained the hairy guy behind the counter. I ran home and consulted one of Pete Frame's Rock Family Tree wallcharts for the unenlightened: Krautrock bands shared a branch with early Roxy Music. But while English groups could be complacent or, in Roxy's case, divinely decadent, German bands were motivated by the urgent need to exorcise their country's recent past, hence the unholy racket. I ran back to the shop and so began a fascination for commune-dwelling, pneumatic drill-strumming, terrorist-fraternising German crazies that endures to this day.

For this trip I have compiled a Krautrock playlist on my iPod featuring Can (whose Michael Karoli was the brother of Constanze and boyfriend of Eveline), Kraftwerk, Neu! and Tangerine Dream as well as Faust and Amon Duul II. If the football goes awry, if this England team bore me or, worse still, threaten to thrill me, maybe I'll take off through Germany on a rock heritage tour of the studios and hang-outs where these bands held the standard, three-minute, verse-chorus-verse pop song captive and tortured it.

But I must remember the job in hand; I must try to 'dig' England. To that end, I've compiled an English playlist as well, a sample selection of which is:

1. 'Jerusalem' – Emerson Lake & Palmer ('And did those feet in ancient times . . .').

2. 'The Village Green Preservation Society' – the Kinks ('We are the Custard Pie Appreciation Consortium, God save the George Cross and all those who were awarded them').

3. 'When An Old Cricketer Leaves The Crease' – Roy Harper ('When the day is done and the ball is spun').

4. 'The Musical Box' – Genesis ('While Henry Hamilton-Smythe minor ((eight)) was playing croquet with Cynthia Jane De Blaise-William ((nine)) . . .').

5. 'Sport (The Odd Boy)' – Bonzo Dog Doo-Dah Band ('Sport sport masculine sport, equips a young man for society . . . it's an odd boy who doesn't like sport').

6. 'Thick As A Brick' – Jethro Tull ('Where the hell was Biggles when you needed him last Saturday?')

7. 'Beechwood Park' – the Zombies ('When all the air is damp and warm in the green of summer lanes').

8. 'Moonchild' – King Crimson ('Talking to the trees . . . playing hide and seek with the ghosts of dawn').

9. 'Refugees' – Van der Graaf Generator ('South was birth to pleasant lands . . . we were at peace and we cheered').

10. 'Elspeth Of Nottingham' – Focus (No words here, this is instrumental English medieval folk at its best, performed by Dutchmen: absolute harpsichord-playing from the total football nation).

There is no Vaughan Williams, Elgar, Purcell or indeed Sir Clifford of Richard. I can only go with music that moved me in those formative teenage years, when football had its only serious rival for my affections. The emphasis is on the pastoral and the whimsical (with a touch of the fey). I spin through the selection and imagine a Merrie Englande of lazy sunny afternoons and shadows lengthening in churchyards in the time-honoured clichéd way . . . just before a giant boot descends from the sky and crushes the vicar's wife, sending her prizewinning scones flying.

I say '*skon*', they say '*skewn*' – let's call the whole thing off. A Scot joining up with the whiteshirts. It's never going to work. No, let's soldier on. I've bought my air ticket and, being Scottish, I'm damned if I'm going to waste it.

A lot of these rock acts – with Gentle Giant, Caravan, Soft Machine, the Strawbs and Lindisfarne all waiting for their chance on the subs' bench – are now deeply unfashionable, but they are firmly from a time when, without realising it, I was just about the most pro-England I've ever been.

Until now.

*

With arrivals/departures boards as big as football pitches, Frankfurt is one of those ginormous travel hubs you can reach in one hop from just about anywhere, even the capital of non-WC-participating, fallen-off-the-edge Scotland.

The train journey from the airport to the main railway station, the Hauptbahnhof, is quick and effortless; staff everywhere are alert to the disoriented dithers of the just-arrived and are extra patient with fools. At last I've made it to Germany. And the first thing I want to do is apologise for Paul Lambert.

The former Scotland captain's crime was not grave. Simply that when he quit playing for Borussia Dortmund, he ran round the pitch with a banner reading 'Thank's fans'. But this is the land where, thanks to gold-standard efficiency, everyone is punctual. I am a representative of the country of poor punctuation. I've got to say sorry for something.

The regular transport teams are backed up by special World Cup squads of multilingual students in special World Cup livery. Virtually every German, it seems, is putting on his or her most efficient smile for the tournament, everyone is up for the *fussball*. The WC mascot, a cuddly lion called Goleo VI, is prominent, as is the WC slogan: 'A time to make friends.'

Who are going to be my friends in Germany? Who are going to be the first English friends I've had in my life? There were no English kids at either my primary or secondary school; none in my neighbourhood growing up.

The world outside my window as a boy was unmistakably Scottish. This was in sharp contrast to that of my father, who at the beginning of *This Is My Country*, listed all the different nationalities represented in the Edinburgh of his youth, including the 'pickled walnut under a turban who peddled brushes and rugs round the doors' (steady, Dad) and the 'yah-yah English family who lived across the street'. By the time I was working for Edinburgh's *Evening News*, English reporters were being lured over the border by the higher provincial-paper wages on offer in Scotland. But they were colleagues, acquaintances. We drank in the pub together on expenses day and kicked lumps out of each other at five-a-side football. Then we all moved to other papers and failed to keep in touch.

Around this time I had a girlfriend, Barbie Dutter, who was half-Austrian and half-English. But her family home on Ilkley Moor never felt very English. For one thing this was the heart of Yorkshire, that most cussedly individual of counties which was the first in England to follow Scotland's example and demand an assembly of its own. For another, her mother had recently married a Scot, Peter Cheney, who flew the Saltire from the house, took great delight in putting the local newsagents to the bother of ordering him the *Daily Record* and tried to stand in local elections as a Scottish Nationalist, justifying his position thus:

> Scots made Yorkshire what it is today. This goes back to Jamie the Saxt when he was trying to take the English throne. His men ran out of shoes so a message was relayed back to Edinburgh: 'Send 500 brogues.' But Edinburgh thought he said rogues and emptied all its jails and asylums. When the king heard about this he ordered the maddies and baddies to be halted in their tracks. And the place they stopped was Yorkshire.

So, let's recap: in almost half a century, I've had little direct contact with English people, hardly any that's been meaningful and none at all of a lasting nature. If I wasn't about to marry an English-type girl, I might feel like a racist.

Germany have always been great at comebacks: last-gasp equalisers a speciality, missing limbs no impediment (Karl-Heinz Rummenigge using just his left leg being typical). Then there's the comeback that was the German post-war economic miracle, with Frankfurt the financial powerhouse playing deep-lying centre midfield. But these days the tourist board are keen to stress that 'Bankfurt' has its share of flair players – it's the birthplace of Goethe – so there's been a bit of a comeback for culture as well.

On this blisteringly hot day, the city's tallest office block has been adorned with the face of the German captain Michael Ballack, the Teutonic talisman. But it is the Hauptbahnhof – the second busiest train station in the world – that is the centre of the universe. It's the start of the tournament, and many of the three million visiting fans must begin their World Cup adventure from the platforms under the big, yawning, triple-arched structure.

Maybe a lot of prostitutes too: some 40,000 are expected in Germany over the next four weeks, swelling a legalised sex industry which already boasts the world's first drive-in brothel, in Cologne. Over in Berlin a 3,000 sq. ft mega-knocking shop with space for 650 customers has been, er, erected next to the stadium. With Sven-Goran Eriksson for a role model, randy English fans are being encouraged by Superdrug to come prepared – with condoms emblazoned with the legend 'Lie back and think of England'.

My hotel, the Excelsior ('*Ja*, minibar is *frei*') is just across the road and after dumping my rucksack I head straight back to the station, grab a coffee and a copy of the *Sun* (this just in on England's opening-match opponents: 'Duelling is legal in Paraguay, provided the combatants are registered blood donors'), and count in the different nationalities. Every few minutes, a big silver bullet train offloads another group.

There are fans from the football superpower Brazil, whose 'golden jockstrap' deal with Nike keeps the national team playing anywhere but the homeland (since 2002 just two of their friendlies have been down Rio way). There are big men from Sweden, all of them blond, and small men from Argentina, all weighed down with a heavy fringe. The Poles come with a fearsome hooligan reputation. The Costa Ricans have brought a drum.

Most are sporting a team colours/national dress combo. It's

clogs for the Dutch, cork hats for the Australians, fedoras for the Ecuadorians and red, yellow and green robes for a big, grinning contingent from Togo. Everyone is whooping and chanting and making good use of the acoustics of the Hauptbahnhof.

Even a casual coffee-shop observer like me, even a non-person like me from a country deep in the World Cup wilderness, feels involved and starts to think in Whickerisms, in the style of Alan, the great, blazered TV globetrotter ('City within a city, world within a world') or underrated, mid-period Prince albums ('Around the world in a day').

And look, over there: here come the English . . .

Half a dozen of them, and not a knee-bell or fluttering handkerchief in sight. They've rejected the nearest England has to national garb, the Morris dancer's attire, but also the smiles, the sheer outward expression of pleasure at being at the party, that is every other fan's calling card on this day of brimming anticipation. Among the small English detachment, brows are furrowed, chins are grimly set and shoulders are thrust, forging a determined, joyless path through the crowded concourse.

They are dressed identically in light blue polo shirts. They pass me, revealing the inscription on the backs of their tops – 'No surrender, never forget'. The first part of the slogan is a warning to the IRA, the second a promise, re the sacrifices of two world wars. I follow them into the newsagents with the intention of eavesdropping on their chat, maybe even joining in and, like the tournament slogan says, 'making friends'.

One of them picks up a tabloid and reads from a back-page story about Manchester United manager Sir Alex Ferguson giving Sven-Goran Eriksson a 'hairdryer-style blast' (he'll be the one who decides on Wayne Rooney's fitness).

'Fuckin' Scotch git,' says one of his friends.

'Fuckin' Scotch *cunt*,' corrects another.

'It is never difficult to distinguish between a Scotsman with a grievance and a ray of sunshine.' – P. G. Wodehouse

'The Scotch as a nation are particularly disagreeable. They hate every appearance of comfort themselves and refuse it in others.' – William Hazlitt

'There was very little amusement in the room but a Scotchman to hate.' – John Keats

In *This Is My Country* my father called on the help of many great English wits and grumps in an attempt to best sum up the Scot, to encapsulate him like you would a spider in a jam jar, shortly before decapitation.

These days Sir Alex would be many an Englishman's idea of the archetypal Scot. In his playing days in Scotland he was a nasty piece of work: all sharp elbows and Rangers attitude, and he had few admirers, even at Ibrox. But I love him as manager of Man U, I absolutely love him.

Icons of English football such as Kevin Keegan and David Beckham have tried to take him on and they've lost. There may be few Scots of influence in the English game now but with Fergie around it never seems like that: he could start an argument in an empty dressing room. If there's some kit on the floor begging to be kicked, and an underperforming, over-groomed right-sided midfielder sitting in the corner as an ideal target, all the better.

With the Scotland-England fixture dead, Fergie provides a vital service. The fallout from 2003's 'Bootgate' – with Beckham in his car, driving very slowly, windows down, then walking around the bustling centre of Manchester with his hair scraped off his forehead with an Alice band *so that no one could possibly miss his prissy wound* – was hilarious. And Fergie's psychological demolition of Keegan was genius.

A peerless teacup thrower, Ferguson winds up everybody and fears no one. He chews hard on Bazooka Joe bubblegum all game long then emerges for the post-match interviews to chew just as hard on his interrogators. He dares them to ask an interesting question. Too interesting, though, and he'll roar: 'Yooz are all fuckin' idiots.'

When Fergie is bad-mouthed in Frankfurt today, I want to defend his honour but I manage to restrain myself (not hard). There will be other battles (battles of the mind, I hope). There will certainly be other England fans. Around 100,000 Ingerlanders are expected in Germany, for starters 70,000 in Frankfurt.

To aid recognition and acceptance, I nip back to the Excelsior and put on my Nobby Stiles T-shirt. I can't wear an England strip; at least not yet. I haven't squared that with the man who wrote *Jock*.

Why Nobby? Well, he was missing his front teeth and seemed to be suffering from rickets. With the possible exception of Alan Ball and that hair the colour of Irn-Bru, he was the hero of 1966 who most resembled a Scot.

An underground train takes me downtown. There are no ticket checks (*Frei* minibar? *Frei* train travel? *Ja*, so this is German efficiency!) and I'm disgorged onto a bustling shopping thoroughfare, a dull main drag that reminds me of Reading, where my sister lived for a while, shoe-shop dominated and the most anywhere-and-nowhere part of England I know.

Now I'm jotting down the names of the streets, in case I want to do an about-turn and head back to the station. This is Schumacherstrasse and soon I'm wondering where the West German goalie Harald Schumacher's unpunished attempted beheading of France's Patrick Battiston in 1982 would figure among the Great World Cup Outrages (others in the series: West Germany playing out time – all eighty minutes of it – with Austria to deny Algeria qualification, also in '82; the murder of Colombia's own-goal victim Andres Escobar in '94; and . . . The Goal That Wasn't A Goal).

How did that happen? I was thinking about something completely unrelated. Am I going to contrive grudging, spiteful gibes at England at every turn? That would be very tedious, not to say dangerous, should I let slip a snide aside. Anyway, where are the Barmy Army?

Then I hear a song, a lilting melody:

> There were ten German bombers in the air
> And the RAF from England shot them down
> There were ten German bombers, ten German bombers
> Ten German bombers in the air

It is the opposite of a mirage. It is the flipside of that sensation when you're delirious in the desert and fooling yourself into believing that up ahead you can see a well. Here I'm stumbling towards what I know to be my quest but am desperately trying to convince myself it isn't there, that it doesn't actually exist.

It's no use . . .

> There were nine German bombers in the air
> And the RAF from England shot them down
> There were nine German bombers, nine German bombers
> Nine German bombers in the air

These are real England fans, all right. In a square called the Romerberg, about a hundred of them are drinking Lowenbrau by the litre and singing about the war. I am right in the middle of them. All I can see is white. I am standing on the beach at Dover, gawping at the cliffs. No, I am Ronnie Corbett again, trapped in the gully between No. 2 English Pin-Up Madeline Smith's giant snowy peaks.

The Romerberg is the most famous square in Frankfurt. It is 1,200 years old and kings and kaisers have been crowned here since the sixteenth century. I know this because I'm reading the information post at the square's entrance. Then a shaven-headed fan with piercing blue eyes blots out the rest of the info by draping a giant Cross of St George between the post and a pub which his friends have commandeered.

'Yes, mate,' he says. 'Built by so-and-so donkey's ago. Bombed to fuck by the proud boys of the RAF in 1941.'

His pale blue eyes are striking, almost ghostly. They remind me of Alan Hansen's, before his were watered down with age and too many insipid England performances viewed from the pundits' perch. The inscription on the lad's flag confirms he's a Queen's Park Rangers fan. I'm about to quiz him on certain matters (did he ever see Stan Bowles pass a ball but – *boom boom* – never a bookies? These Three Lions he's just tethered to the mast, does he know – and the FA's historian confirms this – that they're actually leopards? And St George, did he know that his great foe was mythical, that the ye olde monsters inspectorate could find no dragons of mass destruction?) But before I can do this, he rushes back to join his pals for some staged bouncing for the benefit of a German TV crew.

Rebuilding of the Romerberg was only completed in 1986. There's a fountain in the middle, an old church, the Alte Nikolaikirche, and a town hall, souvenir shops and bars. For obvious reasons, it's quaint rather than classic. But the England fans don't mind. Every single corner has been claimed by them. The shirts are off and the banners are hoisted. This is how you *let the opposition know you're there.* You plant a flag and you sing your songs ('Keep St George in my heart . . .'). When other fans show themselves, you acknowledge them ('Who are ya? Who are ya?') But you're not moving; not for anyone, and you dismiss rival chants with a sneer: 'What the fuckin' hell was that?' Suddenly, all those jokes about the Germans nabbing the sunloungers that have been around since the advent of mass air travel are redundant.

From a safe distance I grab a frankfurter with 'green sauce' and another local speciality, *Apfelwein*, a kind of cider, and watch the malarkey. Then two unthreatening-looking lads in their twenties sit down at my table and finally we get talking, me and *the English.*

Christian Gladdish and Gary Rushgrove, from Canterbury,

were lucky enough to scoop thirty-five-euro tickets for the Paraguay match from just 5,000 made available to England fans in an online draw.

They think England are going to win the World Cup – 'We'll do it the hard way, mate: Poland in the second round, then Argentina, Brazil and Germany in the final,' says Christian, a charity worker who supports Arsenal. 'And then I want to see Becks get a knighthood and Sven do the Crouchy dance!' These guys are having the time of their lives and Scotland barely registers in their world.

'It's sad [that Scots are not supporting England] but I can kind of understand it – football's football and rivalry's rivalry,' says Gary, a golf professional who follows Spurs.

'After Germany and Argentina, you're our biggest rivals,' adds Christian. 'But we've not played you and whipped you for a while and where are the great Scotland players now? Barry Ferguson [the current Scotland captain] couldn't hack it at Blackburn and sneaked back home.'

Christian says he's always backed Scotland in games not involving England, although maybe this support is on borrowed time. 'I'm English, mate,' he affirms. 'I don't believe in Great Britain. I hate that my passport says 'British citizen' and I hate having to write 'British' on anything. England till I die, mate.'

I'm simultaneously cheered and depressed by meeting Christian and Gary. They're friendly and full of hope, but they're not especially devastated that Scots everywhere are currently swotting up on the USP of Paraguay (boasts the largest navy of any landlocked country). They don't appear grateful that I'm prepared to break rank and support England, and I detect a patronising tone as well.

I feel like giving the boys a history lesson. Scotland sent John White and Dave Mackay to North London, and if the last world-class Scot to play for one of their teams got homesick and headed home from White Hart Lane before they were even born, then at least Graeme Souness went on to fulfil his early promise as both a midfield enforcer and possessor of the second greatest football moustache (after Brazil's Rivelino).

But where would history lessons get me? What's the point in behaving like I am back in the playground, or the debating society? It would be like: 'My dad's bigger than your dad.' (Though in the case of mine he was.)

Once again I have to reprimand myself for being chippy. This is harder than I thought, being among fans with a sunny, hope-filled present when all I have with Scotland is a past.

I'm a hawker in this square, selling tat – brushes, encyclopaedias, insurance – that no one wants. Scottish achievement in English football is lost in the mists of time, and this lot certainly don't want to hear about 1967, an achievement this Scot managed to miss. Robert Louis Stevenson's quote at the beginning of *Jock* seems relevant: 'For that is the mark of the Scot of all classes: that he stands in an attitude towards the past unthinkable to Englishmen . . .' Thirty-five years ago, when the play was written, Stevenson's words filled me with pride. Now they just make me depressed.

And maybe trying to soundtrack this trip isn't such a good idea after all. These dusty choons could end up giving me a midlife crisis, in Germany, surrounded by England fans. The iPod is a great gadget but I am only using mine as a historical document. In the event of my death, it would tell the authorities all they needed to know about me: 'He liked the 1970s best.' Then my digital DNA plays 'Mr Slater's Parrot' by the Bonzos, featuring on bass guitar – and I used to think this was another posh English joke name, but it's real – Vernon Dudley Bohay-Nowell.

Looking around, I'm positively ancient. Most of these fans are not old enough to have had a father who was too young to go to war but faked his age to enlist, saw no action but pretended to his son he was jabbed in the neck by an incongruous cutlass (thanks, Dad). More relevantly, these supporters only started watching football after Bradford and Heysel and Hillsborough.

In the wake of those disasters, the Premiership/Sky TV/Bosman triple-whammy changed English football out of all recognition. It made the sport safe, respectable, aspirational; expensive, sexy and an arena of diminishing Scottish influence.

Flame-haired imp imperial Gordon Strachan inspiring Leeds United to the final First Division title in 1992 on a diet of bananas at the age of thirty-five really was the last hurrah of any deep significance for Scots players in England. The bulk of the supporters here in the Romerberg today probably know very little about the influence Scotland used to have on English football.

I seek out fans of a mature age and eventually find Philip Sudbury from Mold, an estimator for a building firm and a Nottingham Forest fan. He reminds me about Scotland's single, shining moment in the 1978 World Cup: 'I leapt so high when Archie Gemmill scored that fantastic goal against Holland that I burst the sofa on the way down.' It was a fantastic goal, but I suspect I'm being patronised (again).

Then Philip's group including his son Nathan join in and I'm patronised about the tremendous tartan triumvirate of Bill Shankly, Matt Busby and Jock Stein, about *Gregory's Girl*, Tunnock's Teacakes and the West Highland Way. This long-distance walk finishes slap-bang in the middle of the grim town of Fort William. Even though I've twice almost been caught up in fights there, my Scottishness compels me to accept this end point as a necessary hardship. I ask this bunch what they think of dark plans to create a new finish in a countrified setting and Nathan, the southern sap, says he heartily approves.

Leigh Nugent ('as in Ted and Emily') is a construction worker, Swindon Town fan and man of the world. His professional-traveller credentials are obvious from his deep tan and unironic 'Welcome to North Korea' T-shirt (he's actually been there). Almost alone today, he sports no England paraphernalia. From him I'm anticipating a wider perspective, on Anglo-Scottish relations and everything else.

With his friend Joe Perkins, Leigh left behind an England thick with bunting and delirious and one that clearly *believes.* 'It's mad at home,' says Leigh. 'There were England flags all along the A4, guys stencilling the Cross of St George on their garage doors and even one painting his lawn red and white.' The madness of St George, but Leigh and Joe seem to stand apart from it.

Joe works for Nationwide, sponsors of DestinyEngland, but has yet to feel the benefit of the deal. Faced with having to watch the Paraguay game on one of the giant in-town screens, he grumbles about how few match tickets are made available to company employees at his level. He's got to get back to the office after England's opener but Leigh is in Germany for the duration.

'I've taken the month off to do the World Cup in a mobile home,' he says. 'My girlfriend works for BBC Radio in Swindon and she wants us to file regular reports. I'm going to Italy vs Ghana in Hanover, and Brazil vs Croatia in Berlin should be amazing – I'll take loads of photos on a fast shutter speed. Then I'll head up to Hamburg to hook up with some friends I met recently in Thailand.

'That trip was typical of what happens to me abroad. Everywhere I go I have to justify myself as an Englishman, apologise for it. I don't get into fights, but the arguments can get pretty heated. I'm like: "Uh-oh, here we go again. How do you want me to repent?" My mum's always saying: "You look German, you speak the language – why don't you just pretend that's what you are?"

'The time I went to Goa it all kicked off. I was on a beautiful beach with a Greek, an Argentinean and two Frenchmen. We were standing up to our waists in water and . . . what were we talking about again? Guitars, marine national parks, fine wine, getting the work-play balance right. We were talking about nothing, we were talking about *life.*

'But before long I was having to apologise to the Greek guy for us nicking the Elgin Marbles, the Argie for us sinking the

Belgrano, the first Frenchie for us opening our legs for George Bush and – this bit went on the longest – the second one for the films of Richard bloody Curtis.

'Jean-Claude worked himself into a rage about *Four Weddings And A Funeral* and *Notting Hill* and *Love Actually* and how improbable they were – the amazing coincidences and the fact that in every Curtis movie there's this ridiculous race against time. He was jabbing me in the chest and shouting: "Does it *always* snow in England on Christmas Eve, does it, does it?"

'Then his mate joined in saying the films were just made for America and yet another example of how we were always sucking up to the Yanks. The thing he seemed to hate most about them was the "posh hair" on all the men. Mind you, he was bald.'

I tell Leigh that I'm with the French guys; I can detect the hand of Richard bloody Curtis in this England World Cup 'production'. For instance, David Beckham is a pretty boy who gets tongue-tied, just like Hugh Grant. Eriksson in the role of sex god is as improbable as America's biggest star – played by Julia Roberts – pitching up in a second-hand bookshop in West London (the 'plot' of *Notting Hill*).

There's the obsession with hair and the obsession with swearing (only English public-school types curse as much as footballers) and Beckham's obsession with the American market. There's Team England's relentless branding and CurtisWorld's relentless blanding.

Then there's the overbearing romances with the players' wives and girlfriends when this should all be about football (actually). The blaring jingoism and the feel-good tyranny . . . the crazy optimism despite evidence to the contrary (emotional constipation in the films; footballers who can't keep it up past the quarter-finals). The outrageous conceit (nine separate love stories in *Love Actually*; five separate 'My Stories' chronicling the World Cup, the players' book deals being signed before a ball is kicked).

There's the touchiness about criticism (previously monstered by Sven-Goran Eriksson body double Bill Nighy for daring to suggest that not everyone shared Curtis' fairy-tale vision of England, I've niggled some fans today for not being completely on-message about the World Cup). And let's not forget the smug certainties that surround Curtis and the England football team; that they believe themselves more in tune with the national mood than any political leader, indeed than anyone else; and that they and they alone can deliver the happy ending the country wants.

Leigh thinks England have a chance of glory but is nervous about how such a triumph would be received by the rest of the world, especially if his countrymen turn out to be completely insufferable about it. (Not much chance of that, surely?) There's a lot of the planet he hasn't yet seen and he'd like to be able to continue on his travels without being further called to account for his Englishness.

But Leigh doesn't rule out the possibility of David Beckham and the boys wimping out. 'Either the team will lose on penalties in the quarter-finals or this lot will turn nasty. Look . . .' Outside the town hall, a newly married German couple are trying to pose for pictures on their special day against a backdrop of England flags, flabby white flesh and a plastic ball being battered with stunning inaccuracy across the square.

Observant fellow that he is, Leigh has spotted the tabloid news reporters hanging around the fringes, trying to blend in, waiting for the situation to overheat. A film crew from the Nickelodeon satellite channel are making a programme which according to the stickers on their cameras is called *World Cup Of Scum*.

'We're an arrogant race,' continues Leigh. 'Because English is spoken just about everywhere – half of Germany is fluent – we're lazy about learning other languages. That puts us on the defensive and from there we start to lord it.'

Leigh tells me he's a mixture of German, Jewish, South African and English. Lots of the English people I'm encountering are a bit of this, that and the other. They state the exact mix, right away, as if it was a criminal's plea in mitigation: 'No, no, I'm not *one hundred per cent* Anglo-Saxon, perish the thought.' Americans do something similar, of course. Well, we're all God's mongrels. But Scots don't apologise for being Scottish, even though sometimes they should, and surely as many of them have ancestors who were born on the wrong side of the bed.

I'm thinking that it might be fun to travel Germany with Leigh; he seems to have just the right amount of cynicism towards England. Unfortunately, he also has a fair degree of cynicism towards Scotland.

'My dad always hated the Scots – he had a steel business, but you lot wouldn't let him trade north of the border – and I think I've picked up a bit of that from him,' he says.

'I love Scotland for Billy Connolly, Franz Ferdinand, the great sailing on the west coast and the bonnie lasses. It's a beautiful country but I just don't feel welcome there. I've watched England games in pubs in Edinburgh and Glasgow when I've been on building jobs and felt like a) a spy, b) a condemned man, c) the loneliest bloke on the planet.'

I can empathise with Leigh. The Romerberg is wall-to-wall England now. The 'Ten German bombers' chant has started up again, despite Eriksson, in the handy fans' guide *Free Lions*, appealing to fans not to sing it. Only when another wedding party emerges from the town hall does the singing stop. But then someone starts whistling the theme from *The Great Escape* and pretty soon the whole gang has joined in.

Germany's police have warned that even whistling, if done with malicious intent, will result in arrest. Doubtless these supporters would claim that no offence is intended by the World Cup/World War Songbook; that it is all about identity and 'your actual history, mate' – topped off with some jokes. (Eriksson insists he meant no offence when he included 'The Dambusters March' on his classical CD, then removed it.)

But I can help feeling sorry for these newly-weds. While my own marriage will be witnessed by people completely antipathetic to football, this couple have had their ceremony hijacked by some five-bellied blokes from Crewe, and every time they dig out the photo album to remind themselves of their happy day, they will see it: the banner flown from the town hall steps, obscuring heads in the family group and the mother of the bride's hat: 'British by birth – English by the grace of God.'

I think I've had enough Ingerland for one day. I head back to my hotel, order room service and watch some TV. One of those English-style light entertainment shows disturbing the ghost of Benny Hill has to be endured before the opening-day matches are analysed by the great Gunter Netzer – midfield choreographer, in green change-strip and size thirteen boots, of a stunning Wembley triumph by West Germany in 1972.

Now I'm drifting off to sleep and dreaming of Gunter, and Eveline Grunwald and Constanze Karoli from the *Country Life* cover. They're dripping with sweat, Netzer's shorts eight shades darker, the girls' surviving underwear even more see-through, and they're all sated and delirious after giving the English a football lesson, a sex lesson and an efficiency lesson.

Saturday, 10 June. Finally it's here, England's opening game, the Group B encounter with Paraguay at Frankfurt's Waldstadion. Kick-off 3 p.m. local time. Sven-Goran Eriksson, musical director of *The Sven-Goran Eriksson Classical Collection* (RRP £14.99), is ready. What about the players? Rio Ferdinand – the star, let's not forget, of *Rio's World Cup Wind-Ups* – takes time out from his hectic schedule and says: 'Let's do it.' And then the men entrusted with the country's dreams board the team bus emblazoned with the legend: 'One nation. One trophy. Eleven Lions.'

I contemplate the opposition. What do Paraguay mean to me?

A table. Next to my father's armchair – the one from where he shouted 'Bloody bastardin' shite!' in 1966 – there was a small, glass-topped occasional table. Underneath the glass were lots of stamps, all of them Paraguayan. This crucial piece of furniture meant Dad could keep within easy reach his whisky glass, snuffbox, *Radio Times* and other missiles to throw at the TV.

Yes, I'm ready, too.

I spin through my iPod in search of something appropriate. On King Crimson's 'In The Court Of The Crimson King', you hear the very English voice of Greg Lake: 'I walk a road, horizons change/The tournament's begun.' But on the Zombies' 'This Will Be Our Year' there's the even Englisher Colin Blunstone: 'This will be our year, took a long time to come.' Blunstone shoots, and scores.

Even the serious press is casting off its calm, objective speculations to reveal podgy pink English flesh wobbling with anticipation, just like the rest of us. In the *Independent* Sam Wallace plots England's route right up to the final, where he confidently predicts they will beat Holland to bring home the World Cup.

New arrivals at the Hauptbahnhof will swell the Ingurland ranks far in excess of any other visiting nation and each and every one of them will *believe.* So naturally I head out early to the Goethe House. Well, I want to beat the rush.

Johann Wolfgang von Goethe's birthplace is now a museum to the man many consider the greatest writer in the German language. A leading light of the Weimar movement, he was a true polymath: poet, novelist, dramatist, scientist, painter, politician . . . and football pundit? Many of the Goethe quotes adorning souvenirs in the museum shop could invigorate the anodyne debate taking place in many a TV eyrie high in the stadium rafters:

> 'We usually lose today, because there has been a yesterday, and tomorrow is coming.' (This could be Goethe on forty years of England yesterdays, and the weight of expectation ever since 1966.)

> 'Against criticism a man can neither protest nor defend himself; he must act in spite of it, and then it will gradually yield to him.' (Never mind whinging about bad press, Frank Lampard, you said you were going to win the bloody thing so get the finger out!)

> 'The man with insight enough to admit his limitations comes nearest to perfection.' (Can you look in the mirror, Rio Ferdinand, and for once *not* pull that smouldering, scarred, 'this is for da bruvvas' look . . . Can your peer into your soul, can you dive into your vast reserves of self-belief, right down to the murky ocean floor where the fish look as ridiculous as you, and finally acknowledge that maybe your concentration needs sharpening . . . *can* you?)

A mural on the museum wall has Goethe playing keepy-uppy and I want him represented on the streets of Frankfurt with a bold T-shirt slogan. 'That one,' I tell the girl behind the counter: *Divide and rule a sound motto; unite and lead a better one.* 'And don't bother wrapping it, I'll wear it.'

Every shop in Frankfurt has entered into the World Cup spirit, and while the most exclusive boutiques staffed by beautiful, bored Heidi Klum lookalikes – Heidi Glums – playing Depeche Mode remixes over the sound system are too cool to offer shelf space to the toy lion mascot, they will happily give prominence to Germany's national colours.

The host nation are up for it. So are the Mexicans, who've just arrived in great numbers to swear green, red and white allegiance. Ponchos a prerequisite, none of them over five feet two, all built like small armoured support vehicles chanting: 'Meh-hee-co! Meh-hee-co!'

Italians, Spanish and some rumbustious Croats have joined the crowds since yesterday but on the *Strassen* of Frankfurt on another sweltering day, each and every competing nation is outnumbered by the English. And back in the Romerberg, they are outnumbered by cockneys alone:

Steven Gerrard, Gerrard
He's big and he's fuckin' hard
He can pass the ball forty yards
Steven Gerrard, Gerrard

A Scouse icon, trumpeted by voices that will never stray out of range of the Bow Bells? Well, we're all English, *mate*. Indeed, *we* are. From Goethe to 'Gertcha', that's been my journey in just a few short minutes, and we're still five hours from kick-off.

I don't have a ticket for the Waldstadion. I could probably blag a press-box seat but what would be the point? I wouldn't be among 'my people' – though it has to be said my presence would not be missed.

The sheer mass of Englandkind is truly a sight to behold. Because this is match day, replica tops must be worn. You can get away with a T-shirt on eve-of-match, as long as it makes pointed reference to English superiority – 'Two World Wars And One World Cup' – and you can wear the red 1966 strip for the game (though today this risks you getting confused with, and possibly recruited by, the 'Know God Now' religious group who are in town for a convention). But the preferred option is the classic white, in real synthetic.

No other country represented here is more regimented when it comes to appearance. The shorts complement the top or they're camouflage-patterned (keep those war references coming, lads). The trainers are always white, and many fans will have acquired their gear from the same chav chain, JJB Sports, ironically founded by a Scot, Tom Hunter. Baseball caps are optional, but useful protection if the head is shaven, as many are. England are also the most tattooed nation, and in inking the Three Lions onto an arm or ankle, the supporters are apeing David Beckham, The Painted Fool. Flags worn round the waist recall Becks' sarong period and there are plenty of Rio Ferdinand-style skinny beards, in honour of the *super-baaad* centre back. The white, white polyester – with the single gold star denoting ex-champion status – completes the look.

One gold star, but in their 'Made In Honduras' garb, the English are acting like they own the Romerberg. Chins are jutting, arms are rigid, in readiness for the 'carpetfitter's walk'. There are more flags than the day before ('Oldham Loyal – 100 Years at Boundary Park', 'Walsall Till I Die', 'Locksheath – Stone Island', a rare namecheck for the clothing brand favoured by 1980s football casuals) and some fans are now firmly on a war footing, chucking plastic Spitfires across the square. Then a red double-decker bus shows up.

This English icon comes courtesy of another one – the *Sun* – and presumably it's parked up in the Romerberg to keep spirits buoyant. You could say the same of *Sun* reporter Tim Spanton: he's walked the 529 miles from London to Frankfurt with the bus as his support vehicle. But the fans are much more interested in the buoyancy on display from the two *Sun* glamour girls dancing and pawing each other on the top deck. 'Get your tits out for the lads!' is the chant.

Now a giant Cross of St George is being unfurled on the cobbles. It has travelled all over the world with the England team and been autographed by hundreds of fans. In charge of the official felt pens is Chris Hull.

'The flag is designed to promote goodwill and friendship,' explains Chris. And promote Nationwide: the building society's name is biggest on the flag. 'It's a unique relationship, England and Nationwide,' he says, and the company must be proud of their boy, in his Nationwide top, being interviewed by foreign media as the acceptable face of England fandom.

I ask Chris about the unacceptable faces, over there, singing about the war. 'What you have to remember, Aidan,' he says, 'is that the vast majority of England fans are culturally sound, with quite broad horizons.'

Chris has the too-severe haircut and burning eyes of a door-to-door evangelist. He's also reminiscent of an ingratiating politician in the way he keeps addressing me by name.

'Look, Aidan, there are 100,000 England fans expected in Germany for the World Cup. A small minority will have too much to drink. The problems we will experience with them will be no different to what we see in most town centres on a Friday night. I'm not condoning that tiny minority for singing about events that happened sixty years ago' [he's careful not to mention the war by name] 'but they comprise only one or two per cent of our number, and we're not going to have our image tarnished by a few idiots who have not been on the cultural journey.'

The way Chris talks, you would think a small group of troublemakers had barnacled themselves onto the good ship England only recently, when in truth it's the law-abiding whiteshirt that is the newish concept, and he's still feeling his way in major football tournaments. But you have to admire Chris' devotion to Nationwide's cause; also his devotion to their equipment. He breaks off from our chat to alert a colleague to a matter of some concern. 'Paul, quick – one of our pens is rolling away!'

He wishes me well in my efforts to integrate with 'the England family' and mentions – as one whose mother knows the former Celtic and Scotland winger Bobby Lennox – how much he misses the Home Internationals in summer's early promise (eg. Kevin Keegan scudding a shot past George Wood, a hapless Scotland goalie I'd completely forgotten about). 'But the thing is, Aidan, with all the fixture congestion, it would be almost impossible to fit them in. Shame. I really hope Scotland can get back to qualifying for the World Cup again. Very nice to meet you. Now Paul, when are we sending out that news release?'

With the help of people like Chris, and slogans like 'Pride Passion Belief', England fans are being rebranded. This is happening in just about every area of life, so resistance is probably futile. It is easy to sneer at the sanitised, emasculated, bowdlerised, made-over football supporter, but in England's case I guess you have to remember what came before him, the mayhem the old version caused, and the damage it did to the country's international reputation.

Just then, a new song starts up in the Romerberg. It's being sung to a backing tape, by possibly the oldest boy band in the world – certainly the only one in 36-inch-waist jeans. They're frugging around in an embarrassing manner on the top deck of the *Sun*'s bus and I guess they're supposed to look like regular guys – possibly regular Nationwide guys. The lyrics are jaunty drivel and may also be a sponsors' creation, in collaboration with the FA's 'creatives'. (I'm imagining a meeting of the 'song committee' – convened at the same FA table in Soho Square on which the Eriksson lookalike, in *Sven: The Coach, The Cash . . . And His Lovers*, bonked his secretary. I just can't stop thinking abut 'Sven', trousers round his ankles, Threadgold's Thorough-grip Garterettes *in excelsis*.) 'Keep on dreaming,' the song goes, 'sing it for Eng-a-land!' The square is jam-packed but no one pays much attention, or bothers applauding at the end. So a few minutes later these 'official' fans sing the 'approved' song all over again.

Now I'm wishing someone would fling a plastic pub chair and start a good, old-fashioned riot.

For the ticketless, and that's most of us, the good burghers of Frankfurt have plonked screens in the Main, the fat, slow river running through the city. They're massive. In the 1980s, middle-class snobs deemed big televisions common and dubbed them 'drug-dealer TVs'. These are drug baron-sized, and this is the FanFest.

Queues for the temporary grandstands on the river's banks began three hours before security guards opened the gates. All the seats were quickly snapped up. The next best vantage points – walls, statue plinths, electrical control boxes, even trees – have gone. In a pub on the north bank, England fans have commandeered all the windows. In the window frames, standing on the ledges, they look like an angelic chorus, arms outstretched, until you realise they're impersonating fighter planes. And as some Germans pass, happy enough to watch England in action, some even happy enough to wear England shirts for the day, the English show their gratitude by singing the *Dambusters* theme:

> Proudly with high endeavour
> Those who are young forever
> Won the freedom of the sky
> They shall never die

As I cross the Main by bridge, the patrol boats are already hard at work fishing England fans out of the water, prompting one of the bilingual policemen – identifiable by their blue bibs – to shout through his megaphone: 'HEY ENGLAND! STOP JUMPING IN THE RIVER! YOU'RE FUCKING MAD!'

It's early days, of course, but what a fine job Germany is making of this World Cup. Transport in Frankfurt is run on the honour system. The police survey the fans from a distance, cut them a bit of slack and occasionally join in the banter. They will only intervene if things threaten to get out of hand: 'HEY ENGLAND! DON'T BE ANTISOCIAL BEHAVIOUR! LET'S JUST PARTY!' And the FanFest is well run and friendly and the atmosphere must be on a par with being in the stadium. Indeed since there are no corporate whores here, it's almost certainly superior.

And yet . . .

'Piss poor,' mutters the England fan next to me as we jostle for position on the south bank. He's not impressed by German organisation. Euro 2004 in Portugal was much better, he says. Even when he stands on his coolbox he can't see the screen. But I reckon that's nothing to do with substandard German planning and everything to do with him being a short-arse from

Bolton. Teutonic efficiency makes England fans jealous and even scares them, so they refuse to acknowledge it.

I don't feel like starting up a conversation with this man and his wife and so I never get their names, but let's call them Terry and June. They make me think of the Bonzos' song 'My Pink Half Of The Drainpipe', and its suburban bragging about tomato plants, the latest power drill, foreign holidays and how 'it's life, not books, that's taught me what I've learnt'.

Three minutes into the match the considerably taller June passes down the information to Terry that England have scored. 'Tor!' shout some young Germans next to us. 'Beckham,' says June, but action replays confirm his free kick – delivered with a right boot smeared with gel for extra purchase; is that allowed? – got a touch off the Paraguayan captain, Carlos Gammera. No matter: DestinyEngland are on their way. I stifle a cheer. And I hope you appreciate this, Terry and June, because today, right now, is officially the most English I've felt in my life, *ever*.

That's as good as the match gets. Eriksson's reading of this poor start will doubtless be along usual lines: 'First half good, second half not so good.' But England are extremely fortunate to be playing a team who will ultimately be rated one of the poorest in the competition.

During the 'not so good', downright soporific second half, students with whistles run along the streets just behind me. I stop a girl and ask what they're protesting about; she is a younger version of Constanze Karoli and so not revolting in every sense. 'Neo-Nazis,' she says, 'but we're getting into trouble for disrupting the World Cup.' I tell her that some of us are grateful for the distraction, and by the final whistle, having sweated over the win since the third minute, and with Eriksson using the extreme heat as an excuse, we're all in urgent need of rehydration. It's back to the Romerberg for more beer.

I get chatting to some young German fans. I ask them what they think of all the war references and immediately wonder if my questions are almost as offensive as the songs. 'No, we're not offended, we think they're funny, we're relaxed about them,' says Leif Lengelsen from Dusseldorf, who is much more interested in talking about his favourite German punk rock band, Totten Hosen, and telling me a German football joke – 'What's green and smells like fish? Werder Bremen' – that possibly only means something to supporters of Fortuna Dusseldorf.

Matthias Munzer from Berlin also thinks the songs are 'funny', though he says Germany cannot apologise for Hitler for ever. He shows me his ancient 'Bonnie Scotland' T-shirt – red and yellow and so two thirds German in colour – and tells me how much he loves Scottish beer: 'Deuchars, *ja*?'

Andrew Schaffer from Frankfurt is a bit more expansive. 'The English think about the war a lot because it reminds them of a good time when the country was brave,' he says. 'Germans don't conform to the past but still for us it's been difficult to be patriotic about our country. For a long time we were forbidden from displaying any kind of insignia. We're trying to be patriotic now and the World Cup – because we're good at *planen*, at planning, yes – is giving us the pride.'

Even Andrew, though, is amused by the songs. And they say Germans have no sense of humour . . .

The games come thick and fast in the early days of the World Cup and today is a triple-header. The down-time before Argentina vs Ivory Coast gives me a chance for one last wander round Frankfurt. A blind Brazilian fan juggles a ball on his crutches in the hope of securing a ticket for his country's opening match. His optimism and skill amuse passers-by until the arrival of an English contingent, one of whom mildly abuses him.

I have not seen many incidents like this. A scuffle in the station, the aftermath of another in a bar leaving an Argentinean with a sore face, a black fan being harassed into giving up his vantage point for England's limp performance. Tame stuff compared with the excesses of past tournaments.

Chris Hull says behaviour has improved. I expected to encounter lots of veteran hooligans from the bad old 1970s and 1980s, but apart from the odd gnarled skinhead, buttressed by young louts in awe of his legend, the real bad guys seem to have left this World Cup to the binge drinkers and small-town malcontents.

Doubtless the authorities will point to the number of known troublemakers they've successfully stopped from entering Germany. Still, it seems a bit early to be talking about 'cultural journeys'. The tension is there, it's just underneath the heat-haze.

If real aggro is to be avoided, you sense that others will be required to step into the breach. Rival fans must resist the English provocation. And David Beckham and Co. must keep winning. No pressure, then.

Down by the Main some England fans are willing to acknowledge the brilliance of Argentina, but the Romerberg regulars won't be budged. These neocolonial neds have claimed this square for England. They're not about to give it up to watch some slippery Argies. The last chant I hear as I catch the underground back to my hotel is: 'I'd rather be a Paki than a Kraut.'

At the other end, with the Hauptbahnhof pointing the direction home, I decide to have one for the road in an Irish bar. It's still warm and the punters have spilled onto the street. Because O'Reillys greets new arrivals at the station, the bar is in a highly strategic position. The place is swamped with flags and the songs are sung with extra venom.

'You can stick your al-Qaeda up your arse!' indicates that these fans have bothered to look at the front page of a newspaper in the last twenty-four hours. (The chant refers to Abu Musabal-Zarqawi, top of America's hit list in Iraq, killed after a three-year hunt.) But the sullen, mistrustful, one-eyed perspective is all too apparent: the supporters bang on passing cars flying German flags, bullfight with buses using their plastic *Believe* banners, abuse a smiley-faced Trinidad and Tobago contingent in Red Indian headdresses – and then sneeringly inform the staff of the adjacent ethnic foodstore: 'This is England now.'

Very few England fans wear sandals. I've just noticed this. Presumably they're too Continental, too meterosexual, and never mind all those swords-and-sandals epics, they're no good for armies. Or lads with army fixations.

Other supporters relax (in sandals) and enjoy the cultural difference. Their nationality almost becomes irrelevant. For the England lot, however, it's all about the uniform, the war, reminding everyone who won it, standing proud (in sweaty trainers), chins *still* jutting umpteen beers later, not conceding any ground, never going off duty, refusing to show weakness, being ready for the call.

Thankfully the call never comes. A plucky Paraguayan approaches an England snarler and suggests an exchange of shirts. All over Frankfurt today there has been a steady trading of team colours. This has been the most popular form of greeting, and confirmation of brotherhood, at the start of the great festival.

'Nah, you're 'avin' a laugh mate,' says the Ingerlander, 'I'll *never* swap.'

The Ingerlanders I expected. The other guys were a bonus. On the flight home I revise my opinion of England as represented by Leigh Nugent, Christian Gladdish and the rest – even Chris Hull. They could have ignored me. Instead they tried to make me feel welcome. I thought I was being patronised. In fact, they were merely sympathising with me for Scotland's no-show at the World Cup, or anywhere on the football radar.

So who's conformed most to their national stereotype? The England fans, in the end, weren't stand-offish. But I was certainly a bit chippy.

What, then, of the England team? I turn for the last time to my favourite Frankfurt philosophers. There's Richard Curtis, who in *Love Actually* had Prime Minister Hugh Grant describe the country thus: 'Land of Shakespeare, the Beatles, Harry Potter, David Beckham's right foot [he's struggling now] . . . David Beckham's left foot.'

There's Johann Wolfgang von Goethe: 'Everybody wants to be somebody, nobody wants to grow.' Goethe could be talking about the England players, talking up their destiny, over-talking it, then turning out to be more or less mute out on the pitch.

The Bonzos' Viv Stanshall seems to concur: 'Whisky wow wow I breathed . . . *I am a big shot.*'

But maybe that cop with the loudhailer summed it up best: 'HEY ENGLAND! DON'T BE ANTISOCIAL BEHAVIOUR! LET'S PARTY!'

‘Dinnae Forget, I Have to Work Down Here’

After meeting so many English people who care so little for the ancient rivalry, I need, as an antidote, to talk to someone who cares a lot. And because I’m curious as to whether the reminiscences of my generation of Scots are worth anything more than mere nostalgia, this person will have to be a proper football man. I call Sir Alex Ferguson.

‘Aye, whit is it?’ he says down the phone line when I get through to Manchester United’s training complex at Carrington at the prearranged time. Stumbling through an explanation, I feel as small as Kevin Keegan in very big headphones, the day the then Newcastle United manager was freaked by some typical Govan voodoo.

Sir Alex warms to the theme. ‘A fantastic rivalry, fantastic,’ he says. ‘And I don’t know why Scotland vs England doesn’t still happen every year because financially the FA are struggling.’

His first Home International could have put him off for good – 9-3 to the Auld Enemy. ‘Me and four pals from Govan went down by train. It was a long journey in those days but you didn’t care. You were young.

‘Aye we got slaughtered that day but the thing is – and I keep pointing this out – we got the score back to 3-2 and their fourth goal shouldn’t have been allowed. They were fly with a free kick, too quick.’ Sounds like this still niggles him. ‘Brian Douglas put the ball in the net. The referee was Leo Horne, a Dutchman. Aye it does.’ Another year he remembers being landed in a tight spot by his best pal. ‘His wife wanted to know why, on the Thursday after the game, he still wasn't back from Wembley. That was Billy. He died a couple of years ago.

'Wembley was a fantastic adventure for a young Scot but Scotland-England games were also great character-building experiences for young England players. Bobby Charlton didn't exactly go backwards after having a 135,000 Hampden crowd baying for his blood.'

Then there was the time Sir Alex was walking up Wembley Way and he heard a jaunty rendition of 'Hi-hoh, hi-hoh . . .' He explains: 'We turned round and there were these Scottish guys, obviously without tickets, but carrying oxyacetylene torches. "We're gonnae burn our way in," they said.'

Fergie was a professional footballer so there was no Thursday dallying for him. In 1967, he was in with a chance of playing in the Wembley game that Scotland won 3-2. 'I was top scorer in Scotland [for Rangers] and I was selected for the Scottish League to play the English League at Hampden a few months before. But we lost that match 3-0 and, well, you know what the Scottish press are like.'

Who did Fergie support in 1966? 'England. It was a beautiful evening, very sunny, and afterwards I dug the garden. I supported them in the World Cup because I was a player and I could equate myself to them.' He pauses. 'When I say *support,* that's wrong. I was . . . happy for them to win.'

And what of the England team in subsequent tournaments – did he carry on 'supporting' them? A much longer pause. 'Ach son, I cannae tell you that. Honestly. Dinnae forget that I have to work down here.'

I tell Sir Alex about my father's reaction to England's great triumph and he laughs. 'History dictates that. The Highland Clearances and everything – there's a residual effect.

'A lot of Scots maybe don't understand where the rivalry between Scotland and England comes from. They probably don't know their history as well as they should. They probably don't know about the Clearances and that annoys me.

'It's not enough to wake up, to be born with a dislike of England before you're able to put a hand to a mug. You should know why. The reasons are obvious. And we're not the only country in the world that's been subjected to English rule.'

So how does he get on with English people, does he like them? 'Not a problem. It's fine.' At Man U, Scots are in the minority. 'There's only Darren Fletcher so he has to rely on myself and my coaches, Jim Ryan and Brian McClair.' With that kind of backing, you doubt that Fletcher suffers from an inferiority complex.

'I miss the Scotland-England banter, if I'm honest,' Fergie continues. 'I'm richer now that Steve Bruce and Bryan Robson aren't around to rob me because they wanted to bet on every tiddlywinks contest going. Further back, guys like Alan Ball and Nobby Stiles hated the Scots. I remember Denis Law telling me that Stiles tried to shake his hand in the tunnel before a Scotland-England match and Denis told him: "Fuck off, you squinty-eyed, bandy-legged bastard." That's rivalry. That's why we love football. Without rivalry, football really *is* tiddlywinks.'

Fergie wants his Scotland-England match back – and so does Sir Bobby Charlton. 'Bobby's aye on the FA to reinstate it,' he says. 'England might think they've outgrown it but beggars can't be choosers. The FA are in deep shit with this new Wembley; rebuilding the bloody Taj Mahal would have been cheaper. They need the money and are only going to fill the place if they open the doors to 70,000 mad Scotsmen. And what a wonderful sight that would be!'

Pleasing Frontal Aspect

Wedding update: Lucy's old university chum, 'Johnny Ha-Ha-Cha', can't come and neither can the Cave-Bigleys or the Duke-Willys. That's too bad. But some of those who've replied in the affirmative are wondering if the invites have missed out a significant hyphen in my name.

Imagine being double-barrelled! Like Shaun Wright-Phillips! Or, further back in football-time, Ian Storey-Moore! No disrespect to these guys, but I don't think they're very posh. Not like . . . 'blunder-prone Sloane' Tiggy Legge-Bourke! I'm contemplating introducing myself as 'Aidan Gordon-Smith' when I debut my kilt.

Three of Lucy's girlfriends are getting married before we do. I really should be keeping the kilt for my wedding but Lucy is courteous and considerate enough to allow me to break it in early. She is, after all, a former winner of the Swinton Cup.

I need to wear the kilt and look my best because I'm meeting, for the first time, some important members of Lucy's circle. I've already got a sense of how her world differs from mine. I can often be found in the 'lounge'. Lucy prefers to inhabit the 'sitting room'. I have 'tea'. She has 'supper'.

On childhood holidays, in the but 'n' ben, the 'lounge' was, curiously, a 'parlour'. Even more parlous than the parlour was a musty room with a wheezing harmonium in the corner which, in my young imaginings, was the one played by the great, glum humorist Ivor Cutler during recordings of his epic series *Life In A Scotch Sitting Room.*

Life in my Scotch parlour wasn't as surreal or as spartan as Cutler's but, perversely, I kind of wished it was. Both there and back home in Edinburgh, I wished for more dourness, more cod roe for tea, more tapioca for pudding (when there was pudding), more Sunday School, in a church annexe suffering from a more insidious dampness, sterner lectures on carbolic-soap-cleanliness being close to godliness, longer slide shows of missionary work in the Congo, a tighter hole for your head on the itchy-scratchy sailor's pullover I was required to wear for junior worship. Such was the lot of a Son Of John Knox.

The reward of dancers is to drink in hell

That was the great Protestant noise-abatement officer, in a quote used by my father in *Jock* and also in a follow-up play, *Knox*, which gave full vent to the man's life and work and enduring influence over Scotland. But here I am dancing, in my kilt, with lots of posh totty. Down here in hell, it doesn't seem too bad.

I feel like I'm in the TV adaptation of *The Camomile Lawn*, that gamey Mary Wesley yarn about spirited gels who craved stockings but didn't keep them on for long and lay back and thought of England and had a 'good war'. None of these women doing the leading in the wedding marquee could remotely be called a wallflower; and a couple of them are even starting to resemble Jennifer Ehle and Tara Fitzgerald, the sexy stars of that drama.

A lot of the guests are 'in property' and the father of the bride makes a joke in his speech about his voluptuous daughter's 'pleasing frontal aspect'. So there's Jennifer and Tara but also those bossy, buxom presenters exploiting the Englishman's obsession with his castle: Sarah Beeny from *Property Ladder* and Kirstie Allsopp from *Location, Location, Location*. The marquee resounds to refined whooping.

Some of the guests shoot. Others sail. I'm cowed by chat

about Cowes. I mention the World Cup to my new yachtsman friend and in mere seconds he's staring across the loch. I don't think there's a single football fan here.

Lucy has been teaching me some of the trickier Scottish dances. I'm a sulky pupil because this feels very 'coals to Newcastle'. Actually it's worse and more like 'fanny pelmets and shag-me stilettos to Newcastle'. I'm Scottish, these are *my* dances. These other people here, they're . . . well, what are they?

'*Scottish,*' says Lucy, with mounting exasperation. '*Like me.* My mother is descended from King Duffus, who in 961 became Scotland's seventy-eighth monarch. Her great-uncle founded the *Dundee Advertiser*. Both my father's grannies were full-blooded Scots. Admittedly there was some sheep rustling in the family but I could play football for Scotland, if they were desperate, which they are. I bet if you were to research your family tree you'd discover you qualify to get a game for England.'

I retire to the bar. There I meet a Welshman in denial; he refers to himself as English. This makes me think of my friend Magnus Llewellin who's the other way round: a wannabe valleys boy who's technically, tragically, a Sassenach.

There is Welsh in Magnus somewhere but he was born in Oswestry in Shropshire, on the English side of the border. He tries to make the best of his lot, turning himself into a walking gazetteer of the market town. Everyone whose lives he has touched now knows of at least one famous Oswestrian: war poet Wilfred Owen; Ian Hunter, the singer in Mott the Hoople; Ryder Cup captain Ian Woosnam; cuddly, coke-snorting TV presenter Frank Bough . . . the drummer from Marmalade (he's getting desperate now) . . .

And Alan Ball.

Magnus carries this vital information with him at all times. 'It's like a Kidney Donor Card,' I suggest.

'It's my Oswestry Boasting Card,' he confirms. But even with a 1966 World Cup winner like Ball helping put their town on the map, some people can still lack pride in their Englishness.

Lucy says that when she went travelling she used to say she was Scottish to avoid 'international incidents'. The Englishman abroad, in her experience, was a drunken oaf and it was best to avoid any association with his kind. 'You should be proud that the Scottish identity travels so much better, and that so many people want to call themselves Scots,' she says.

Strange but true: some folk would die for our lineage and what comes with it: the history, the hard-luck stories, the cock-ups. Emboldened, I hit the dance floor. It's the 'Reel of the 51st', a right bastard. To get me through the intricate steps I become highly competitive. This is war! No, more than that: this is Scotland vs England in a revival of the Home International Championship!

The reel ends in a high-scoring draw. 'It's not ownership of the dance that's important,' says Lucy, 'it's the taking part that counts.' She's right of course. And she knows she's unnerved me with that remark about my genealogy possibly extending south of the border. Either I've got some English in me or I'm perfectly in proportion as a Scot, chip on each shoulder – chips with everything. Either way, I shouldn't brag.

I suggest a tiebreaker to Lucy. How about one of the disciplines from Monty Python's Upper-Class Twit Of The Year Show – Taking The Bra Off The Debutantes? She doesn't speak to me the entire journey home.

Toepoke No More

I'm getting used to this now. Another early morning flight to Frankfurt, and before that another taxi ride . . .

'Did you hear him last night?' asks the cabbie, mild murder in his voice. 'He's all "*We* need to push up on the right" and "*We* need to get our shooting boots on". Well, *we* need to remember where *we're* from, Alan Hansen, with your Alan Hansen ringtones and your Alan Hansen modelling contract for Marks & Sparks and your *Alan Hansen opinions about England.* And come to think of it, exactly why did you tackle Willie Miller in 1982 when the situation was under control?'

This is a typical Scottish reaction. We hark back to the past because when it comes to the World Cup – Malaga, Spain, Scotland vs Russia, and the 2-2 draw which eliminated us from that tournament – the past is all we've got.

And when a commentator or pundit gets it wrong, we bear a grudge. Boy, do we bear a grudge.

From the same World Cup, Jimmy Hill's description of David Narey's goal against Brazil – right foot, top corner, pretty brilliant, we all thought, considering it was little old Scotland – has reverberated down the years.

'*Toepoke? Toepoke?*'

An entire nation was dealt a wounding blow by that remark. Hill, the players' terms-and-conditions champ-turned-pundit, had already long been celebrated in song by the Hampden hordes:

We hate Jimmy Hill
He's a poof
He's a poof

It is possible the 'toepoke' comment was Hill getting his own back on Scotland for the incessant taunting. But it is also possible that *no offence was intended.*

The remark's significance in the recent history of Anglo-Scottish relations cannot be overstated. Ask the average Scot what he doesn't like about the English and invariably the answer will come back: 'The football commentators.' Ask for elaboration and you will be told about their arrogance, their triumphalism, their failure to acknowledge the fact that not everyone watching will be supporting England. Ask for specifics and Hill's 'toepoke' will be right up there.

A few years after that vile calumny, Prime Minister Margaret Thatcher decided to abolish domestic rates and replace them with the poll tax. The new system was hugely controversial because it shifted the burden for local services from the rich to the poor, and Scotland got it first. We felt like we were being animal-tested; we felt like beagles forced to puff on Capstan Full Strength. To this day, mere mention of 'poll tax' can cause a collective shudder. But no more than 'toepoke' does.

Are we being oversensitive? If so, I cannot pretend that I rise above the rabble. My father taught me well.

Scots have highly sophisticated antennae for the chumpish, the chicken-counting, the ill-informed, the clichéd, the anodyne, the boastful and the disrespectful in all football talk. That includes scene-setting, prediction, commentary, summarising, punditry, analysis and next-match forecasting. This is especially true when it concerns English teams. Only beagles able to pick up high-pitched whistling can tune in with the same precision.

At the 1998 World Cup, England were beating Romania in a

group match and, late in the game, summariser Kevin Keegan declared: 'There's only going to be one winner now.' Romania won 2-1.

At the 2004 Euro Championships, England were in a similar position against France when commentator Martin Tyler ventured that the Spurs-bound French coach Jacques Santini could look forward to hearing a popular Arsenal chant rewritten for his benefit: '1-0 to the Ingerland'. France won 2-1.

And in 2006, during the Champions League Final, Clive Tyldesley sensed commentator immortality was imminent. 'And it's Thierry Henry! In Paris! For Arsenal! . . .' he shrieked as the Gunners' talisman bore down on the Barcelona goal. This was to be Tyldesley's 'Interesting . . . very interesting!', his 'Just look at his face!', his '1-0!'

Henry blew the chance, and Arsenal lost.

There are Missing Link hunters and Mossad agents and others whose jobs require them to be less driven, less name-in-blood, less permanently *on* than the Scot who's poised, waiting, *daring* an idiot with a microphone to utter something preposterous or presumptuous about the English cause.

I am not this man, otherwise Lucy would not be marrying me, but a couple of years ago, Socrates, the great Brazilian from that peerless 1982 team, was in Edinburgh to promote a skills school for kids. Some tabloid reporters were there but all they wanted to ask this genius in their midst was whether he thought the much less gifted Brazilian, Juninho, could improve on his poor start for Celtic.

How typically parochial, I thought. How typically Scottish. For my broadsheet, *Scotland On Sunday*, I suggested that this exchange seemed to sum up the small-minded, stagnant state of Scottish football.

And after the Old Firm-obsessed tabloids had scurried off with their updates on the SPL's 'samba boy', I got to ask Socrates *the* question of the age: 'That Narey goal – two whole decades and six World Cups ago, the one that annoyed Brazil and provoked them to score four in response, two of them mystical – was it a toepoke?'

'Yes,' said Socrates, 'but that is good. To hit with the toe is *bico*, a classic play. Look at Ronaldo, how he shoots with the toe. Remember his goal against Turkey [2002 World Cup semi-final]? And Romario. Half of all his international goals were with the toe. In *futebol de salao* [the short-form version of Brazilian football dating from the 1920s which was played by all the canary yellow legends], *bico* is classic because of speed and surprise.'

The man with the worst beard in football – Jimmy Hill – got it wrong. The man with the best told us so. David Narey – *bico*. Hill – *berko*. Parochial journalism? *Dinnae knock it.*

Nazis Are Sexy

On the journey to Nuremberg, via an internal German flight, I spare a thought for the poor buggers at home watching the World Cup on TV.

The previous day on ITV1, Clive Tyldesley remarked: 'By now you're probably in the habit of popping over to ITV4 for a *WorldCuppa*. It's a bit off-the-wall . . .' I've never seen *WorldCuppa* but I bet it's nothing of the sort. ITV don't do off-the-wall. They are the most wall-based network in the entire history of television.

Their World Cup theme is a hysterical version of David Bowie's 'Heroes'. You imagine it to be the work of a tribute act who learned about understated political messages in music from *Spinal Tap* and reckon this song, from Bowie's Berlin period, would be enhanced by some of the Nazi saluting Dame David tried out during the mid-1970s.

The World Cup is still, just, one of the televisual events in which we place our faith in the BBC, for which the bold Alan Hansen is the pre-eminent pundit. Hansen's position right now is interesting. He's not just a *talking heid* on the subject of football; he's emblematic of top Scots working in England. The debate is no longer about how well they do their job, rather how they're viewed by their countrymen on the issues of nationality and loyalty. Increasingly now, it's about how English people respond to them.

A highly successful Scottish footballer in England, Hansen

slipped effortlessly into the pundit's chair, stretched out his legs and made 'Diabolical!' his watchword.

The Scottish reaction was: 'Goan yerself.' A few were suspicious, but these were doubts of the perverse kind, like: 'Ach, he never got his shorts very muddy.'

The English reaction was one of approval; people liked his plain-speaking and even his cynicism, because at that time, when it came to the international team, the English public could be cynical too.

But the lie of the land has changed. Since Euro '96, England has become more English. These days, a team of pundits assembled for England duty probably wouldn't include Hansen. There would be no concessions to 'the regions'. Football debate would be dumbed down to faintly yobbish pub banter. There would be more guys like Ian Wright. This, the BBC believe, is what the England armchair fan wants.

Hansen isn't stupid; he saw this coming. So *he's* become more English. He's too nice; he doesn't want to offend. He's that mythical beast: a Scot who patronises the English. This hasn't gone down well in Scotland.

Despite his critics, I don't think he's sold out, not yet. I've always admired him for not waving a Saltire or swinging a kilt for the benefit of the Scottish tabloids but I do worry that he's losing his edge. I wish he was more provocative, more *Scottish.*

Hansen is in a hopeless position. He's the Scottish No. 2 to the smug git on his right, the *Match Of The Day* chancellor. He's like another Scot who's successful in England, the most successful in his field, but one who's wondering how the cross-border disaffection concerning DestinyEngland is going to play out – Gordon Brown.

14 June, the day before the second group game, and I can just about do the 'Ingerland in Germany' routine in my sleep . . .

You turn up in a new town the day before, check into the hotel, and drape your flag from the bedroom window. The

Cross of St George confirms the name of your diddy club (Rotherham United, Exeter City, Chesterfield). There are design variations because – too right, mate – you're not sheep. The RAF insignia in the top left-hand corner is proving especially popular this year, though between 'Derby' and 'Loyal', the Red Hand of Ulster can still sit proud. And – hello darkness my old friend – the Rangers crest, all the way from Unbonnie Scotland, puts in the occasional perky appearance.

Then when you're ready – Three Lions, collar up, and don't forget those Reeboks, for even the executives and the grey-haired grandads must wear them – you will hit the bars.

There you will drink and drink. Publicans will be run off their feet and, even in a proud beer nation like Germany, the reaction of the dachshund-walkers to the pyramids of empties will be one of astonishment.

You will sing the entire World Cup/World War Songbook. 'England Till I Die' contains the line 'I know I am, I'm sure I am', which sounds convincing the first time, but on the forty-third run-through suggests you're trying to persuade someone of your identity – possibly yourself, or a genealogist, or even a psychiatrist.

Humour in football songs ain't what it used to be, but '5-1 and even Heskey scored' is a good effort. (Emile Heskey was the clodhopping centre forward in a rare and outrageous victory over Germany.) Then, like Airfix kids, you will reassemble the Luftwaffe and start all over again with 'Ten German Bombers'.

All that drinking and jumping on the spot gets knackering after a while so you grab a seat (all together now: 'Sit down if you won the war!') and order – cheers! – more beer.

But the break doesn't last long. Someone will produce a football and you will embarrass yourself with your rubbish control as it is booted higher and higher, scudding off faux-medieval balustrades until the ball is finally confiscated by the ever-tolerant *polizei*.

Finally, in an echo of the pay-off from the most memorable

episode of *Fawlty Towers*, an elderly German will shake his head at this thuddingly inept display of the game you claim to have invented and sigh: 'How did they ever win the World Cup?'

This is what happens in Nuremberg within hours of my arrival from the airport. It was pretty much what happened in Frankfurt the week before, except the latter city was the starting point for everyone's World Cup adventure so it was a riot of colour and convergence. Five days in, you only pitch up in Nuremberg if a) you're an England fan, or b) you're interested in Nazi history.

There's obviously a worry that Nuremberg is attracting some who are both. On 9 June, the day the tournament began, the headline above the *Guardian*'s upbeat report of happy mingling and pictures of painted faces was: 'England fans join football carnival'. On 15 June, on the front page this time, it is: 'Quit the Nazi thing says our man in Berlin'.

Sir Peter Torry, Britain's ambassador to Germany, is appealing for fans to behave after six were arrested by police for giving '*Sieg Heil!*' salutes from the grandstand at the Zeppelin Field parade ground where Hitler mesmerised the masses. Said Torry of "Ten German Bombers': 'If only the people singing it could see themselves – great, fat, uncouth, bad-mannered people.'

But, according to some observers, this seems to be merely the great, fat, uncouth, bad-mannered articulation of what the English instinctively think and feel. Until recently Matthias Matussek travelled in the opposite direction from Torry: he was London correspondent of *Der Spiegel*. His perspective on English life made for dispiriting reading. For two years, according to the *Sunday Times Magazine* in a World Cup preview piece, he ranted about how the 'stoicism, education and humour of the British were being devalued by *Big Brother*, binge drinking and happy slapping'.

(This doesn't sound much different from the character description in a new edition of the *Rough Guide To England*: 'A nation of overweight, alcopop-swilling, sex- and celebrity-obsessed TV addicts'. Or that of A. A. Gill in his book *The Angry Island*: '. . . the lumpen and louty, coarse, unsubtle, beady-eyed, beefy-bummed herd of England'.) Now back in Germany, there's still exasperation in Matussek's voice when he remarks: 'You Brits dwell on the war because it was your finest hour. The war defined modern Britain.'

There's recent statistical evidence to support this opinion. After the 7/7 London bombings, a YouGov survey asked Britons to sum up Britishness from a choice of phrases. In first place was 'Our right to say what we think'. In second place was 'Our defiance of Nazi Germany in 1940'.

For Britain and Britishness, read England and Englishness. The fans on their tour of duty in Germany are obsessed with the hosts. They are frighteningly excited about the prospect, at some stage in the tournament, of having to play the inheritors of the iron-willed legacy – 'Penalty shootout? *Ja*, no problem!' – of Franz Beckenbauer, Gunter Netzer and Jurgen Klinsmann. Beckenbauer is an omnipresent president of the WC organising committee, leading the applause at every match. Netzer is just as relentlessly German as he punditises on TV every night. But Jurgen Klinsmann, now the national coach, is the possessor of an effeminate, skipping goal celebration which might suggest to England a character weakness and give them some hope. England-Germany is *the* great rivalry of this World Cup and while that's hard for a Scotsman to accept I have no option.

Second game in, I think I'm becoming inured to the war songs. Maybe the bombardment makes you deaf to them. But, in the context of this desperate slug-out between two once-great powers, they're all England fans have.

That 5-1 win in 2001 was a mere World Cup qualifier. Since 1966, Germany have won the games between the two teams that really mattered – 1970, 1990 and 1996. So the English cannot sing about football.

There *is* another triumph they could celebrate in chant-form:

the economic one. Germany, for so long the champs in this arena, have been deposed. Matthias Mattusek says the English currently display 'the same smug, self-righteousness we saw in the Germany of the 1950s, the era of the economic miracle' but as yet, the smugness has yet to translate into a song goading Willy Brandt and the Bundesbank. Chants, they just ain't what they used to be.

In the mid-fifteenth century the future Pope Pius II wrote of Nuremberg: 'Nothing more magnificent or splendid is to be found in the whole of Europe.' The city was the unofficial capital of Germany at that time, a great trading hub and a centre for artistic excellence. 'In truth,' the testimony continued, 'the kings of Scotland would be glad to be housed so luxuriously.'

You get a vivid sense of Nuremberg's glorious past from the moment you wander through the massive gateway in the medieval fortifications which still enclose the centre, the Altstadt. Eighty towers stand sentry round the Altstadt. Anywhere you turn down the cobbled streets, the castle – the Kaiserburg – hoves into view. Of course it's an illusion, a very clever one. Ninety per cent of the centre was reduced to rubble during the war.

Nuremberg's less than glorious past is located in the southern suburbs. Mention the city's name and the first thing most people think about is the Third Reich. That's if it isn't the war-crimes trials. Not only English football fans do this. Matthias Matussek recounts the story of a group of English history teachers on a visit to Germany. Their hosts laid on a wide and varied cultural programme but the teachers only wanted to discover more about Hitler. 'Nazis are sexy, evil is fascinating,' was how a colleague summed up the trip.

The football stadium, the Frankenstadion, is near all the monuments to Nazism – the ground itself used to host Hitler Youth meetings – and the England hordes will encounter them soon enough. I don't have a ticket for tomorrow's match but the

FanFest is down by the stadium. Already the prospect is filling me with apprehension. The city centre is currently under Ingerland rule. 'Ingerland, Ingerland, Ingerland . . .' is the chant of choice in the late afternoon. Call me a musical snob – call me Scottish – but the ditty really wouldn't count as one of Mr Noël Coward's better efforts. There's a beautiful fountain in the Altstadt called, according to my guidebook, 'The Beautiful Fountain', but it's been swamped by a massive banner proclaiming 'Dover Whites'. Nearby, a different song is being sung, but this turns out to be a Mars promotion featuring buffoons in monks' habits, another piece of contrived jollity from our sponsors:

Believe (England)
Believe (England)
If we all just believe
We're gonna win the World Cup this time
Believe!

My hotel is some distance from the city centre, and after getting off the train at Furth there's a rare flaw in German transport super-efficiency. I decide to kill the wait for the connecting bus – a mere ten minutes – in the terminus bar. When I emerge into the bright sunlight again, three hours later, I have a woozy head but a better understanding of what being an England fan is all about.

Two big, burly men are fiddling with the tiny speciality sausage, the Nuernberger Bratwurst. Bill Butler and his friend Woolwich – not his real name, but the nickname he acquired from a spell living in the London district – are West Ham supporters, fortysomething veterans of hundreds of internationals in England campaigns spanning two and a half decades . . . and reformed hooligans.

Woolwich is shaven-headed. Bill is just as imposing, but at least he has hair. However, parts of his face seem to have been rearranged. One eye peers at me strangely.

We're drawn to each other by our lack of Englandwear – me because I'm Scottish and them because they still adhere to old-skool football casual traditions.

'So what you doin' here then?' asks Woolwich. While Spain thump the Ukraine on TV, I tell him. 'Christ, that would be like me supporting Millwall. I'd rather die than do that.' Like everyone I've met, Woolwich supported Scotland at World Cups that England missed. Like everyone I've met, he thinks that 'the way fings have gone' Scotland couldn't count on that backing now.

'Why's that? Well obviously I'm going to apportion the blame elsewhere. I think there's been a counteraction to Scotland betraying us – maybe that's too strong a word but you know what I mean: this "Anyone But England" fing.

'I was at Hampden when we beat you 2-0 [1999, Euro Championship qualifying play-off] and the Jocks were shouting "Malvinas! Malvinas!" How's that getting at just England? Scots soldiers as well as English died in the Falklands War. When we go off to fight we're side by side.'

Woolwich is a taxi driver. Every morning he buys his copy of the *Sun* from a Scottish vendor at Piccadilly Circus. During the countdown to the World Cup, the paper-seller took to wearing the blue and white of Argentina. 'That's wrong,' he says. 'You shouldn't earn your living in England then slag us off. If I was to move to Scotland – though wild horses wouldn't drag me – I wouldn't do that.

'Don't take this personally, but I think you've got little man's disease. When a bloke's little he shouts to make himself big. I put the Scots in that category.

'It's not always England's fault when you get disrespected. Most Americans are quite uneducated and they'll say "English" when they mean "British". But fings have changed between us now – for the worst. In the past, you would slag us off and we wouldn't notice. Now when we go to tournaments we sing songs about how crap you are and you're not even there.'

Bill is East End born and bred. He grew up in a multicultural community where there were lots of Scots, so has long experience of Scottish attempts to burst England's balloon. He says that English people who have not had the dubious honour of living next to Scots will be the ones surprised and possibly upset by Scotland's reluctance to swoon at David Beckham and Co.

Bill now works for a charity which helps immigrants adapt to life in Britain. He remembers recruiting Bobby Gillespie of Primal Scream for a fund-raising five-a-side football tournament. The Scottish rocker turned up in an Argentina strip. Underneath was a German one. 'Bobby hates us and I assume you do too. No fucker can tell me why, though.' Bill will ask me the question a few times, and to be honest this fucker is struggling for an answer. Forty years is a long time to be carrying a grudge about a game I only half watched while recreating the Battle of El Alamein with my toy soldiers on a swirly-patterned rug.

In his wild youth Bill didn't much care for his national team. 'In the 1970s it was very uncool to support England, especially coming from where I did with all the connotations with the National Front,' he says. 'But it was also quite a speccy fing – trainspotterish. If you were a West Ham fan, that's who you supported. I didn't really *get* England as a kid. How was I supposed to like all those different players? I hated Emlyn Hughes. I really hated Kevin Keegan. Them wearing white shirts wasn't going to change that.'

But football for Bill has always been a means to an end. Early on, back in the 1970s, he would organise West Ham awaydays round Northern Soul all-nighters in places like Leicester and Wolverhampton; the music came first. That continued through to the late 1980s and the explosion of rave.

Then, during a slump in West Ham's fortunes, he started travelling abroad with England. 'We'd go to Spain, France, Italy on £15 awayers and these trips would be great for feevin'. Mostly we nicked clothes. I appreciate football more now but when I was sixteen I just wanted to go fuckin' mental. Although we were all supposed to be supporting England there was a lot of rivalry between the clubs. West Ham were disliked by most teams so you went mob-handed. It's still the case now. In a group of 600 England fans here, 450 will be Northerners and ten to twenty per cent of them will fuckin' hate cockneys.'

Bill and Woolwich don't have much time for their fellow England fans, especially these days, which explains why they're here, in the suburbs, far from the platzes and their drinking games. Woolwich reckons that lot are spoiling the good-bad name of real hooligans.

'The guys who are perceived as hooligans now are just drunken idiots,' he says. 'I'm not claiming it's clever being a hooligan, but in our day you only fought people who wanted to fight you. Honour among feeves, if you like. You didn't throw furniture and hurt innocent bystanders. These idiots need locking up.

'They can lift a ton but they can't spell it – there's not a lot of intelligence among them. It's like Guildford on a Friday night down in those squares; you can see what a mass drinking culture England has got now. In our day we didn't drink much and we don't now. I'm not saying our era of hooligans was *Mastermind* class but quite a lot of the guys I used to hang about with are millionaires now.

'The reasons people get into football are different today. When I was a lad it was all there was. The fighting came later – we went to away games which weren't policed and at first we were defending ourselves. Then you become the aggressors. I'm not saying I didn't enjoy the fighting, I did. And I got pretty good at it. But there's a fallacy that hooligans are all extreme right wing. Most of us thought right wing meant George Best. We were fans first and foremost who loved our clubs.'

Ah, the good old days. Woolwich might be accused of looking back on his youth through beige-tinted specs, that being the 1970s shade of choice. But you would find it hard to argue with his claim that there is less true feeling for the game among these recent converts: the corporates, the Loserville lager louts and the middle classes who view England trips like stag weekends, with the chance to 'slum it' among ruff, tuff guys keeping football a rung above paintball.

Bill's and Woolwich's working-class credentials are impeccable – they even travelled to Germany in a white Transit. Bill is less into football than Woolwich – when I correct some dates and scores he confers on me his epithet for the colour-coded fact-obsessed: 'speccy' – but Woolwich leaves the political/sociological matters to him. Bill, it turns out, attended – where else? – East London University and blagged himself a degree in popular culture.

So what does he think of the flags, the team colours, the great spewing forth of national identity? 'Well, I'm a Londoner first, an Englishman second – but I've never called myself British. To me the Union Jack means all the land-grabbing that went into making the Empire and the repression of the working classes. It's the Butcher's Apron, innit? No, *never* British.

'It was nice to see so many England flags at home before we came over but wearing the strip in Germany, it's a bit tacky. Football shirts only look good on a football field. It's obvious we're England and it's obvious why we're here. Maybe this is the casual in me but when you go away you should look your best. You're representing your country. Sadly England these days is just full of muggy boneheads who wear their football shirts to go out for Sunday dinner.

'In the 1970s fans were proud of their regional differences. If a skinhead walked into your pub you knew he must be a Northerner because there were very few skins in London. If he was wearing a deerstalker he would be a Scouser.

'England, our country, doesn't have its own borders or institutions or national dress so we don't have a national identity. There's a Starbucks on every corner and Clinton Cards across the road. If I was to go clubbing now it would be "Music

Sounds Better With You" and all the latest indie summer hits ["Music . . ." was a club anthem seven years ago but I get Bill's drift]. And these kids from the nowhere places where nothing happens buy into the mass culture, buy the badly stitched England strip and dress the same and follow each other around and copy each other's rotten chants and never stop to think and look about them and wonder if maybe they're being conned and they're just so . . . *lumpen.*'

Woolwich might insist he 'ain't no culturalist' but he does not lack insight. A lot of his friends are 'racialist' – blokes who question the right of non-whites to wear the England strip. He admits that fans without white faces are few in number. But he at least commends those who are brave enough to declare their support.

Wisdom came to him in the nick of time. 'The sentences being handed out by the courts were getting tougher. Maggie Thatcher decided that the hooligan was Public Enemy Number One. For punching some git in the mouth at a match I might as well have done an armed robbery for thirty grand. Not that I did, mind.

'Sadly, for a long time being a hooligan was central to my life. My dad didn't understand the fighting and was always asking me: "What's it all about son?" The penny dropped when I got married and the kids came along. My horizons broadened. Before, every friend I had was a West Ham fan – that's English football for you. But with the wife came an Arsenal-supporting brother-in-law. I couldn't hate him. Now – get this – I help coach Arsenal's Under-10s.

'I still go to West Ham and when I see rival fans who were high up their clubs' hooligan hierarchy – guys at my level, which was pretty near the top – we just nod at each other as we pass. And every day on the cabs now I have my tea break with this Millwall geezer who I used to absolutely fuckin' detest.'

It's time I was going. Spain's 6-0 win has been heavily analysed, the evening match will start soon and I still haven't found my hotel. I seem much more drunk than Bill and Woolwich and I'm pretty sure I must have been giggling like an idiot most of the time. This is what middle-class boys do when they get the chance to hang out with hard men and think themselves terribly brave. Bill and Woolwich stressed how much they dislike this kind of fan but I failed to take the hint.

Nevertheless, the lads give me their phone numbers and suggest we meet up later. This emboldens me sufficiently to ask Bill how he came by his scars.

'Leeds away,' he says, starting with a gouge on his right arm. 'And the one next to it was Old Trafford. I'm the unluckiest fan ever. If Newcastle threw a bottle at 20,000 West Ham fans, it would hit me. At our local, the Green Man, we used to play a game called "Guess My Wound" because every other week I'd come in with a new one.'

So what about his face? I've been trying not to stare at this miracle of surgical reconstruction for the past three hours – what happened?

'Oh that? Nah, that wasn't football. Happened when I was a student. I was walking home one night and went straight into the middle of a gang war. The junkies had taken over the estate and this bloke tried to chop off my head with a samurai sword. Nah, not football . . .'

Phew. For a minute there . . .

My hotel, the Furth Nuremberg West, is so far west of Nuremburg that I think I'm back in Frankfurt. I come down for breakfast on match day number two and, because the hotel is right on the autobahn, assume with some disgruntlement that I'll be stuck among OAPs on a bus tour of Bavaria's castles.

Sure enough, there are two old-timers at the serve-yourself buffet, one of them on crutches, and I guess they must be fighting over the last of the prunes. But Jim Hughes and Stuart Hodgson are arguing about what they always argue about: the great rivalry.

Jim is originally from Carfin in Lanarkshire. He's fifty-nine with a boxer's phizog. Stuart, from Wakefield in Yorkshire, is eight years older and the possessor of a debonair moustache. It's forty years since they left home to begin new lives in Australia: two men from two very different corners of Britain who arrived on £10 'poms package' tickets and quickly became firm friends. Now they run a taxi company together. But all the years and the distances travelled from their homelands have not dulled their desire to see their country win at football and the other lot lose. Heavily.

They have tickets for three games, including England vs Trinidad and Tobago. Jim is far from overjoyed at the prospect of having to watch the whiteshirts. He offers to sell me his ticket: 'The only thing is, you'd have to push this bugger's wheelchair.'

In common with many expat Scots a long time gone, Jim prefers his news from home dipped in sugar, so he gets the *Sunday Post* delivered to Adelaide. Despite the date on the paper's front page, it reminds him of how Scotland used to be. He would like more features on old Scotland football legends like Jimmy Johnstone and Jim Baxter, even though both are now dead. When I ask him what he misses most about Scottish culture, I assume he mishears me because he mentions shipbuilding and steel, now virtually dead industries. Then again, they're probably 'cultural' to him.

I ask Stuart what he thinks about Scotland's refusal to paint a red cross on its face for the England team and he just shrugs, as if there are more important things to worry about. Then he says: 'I like to see Scotland lose every time they play. They only have to take one towel. That's all they'll need.'

Four years ago, in a life-saving operation, Stuart had his toes removed. This doesn't seem to bother him as much as the fact his surgeon, a Scot called Larry Ferguson, played him 'Flower Of Scotland' before administering the anaesthetic.

I know the great rivalry matters but I thought it was only Scots who were preoccupied with it. It's remarkable, therefore, that of all the English people I've met so far, the one who believes in it the most is a 67-year-old expat who recently cheated death.

As I leave the guys to their ritual banter and bickering, Jim whispers to me that his old pal will shortly require another operation; this time he will lose his fingers. 'Don't tell the bugger,' he says, 'but for his sake I really want England to win today.'

At the bus stop outside the hotel, Shamir Jokima is talking to some fellow England fans. A text message from home on Shamir's phone has sparked much hilarity. After just one match, giant screens erected in England's city centres have had to be dismantled because of fighting among supporters. They include the one at London's Canary Wharf, where Shamir would almost certainly be watching today's game if his sister Selina had not managed to secure some corporate tickets. 'Typical England,' he says. 'We try to be Continental. We allow al fresco drinking. And we just muck it up.' Nevertheless, Shamir thinks this team can do something untypical and win the World Cup. 'I know there's a lot of hype but I'm trying to stay objective. I honestly believe we've got the quality to do it.'

Despite the positive spin from the FA about England now having lots of fans from ethnic backgrounds, I haven't seen many in Germany. Neither has Shamir, a twentysomething bank worker, which might qualify him for a free drink from Woolwich – if not his mates.

'This is my first England game and I must say I'm disappointed that it isn't more multicultural,' Shamir says. 'Fans of my dad's generation don't go to football because they remember the 1960s when it was all white. When I first got interested, I had to get my next-door neighbour to take me to matches. At my team Gillingham now you're still lucky if you see two brown faces. But I expected more at England games. The FA are always telling us we're one big happy family.' At least

Shamir believes, though I get the impression he uses the word in its traditional, pre-Mars Inc. sense.

With a population of just 1.3 million, Trinidad and Tobago are the World Cup's tiddlers. Their manager is another wily fox, the Dutchman Leo Beenhakker, but really England shouldn't have any problem racking up a big score. Just look at the number of Scots-based players in the T&T team.

Among the Scottish contingent for whom First Minister Jack McConnell will be rooting are Marvin Andrews, a charismatic centre back and devout Christian who calls on God's help before chopping down opponents with interventions which are anything but divine. Russell Latapy is a dreadlocked, ageless, sand-dancing playmaker who entranced fans of my team, Hibs, for a couple of Caribbean-flavoured seasons before overdoing the Lilt on wild nights with his friend Dwight Yorke, the T&T captain. And let's not forget Jason Scotland, inspiration for his adopted country's alternative WC anthem:

> We can still support . . . Scotland
> What?
> Scotland!
> Eh?
> Jason Scotland!

Once again I don't have a ticket. Bill Butler says he could probably get me one. He knows the touts – 'not the scallies but the actual guv'nas'. But he reckons the black-market price would be 1,000 euros – too steep for someone less than convinced about DestinyEngland who also has a honeymoon to pay for. I need to consider my viewing options.

The heavily scarred popular-culture spokesman for the free republic of Forest Gate has convinced me there is no shame in forsaking the FanFest given its location in the Luitpoldhain, the parkland where much of Nazi Nuremberg stood and venue for the rallies before the war. (Along with the Zeppelin Field, there's the Great Road and what little remains of Hitler's plans for a 400,000-capacity stadium, the world's biggest.) I head back into town where most of the shops seem to have closed in honour of the England fans (OK, apart from World Of Sex) and eventually find a smaller screen in a pretty square called the Hauptmarkt.

The bar with the best balcony views, Alex, has already been claimed by fans from Doncaster, Hull and Halifax. Presumably these are Bill Butler's 'muggy boneheads'. A group of friendly looking Evertonians seems a better bet.

Mike Lewis is in Germany to celebrate his fortieth birthday. He's brought along his brother Nick and their father George, who bears more than a passing resemblance to Tony Blair's father-in-law Tony Booth, 'yer randy Scouse git' from *Till Death Us Do Part*. Right away, they understand the Scotsman's plight.

'We sympathise,' says George. 'Like the Scottish, Evertonians have bigger, more illustrious neighbours who lord it over us.'

I thought the Liverpool-Everton divide was special: a rivalry with less enmity than most, more mutual respect, with fans standing shoulder to shoulder demonstrating that first and foremost they're Liverpudlians. 'Christ no,' says George.

What about the camaraderie of the 1986 FA Cup Final? 'Nauseating,' he says. 'Listen, Everton won the league the year of Heysel. The ban on English clubs stopped us playing in the European Cup and we've never forgiven Liverpool for that. The rivalry is quite bitter now.'

'Mind you,' adds Nick, 'no one hates Stevie Gerrard more than me when he's in Liverpool's colours. But when he pulls on that white shirt I love him.'

Mike appears to be going through a midlife crisis. But this only sharpens the famous Scouse wit. I thought I was bad, never giving England an inch, but then he describes his feelings at around half-past eight on 25 May 2005 – the Champions League Final between AC Milan and the rabble from across Stanley Park.

'That was the night I split up with the wife,' says Mike, 'and we were in separate rooms, packing boxes. I was with my son and we watched Liverpool go 3-0 down. Then she shouts up do I want a glass of wine. I say OK because I'm thinking: "Even you can't fuck tonight up for me." Well, you know how the game went after that.

'I think I finally got to sleep at twenty to three. I woke up again ten minutes later in a cold sweat. I'd just remembered that at work I'd have to face all those delirious bastards.' When life lets you down, there's always your football team – more or less. 'I wish I didn't love Everton but I do, I can't help it.'

The crowd is tightly packed into the square. On a stage near the viewing area, a Soca band plays the traditional T&T music while two buxom women in red bikini tops demonstrate how to sway to the lazy rhythms. It's going to be touch and go whether the women can complete the song before they're encouraged to doff their tops. 'You should have been here half an hour ago,' says Nick. 'A girl in an England shirt got up on stage and starting jigging about. After about a minute the crowd were ignoring her, so she decided to get her tits out. That bought her an additional minute. And she's been the sum total of our cultural contribution.'

But I detect an improvement in the behaviour of the England masses. It's only slight, but they don't seem as edgy as in Frankfurt. There was a 'first day of school' feel to the beginning of the World Cup; everyone was out to impress with songs and wind-ups. Now they know their way around Germany a bit better, the Ingerlanders appear more relaxed. T&T, of course, pose absolutely no threat. The English can claim the town as their own, confident they will not be outsung by other nations. All we need is for the team to start playing better . . .

Not tonight they don't. Indeed, for a large part of this match, a shock looks possible. A team which includes representation from Luton Town, Port Vale and Falkirk (cue my father: 'Not Fal-*kirk* – it's *Fal*-kirk!') are matching the big shots of *The Best*

League In The World – © every English commentator – without much difficulty. Peter Crouch misses a sitter and immediately has the whole square on his back. (I try to recall other great England misses and one by Geoff Thomas of Crystal Palace – horribly skewed forty yards wide – comes to mind. Am I the only person here able to summon up a memory of that shocker? I don't think so . . .) Then David Beckham, who's been playing deeper than Gary Neville, sort of right-back-in-the-changing-room – one of the first jokes I ever heard, and a true classic – fires over a cross and Crouch nuts an unlikely goal.

He's big, he's red
His feet stick out the bed
Peter Crouch, Peter Crouch

What a relief! And as the fans relax, the chants get even funnier – 'We're shit but we're 1-0 up.' The singing is loud and lusty but there's acknowledgement that DestinyEngland is not a given. T&T's brave resistance is over, and Steven Gerrard scores a second.

Back at the hotel, Jim Hughes and Stuart Hodgson are already settled into their favourite corner of the bar and, as usual, they're arguing. Scott Jones is by himself. As a London-based Grimsby Town fan, he cannot be entirely unfamiliar with this situation. The railway worker will be joined by his girlfriend for England's next match in Cologne, but he explains his unswerving loyalty to his club like this: 'It's in your blood, innit?' He'll support the Mariners until he's ancient, even though they've recently lost their best player, Rob Jones, to my team Hibs.

We're joined by more fans just back from the match. England in the World Cup has probably never appealed to 47-year-old metalworking solutions directors before, but Brendan Drummond offers yet more proof of the irresistible allure of Cashley Hole and his fabulous friends.

Aston Villa-supporting Brendan wonders if his brother Andrew was watching the game in exile in Kilmarnock. During Euro 2004, Andrew discovered that even hanging an England flag from a washing line is a provocative act. 'Someone passed comment about it on his doorstep,' says Brendan. 'I think the Scottish word is "keech".' But Brendan is laughing as he tells the story. And he enjoys good Anglo-Scottish relations with his own neighbour back in the Midlands. This is Willie Carr, one of the diminutive, ginger-haired Scottish midfielders who were regulation issue in England during the 1970s, and now Brendan's regular golf partner.

Tommy Eastham tells me he never used to have any time for the England team. And growing up in Sunderland in the 1970s, he wasn't alone. 'I used to not give a toss about the national side,' he says. 'I thought they were a southern phenomenon, London-based, a bunch of nancy boys who didn't award caps to great Mackems.'

There has been plenty to preoccupy him in his club's internecine rivalry with Newcastle United. 'It dates back to the English Civil War, when Sunderland sided with the Roundheads and that lot went with the Cavaliers,' he says.

Tommy understands why Scots don't cheer for England. He envies Scotland its devolution. 'You've got a very strong cultural identity and I think the only way for England to go is to split into regions. I'd love to see a north-east parliament working its socks off for us. When the chairman of the Bank of England says job losses in the north-east are an acceptable price to pay for low inflation in the rest of the country – and by that he means the south – then it's hard for me to rally round the flag.'

Nevertheless, here's Tommy supporting England and surprising himself. 'Well, it was the least I could do.' Then, smirking, he adds: 'They've done so well these past twenty years to get rid of the ponce element in the team, you're bound to agree!'

There's a Huddersfield Town contingent in the bar who share

a similar desire for a devolved England, broken up into lots of little regions surviving on, among other things, pride and wit. This lot give me a nickname. It's the catchphrase of the rasping Scottish voice of Sky TV's football coverage, Andy Gray: 'Free header! Free header!' I'm flattered.

Then Shamir Jokima wanders in, muttering darkly. 'Forget what I said before about us winning the World Cup,' he says. 'That was horrible.'

The one consolation for Shami is that, for the first time in World Cup history, there was a Gillingham player on the field – T&T's Brent Sancho. This was to England's benefit as well – the TV replays confirm that Peter Crouch used the defender's ponytail as a climbing rope to score the first goal – and the German highlights programme relishes the opportunity to expose some classic English skulduggery.

This looks like being my last night in Germany. The wedding gets ever nearer and, much as I'd like to come back to the World Cup, another trip would eat into my honeymoon. I still don't know how to tell Lucy that if England go on and actually win the tournament, we'll be spending the first day of married life waiting seven hours in Trafalgar Square for a severely restricted view of the victory parade in the company of Sid from Sidcup and Steve from Stevenage and some dork from Dorking who won't stop hugging us until we give them our phone number and promise to meet up *every bloody year*.

I've enjoyed Nuremberg. I've met some real fans with a nice line in ambivalence towards Team England and supporters new to the international scene who have not been first in the queue for white, plastic 'Come On England!' German WW2 helmets (£5.95 or £10 for two).

Remarkably, considering the mobility of people these days – and the fact you travel through Berwick in either direction without risk from a boiling-oil tower – the Sassenachs I've met in Nuremberg seem to know as many Scots as I do English people – next to none. Maybe some of these guys could become proper friends.

As the TV analysis of another dismal showing from Beckham & Co. winds down, I tell them that I plan to watch the next game in England and ask them to suggest a pub where a Scot would get a warm welcome.

'Try the Circus Tavern,' says Shamir. 'It's just off the M25 at Thurrock and very into its martial arts. I'm sure they'd love to see you there.'

The next day I phone Bill Butler and ask if he fancies a bus trip. He didn't watch the game at the FanFest so hasn't seen the Zeppelin Field yet. I tell him to suggest it to Woolwich as well but in the end only Bill shows up.

Matthias Matussek of *Der Spiegel* says the Englishman's fascination for sex scandals is matched only by his 'insatiable appetite for Nazi folklore'. Not today, though. It's just Bill and me. And while one of us is as English as 'Exclusive: What The Actress *Really* Said To The Bishop – Pages 2, 3, 4, 5', the other is an impostor. We're walking in the rally grounds. At least we think we are. They don't seem to be very well signposted. But maybe if this was your city's tourism must-see, you wouldn't draw great attention to it either.

Bill works out that we're at the back of the grandstand, and the giant podium. 'He must have spoke from over the other side.' Bill means Hitler. The terraces are constructed from concrete blocks the size of small houses and Bill wonders how they were ever moved into position. The Fuhrer obviously ordered his architect, Albert Speer, to think big. And what the Fuhrer wanted he usually got.

Nuremberg does own up to its horrendous past. Not far from the Zeppelin Field, we find the Dokumentation Reichsparteitagsgelande, a museum telling the story of the Third Reich and how the blocks were lugged around by concentration-camp prisoners. 'The lucky ones died on the building site,' says

Bill. But then he wanders between the exhibits in silence and I'm wondering if I've done the wrong thing in bringing him here.

Afterwards I suggest we get a drink. Bill looks like he needs one. We're back outside, gawping up at the grandstand again. It's another scorching afternoon, but the sun can do nothing to soften the ugly grey monolith, the linden trees can't dull its brutal edges and the techno throb of the FanFest DJ barely registers.

Then Bill says: 'I came to the World Cup hating the Germans because of the war. They bombed my nan's house. They bombed my mum's house. And if it wasn't for people like my mum, Oswald Mosley's blackshirts would have marched up Cable Street.

'In Forest Gate I grew up on bomb sites, those were our playgrounds. Every day on the walk to work I pass the memorial at Waterloo Station to the war dead. In London more than most places, there are always reminders.

'I came here hating the Germans but, you know, they're lovely, lovely people. They've really gone out of their way to welcome us. Someone of my size, the way I look, you'd expect them to go: "Whoa, hooligan!" But on the drive over here, when we got a bit lost, we even had little old ladies without a word of English trying their best to help with directions. Everyone's done their bit to make this a great show.'

They have, and it's not just Bill and the Ingerland hordes who feel a bit sheepish acknowledging this. Scots can hardly act superior towards fans who bang on about the war – the tartan tabloids did something similar when Berti Vogts was Scotland's national coach. Vogts complained about it; I felt bad because I'd been responsible for the odd joke myself. 'Der Terrier' was a lousy coach, but he didn't deserve the treatment he got.

Bill says he always knew the tournament would be well organised. 'It shows you why the Germans lost the war.' Sorry? 'Everything has to be done in triplicate. Germans need orders.

Tank commanders wouldn't turn right at the crucial moment because no one had told them to do it. They lack that vital element of surprise. That's my theory, as a military historian.'

Today's late afternoon game is about to kick off. It's Argentina vs Serbia and Montenegro. The FanFest is quiet, but Bill isn't surprised by the lack of England fans combining football with history at the Luitpoldhain. 'Our lot can't wait to get back to their vans,' he says. 'You'd expect the middle class to be more cultural but compared to the working class they're a lot less inquisitive.'

Class warrior. War strategist. Northern Soulite. Hooligan (rtd). Now: Germanophile. And he could get even more inquisitive before this World Cup is over.

Argentina, England's other great adversaries after the Germans, are playing wonderful football. They score six goals, one of them the result of a twenty-four-pass move. That's seventeen more passes than the build-up to Carlos Alberto's goal for Brazil against Italy in the 1970 final, generally reckoned to be the best of all time.

'Look at that,' Bill says, marvelling at replay after replay on the big screen, which sits under the monument to terror but is not in its shadow any more. 'Have you ever seen such beauty in more bloody awful surroundings?'

'Is There a Game On?'

Lucy's parents are over from France for a wedding, the last on the social calendar before our own. 'What was the score the other night?' asks future dad-in-law Tony. He could be winding me up but he could also be the only man alive right now – English or Scottish, it doesn't matter – for whom football doesn't matter a jot. What must that be like? My friend Simon Pia doesn't trust a man who doesn't like football, and only trusts a few who don't love it. The one and only football-themed conversation I've had with Tony ended abruptly when he said, and I kid you not: 'Who was that great Brazilian again . . . was it Pepe?'

But those who are not round-ball men have the opportunity to become rounded men, developing a wide variety of interests. Tony has had a fascinating life. He started off in newspapers in Liverpool in the 1960s when the city seemed like the centre of the universe and every kid with a Beatles-style moptop was quizzed for his views on life's inner meaning. Like my own father he then moved into television and read the news for Central TV. I wonder, were my dad still alive, what the two of them would talk about. The media, obviously, and how it's gone 'soft' and 'celebrity'. I could imagine them roaring at the goggle-box whenever a newsreader quizzes a reporter about a story, making said reporter part of it . . . or when a reporter files a despatch, live, from outside a closed building long after the last official statement, when there is patently nothing happening, apart from the New Scotland Yard sign, still spinning round and round . . . or when an interviewer asks the now obligatory question, in a manner suggesting that people in this country – and here we're talking England – were never justly famed for their emotional self-control: 'When such-and-such happened, how did you *feel*?' I like watching TV with Tony because when there are pregnant pauses during live broadcasts, he will always shout: 'You're on!' Dad did this, too.

But I don't think Tony and Dad would have got very far discussing politics. Tony is a Conservative and his last job before retiring was masterminding the 'Stop The Euro' campaign in Scotland. Since moving to France, though, he has given up the struggle. 'There are three things I don't do now,' he is fond of reminding everyone. 'Hills, confrontation and politics.'

Or football.

That bloody game. It's the great unifier, the international currency that the euro will never be. But it also stops men talking about other things. Sometimes my father and I talked about football specifically to *avoid* discussing other things, or to prevent deathless silences. Those 'feelings' never got a look-in. The great unifier was also a crutch, security blanket, placebo, sedative, upper, downer and quack-doctor's cure-all.

So what on earth are Tony and I going to talk about?

In Rio

It's the day of the Sweden game and I've got to go to Brighton for the day job. My plan to is be back home in time for kick-off.

I want to watch the match with First Minister Jack McConnell. I ask the Scottish Executive if he wouldn't mind getting in more beers and budging up the sofa at his official Edinburgh residence. But he turns me down. I'm not really surprised. Trying to prove his commitment to the England cause, Gordon Brown requested the presence of the *Mail on Sunday* for the Trinidad and Tobago game and was stitched up.

The Voice of Middle England, Richard Littlejohn, is less than impressed by Brown's stunt. 'Only a politician on the make would think to invite a newspaper to watch him, watching the football,' he writes in the *Daily Mail*. 'This was the Dunkirk of charm offensives . . . how daft does he think we are?'

McConnell, it seems, isn't as daft. Declining my request, and referring back to his stated support for T&T, his aide says: 'The first minister feels he's said his piece.'

Anyway, Brighton. I'm interviewing the Go! Team, a culty pop group based in the seaside town and apparently run along the lines of one of its celebrated junk shops. Their music is a mishmash of shouty girl rap, easy-listening trumpet parps and deranged guitars impersonating motocross bikes. They're all over the place.

Maybe it is too much to hope, then, that the Go! Team keep to a strict schedule. They turn up an hour and a half late, and as a result I miss my return flight. There's a later one but that would mean me being in air during the game, possibly missing the precise moment when David Beckham scuds his first surface-to-air pass across the night sky above Cologne, and that's not going to happen.

What now? I did not intend to be in Brighton for this match and so have no Plan B. No disrespect, I like the place, but it does not seem worthy of my attentions. England may only have one more game in the World Cup after this and if I have to watch them in action from somewhere south of Hadrian's Wall – and I do – then I want the location to be quirky, different, special, football crazy or football ignorant, a defiant outpost of something or other, a law unto itself. Brighton is to be none of these things.

Down on the seafront I check into the Thistle Hotel, with its tartan bedspread and curtains and, under a bright blue VistaVision sky, begin a surely futile search for what makes Brighton special. The usual shops are the usual shops. The local branch of USC, the footballer-wannabe boutique, is selling T-shirts celebrating Eriksson's prowess as a stud and demonstrating in five easy steps how to 'Do the Crouch'. There are some England flags on white vans and taxis but this is not a town gripped by football fever. Brighton appears too self-consciously cool for that.

At least the Lanes represent a sharp detour off Homogenity Street: I expect you can buy absolutely anything in the curiosity shops of this boho district. I contemplate putting this theory to the test. My most desired piece of English football memorabilia is George Cohen, or rather his solid, dependable napper on a silver plastic disc, the great unattainable missing piece in my Esso World Cup Coin collection, given away with petrol when my father filled up the Renault 4. But I have no time for such fripperies; there's a match on tonight.

What do I know of the local team? In a word-association game, 'Brighton & Hove Albion' would prompt the answer 'Gordon Smith', the Scot who is best remembered on the south coast for an ignominious Wembley moment that's rivalled only by Don Fox's sclaffed conversion attempt for Wakefield Trinity in the Rugby League Challenge Cup Final and George Michael and Paul Young at Live Aid simultaneously feeding the world and blowing a great hole in its ozone layer with a fug of hairspray. 'And Smith must score!' shrieked commentator Peter Jones in the final minute of the 1983 FA Cup Final. Smith didn't score, and Manchester United went on to win the replay. With the sadomasochistic humour that's typical of football fans everywhere, Brighton supporters installed Jones' missed call as the title of their fanzine. But they knew their one chance at glory had gone. And it was a Scot they were cursing.

Ironically, as the team slipped into obscurity, the town shot up the league of desirable places to live. The first time I visited, to interview Julie Walters, Brighton was seedy and full of crusties. Then a smarter set started to take over. They included burned-out yuppies from London, tastemakers and cool-hunters with *Nathan Barley*-style gear and jargon ('Totally fuckin' Mexico!') who had reinvented some of the steaming metropolis' neglected boroughs and were looking for a new challenge . . . and representatives from the nanny states of Chelsea and Notting Hill: real nannies, beautiful, slim, eternally flip-flopped.

The showbiz agenda changed, too. Where once I came to Brighton to report on 1980s nostalgia pop roadshows and hear an impassioned argument from Robin Cousins that an entertainment from even further back in time, *Holiday On Ice* (which actually originated in the Ice Age) was still somehow relevant . . . suddenly the superstar DJ Fat Boy Slim and Zoe Ball were holding court in their art deco love nest on the beach.

Brighton may have become trendy, but the hipsters weren't in town for local football. If they liked football at all, then it would be Arsenal or Chelsea. In this I can sympathise. Edinburgh has become equally desirable, but incomers are not swelling the crowds at Hibs and Hearts.

On my travels in Germany I met two Brighton fans, Mark Colburn and Wayne Marmont. Like many, they were amazed to find a Scot following England. 'That would be like us becoming bloody Palace fans,' said Wayne, revealing a rivalry that I didn't know existed.

Fact: I'd never met a Wayne before. This one then detailed his previous encounters with Scots. On a train journey through Portugal during Euro 2004 he was alarmed to see a detachment of the Tartan Army get on. He told me: 'There was a few of us English and I thought: "Uh-oh, trouble." But then one of the Jocks got out his pipes and played the entire *Sound Of Music* songbook from start to finish. It brought water to my eye, so it did.'

Then Mark urged Wayne to tell me his Gerry Armstrong story. The highlight of Wayne's career as a semi-pro was lining up against Armstrong, the former Watford and Northern Ireland striker, at the fag end of his. 'It was the Southwick Seniors Cup and he was playing for Brighton Reserves,' recalled Wayne. 'I called him a donkey and he nutted me. It made the papers. I needed eight stitches.'

With some pride, Wayne showed me his scar. It was barely visible and I imagine he'll be quite sad when it fades completely. It is a football trophy after all. The closest these Brighton fans will ever get to winning one.

Anyway . . . where to watch the Sweden game? There's only an hour to kick-off and I'm starting to panic. I'm stuck in the wrong town. Not my fault, but it seems inevitable I will compound this by choosing the wrong pub.

The Standard in West Street is guarded by two shaven-headed bouncers who are being chatted up by a blonde chavette wearing a red England top with 'Lampard' on the back and 'I love footie' kneesocks. *Footie.* I hate that word. It doesn't mean anything in Scotland but has managed to creep into our language. Same with cockney rhyming slang.

The Hearts nickname is Jam Tarts. My own team, Hibs, are

known by some, though not me and certainly not my father when he was alive, as 'the Cabbage and Ribs'. Dad used to mutter darkly when he heard shouts of ''Mon the Cabbage!' and, aged eleven, I found this hugely embarrassing – though not as embarrassing as when he developed an addiction to snuff. Sinking my head into my shoulders in an attempt to disappear into the fake-fur lining of my parka hood, I was absolutely convinced my father was the only football fan in the whole wide world who spooned neat, nostril-blasting tobacco during matches. I still believe this now. Though if Dad were alive today, the knowledge that there is a Hibs theme pub called the Cabbage and Ribs would surely force him to ditch the snuff and take up crack.

The pace on the streets of Brighton is quickening. People are walking briskly and some are threatening to break into jogs. They must be rushing to get home in time for kick-off or to the pub or somewhere where they can feel part of this great unifying event. It's like an air-raid siren has gone off and everyone is diving for cover.

Further up West Street, Brighton has a Wetherspoons, also a Yates. But so do most medium-to-large towns in England. (Depressingly, more and more Scottish ones do too.) 'Fine wines – the taste of summer' says the sign in the Wetherspoons window. Hmm. Wine and Wetherspoons; that's like the England football team and low expectations or ball retention or penalty shoot-outs without the need for a drastic change of shorts. Some things just don't go together.

This is not a radical statement, I know, but I loathe these giant pubs, modelled on wind tunnels and aircraft hangars. In 1980s England everything was big: hair, shoulder pads, yuppie expense accounts, share issues, extended twelve-inch single mixes, television adaptations (*Brideshead Revisited*, *The Jewel In The Crown*), Aids and football stadium disasters. In present-day England it's just the pubs.

Now I'm back where I started, on the seafront. The Brighton

Centre was where I heard the preposterous Spandau Ballet rhyme 'diplomat' with 'laundromat' and perform a song called 'Highly Strung' to which the only reasonable response was Basil Fawlty's: 'Yes, they should be.' My Brighton Beach Memoirs are beginning to do my head in.

I promise myself that I'll settle for the next watering hole but this turns out to be the Grand Hotel, where the IRA once tried to blow up Maggie Thatcher. 'Welcome to our football-free zone!' proclaim the posters at the entrance. 'Enjoy a glass of complimentary sparkling wine and a three-course meal created by our Executive Head Chef – £35 a head.'

It's tempting. Maybe I'll just give up on England. Then my iPod shuffles up 'Lola' by the Kinks and Ray Davies sings: 'Well I'm not the world's most masculine man.' This gets me thinking: New Romantic ponces, *Holiday On Ice* flouncers . . . I've got it: for that quirky, different, special Brighton experience, I'm going to have to watch the game in a gay bar.

Brighton is the gay capital of Europe. I may be pandering to base stereotypes, but you'd reckon that by sheer law of averages, some in the community must like football, even if your instinct is to think that gays would be unmoved by the sight of Ashley Cole grappling with a blond, square-jawed Swede.

I have no qualms about doing this. I am a Hibs fan so am obliged to be relaxed about my sexuality. All season long, in the domestic campaign just ended, Hibbys have been taunted by Jambos with a repetitive one-line ditty sung to the riff of the White Stripes' 'Seven-Nation Army': 'Oh the Hibees are gay-ay.'

The reason for this is unclear. I don't think any of the Hibs players has a penchant for antiques or reads the *Guardian*, like Graeme Le Saux – which was what prompted Robbie Fowler to dish out homophobic abuse mid-match – but it is possible the club may have contravened obscure Scottish Football Association regulations limiting the number of man-bags per team and the speed settings on the communal hairdryer.

Nevertheless this will be the first time I've knowingly frequented a gay bar.

It takes me a while to find the Brighton Tavern, a small hostelry displaying the St George's Cross and the rainbow flag: English pride and gay pride, fluttering side by side.

'Oh yes,' says John Moralee, who runs the bar, 'we'll be watching. We're the only poofs' pub showing the World Cup. Stick around, you'll see.'

Huge vases of brightly coloured flowers swamp flat surfaces. Helium-filled balloons trapped on the ceiling drape glittery streamers everywhere. And almost every song on the sound system has 'man' in the title: 'I Need a Man', 'It's Raining Men', 'Gimme Gimme Gimme (A Man After Midnight)'.

John, a tanned, bejewelled, well-preserved fiftysomething, reckons the tournament is a true summit of nations. 'It's like the whole world on the same planet,' he says, and I think I know what he means. 'The other night we were watching some country I've never heard of before. Kris, was it Toga?'

Kris, his young assistant in shorts, has a try. 'To go?'

'Togo!' says John finally.

With the match about to start, the pub is filling up. Everyone seems to know each other. The men kiss and hug; one sitting on his own is greeted by his friends with a chorus of 'Three lions on the shirtlifter!' Not knowing I was going to be staying over I don't have a change of top. No matter; every other bloke in the Brighton Tavern smells sweet, the least threatening gathering of males I've encountered in my life.

Snacklets appear. They're tiny, round wafer biscuits with dollops of what I hope is egg mayo. During the national anthems, as the camera pans along the hunky Swedes, John provides Kris with a form guide: 'Not bad . . . not bad . . . cheeky . . . don't think much of yours . . . ah, Freddie, and if I'm not mistaken I'm wearing your pants tonight.' (Ljungberg advertises Calvin Klein.)

It would be easy to be persuaded that the appeal of football for the Brighton Tavern's regulars is the prospect of, if not men in togas, then shorts. To begin with the pub, with its titter-ye-not electronic slogans flashing above the bar ('Have a stiff drink!', 'Plenty room up the back!'), fails to disabuse me of this notion. I ask John and Kris what they think of David Beckham, not really expecting an answer which will prompt a serious debate about his footballing ability. 'A fantastic-looking man,' says John, 'though a bit smooth for my tastes.' John prefers Michael Owen – 'my boy' as he calls him.

Kris is much taken with Rio Ferdinand. 'Look, he's done his hair. Suits his face, mmm.'

'Bet you'd love to be *in Rio* this weekend,' smirks John.

Qualification out of the way, the object of the game in Cologne is avoiding Germany in the second round, and a draw will suffice. This is the ideal time to introduce the player Germany calls '*Wunder-Sturmer*'. If England are going to win the World Cup, they will need all of Wayne Rooney's elemental gonk power out on the pitch and not just painting a red cross on his naked torso and roaring at a *Sun* photographer for the 'sensational poster' free with today's ish.

Rooney stands apart from the rest of the team in so many ways. Says his biographer Hunter Davies: 'He has no personal vanity, doesn't watch himself in the mirror, only shops twice a year, has had the same haircut all his life, unlike say the dear captain of our national team. He lives for football, not attention.'

With what Jilly Cooper calls his 'dear little convict's face', you might think Wazza would fail to endear himself to gay fans but there are excited whoops in the Brighton Tavern at the kick-off as the cameras make him the focus of attention.

Just seventy-four seconds later, however, England suffer a setback when John's 'boy' falls over unchallenged, twisting his right knee horribly. Hand on cheek, mouth agape, John shares Owen's pain. Sven-Goran Eriksson's gamble of challenging for the World Cup with two strikers some way short of peak fitness has blown up in his face.

'Owen's off,' confirms John.

'The wedding's off?' asks the one they call Chaz.

It's fair to say that Chaz is a good bit behind the rest of the Brighton Tavern's aficionados in his football appreciation. 'He doesn't know one end of the ball from the other,' says John.

I try to help Chaz. 'Think of the World Cup as being like a fabulous party,' I tell him. 'England have brought nothing to this party. Not if you don't count a single bottle of cheap plonk and eleven sulky faces. They stand in the corner scowling, crushing Twiglets and Matchmakers into the shagpile. Everyone else is playing lovely football, some of it heaven-sent. Everyone else is having a – in its historical, *Flintstones*-theme sense – gay old time. Apart from England. Who invited them anyway?'

'OK,' says Chaz, 'but you're supporting England even though you're Scottish?'

'Well, yes and no.'

'Now I'm more confused than ever!'

Chaz has never heard a Scottish accent so soft before. 'It's not like *Dr Finlay*,' he says, giving John and Kris their cue for what I assume to be some well rehearsed camp nonsense based round the couthie telly classic.

Kris: 'Dr Finlay, I think I've got heartburn!'

John: 'Och Janet, yer tits are in yer porridge again!'

John says I'm an outsider twice over. 'The only Jock in the bar and the only straight.' He's got a point, and this gives me an idea. Maybe, if England progress, I can try to contrive a similar set of circumstances for other games. I'd be like a double agent.

Then Joe Cole scores a goal which really tests my commitment to the English cause. It's a belter: a volley taken off the chest and thumped left-footed from twenty-five yards. It's the sort players attempt all the time in training, or when a team are three up and showboating. But rarely do you see it tried by such a constipated bunch as this England. From ugliness comes a goal with a beautiful arc; like a salmon leaping from sludge. It's as good as any in the World Cup so far, and the impulse is to acclaim it. If anything is going to make me 'come out' as an England fan, this goal is it. Equally, this goal is the kind that should make me run for the hills and drag the boulder across the cave entrance and cower in the corner and dread, absolutely dread, the whiteshirts going on to win the trophy.

I cannot leave the Brighton Tavern, though. Here is a pub, in England, where I'm allowed to be myself, to wrestle with who I really am, to strip off the shabby disguise and get naked in a D. H. Lawrence kind of way and tussle and tumble in front of a big open fire, free from intimidation and persecution.

'Goal!' I shout. 'GOAL!'

Seconds later, I get a text from Bill Butler, the reformed terrace marauder I met in Nuremberg who's still travelling with England. He's passing on an anti-Swedish chant direct from the stadium: 'We seen your mum in pornos, na na na na.' When we met, among Bill's many regrets in the fings-ain't-what-they-used-to-be category was the decline of the football song. And he's still demanding an answer to the fundamental question: 'Why do you hate us?' I text back to say I've just met some very nice Englishmen in a gay pub in Brighton and right now I don't (ducky).

Behind the bar, John flicks a switch on the stereo. It's 'Jerusalem', the disco version, possibly performed by the Pet Shop Boys or maybe even the Village People, with Randy the cowboy-in-chaps on lead vocals. Next, 'Back Home', the official song of the 1970 England World Cup Squad. 'I *love* that key change in the third verse,' says John, and tonight so do I.

The pub is rammed now; it's as if everyone is starting to *believe* (© Mars Inc.). Apart from two women – one of whom John says went about with Frank Lampard Sr in her youth – it's all men and therefore similar to every other pub-telly football experience I've ever had. Similar, but oh so different.

A short man with darting eyes and an earring positions

himself at the bar next to me. He stands out from the rest because he's the only one in an England shirt. Chris has fled from another pub, the Horse & Wagon. 'It was full of twats – too many male hormones,' he says.

So what's with the strip? 'Well I'm a gay man very centred around peace but I reckon I've a right to wear this top and support my country.' Chris knows that not everyone wears it as politely as him. During Euro 2004 and the angry night of England's demise, a group of Italian students had to barricade themselves in a Brighton college to escape a baying mob who assumed them to be Portuguese.

'England fans like that make me embarrassed and ashamed,' says Chris. 'This newly discovered nationalism of ours concerns me. We're one of the world's richest countries; we should be helping other nations, not beating them up. So I'm careful when I wear my strip. I don't walk in front of cars and I hold doors open for people. The white shirt of England is not exactly a seductive calling card in the world right now so I'm always extra polite.'

Unlike the kilt. Though I tell Chris I think Scots are far too pleased about their national dress. They complacently assume it will make everyone else fall in love with them.

We swap notes on what it's like to be a member of a minority. 'I like being gay,' says Chris, 'but I lose a bit of my brilliant individuality by also being an England fan. One of my friends says that as a homo England supporter, surrounded by these meatheads, I'm caught between a cock and a hard face.'

But small isn't always beautiful and I tell Chris I'm bored with glorious failure. Bored with plucky triers. Bored with the patronising pat on the head. Bored with our most important contribution being our *colourful fans*. You may become less 'special' as part of a bigger group – say England-sized – but I could live with that if it meant more success.

John, who's been listening to our chat behind the bar, says he's just read a book called *Walkers* – about the women who are 'beards' for gay actors that Hollywood keeps in the closet. 'If a few more footballers admitted they were gay that would be good for the sixteen-year-olds who hero-worship them and are confused about their sexuality,' he adds.

'I didn't come out for a long time,' admits Chris. 'I didn't like Kylie Minogue or have a moustache or wear tight jeans. When I was a kid the only gay man in our culture was Larry Grayson. In my teens it was Julian Clary. I couldn't relate to either of them.'

The last topic I expected to be discussing during my flirtation with the England team was gay rights. We try to pick up the game again. 'Go on, Ashley, my son!' roars John.

But England have lost their way after the bright start and Sweden bludgeon their way back into contention. Half-time, 1-1, and Chaz ventures an opinion. 'Sweden are very butch, aren't they?'

'Oo hark at you!' chorus John and Kris, who have reappeared from the kitchen with the interval snacks: not pies, but trays groaning with meringues, éclairs, fondant fancies, *fairy cakes.*

Of course Chaz, fount of all – fondant of all – football knowledge is right. Sweden are very forceful and direct. A number of their players have experience of *The Best League In The World.* The Swedes know that England have a problem with teams playing them at their own game. With their super-muscular approach, they are more English than the English. Their coach, Lars Lagerback, effects this impersonation on the cheap. It takes him a year to earn what Eriksson does in a week, and not surprisingly, he brands his fellow Swede's salary 'obscene'.

England, meanwhile, are 'gay'. The word has a new, third meaning, which has spun off in a derogatory way from the second meaning. If something is 'gay' in playground parlance and, more and more, in adult conversation, it's lame or rubbish. I ask the guys what they think about this and they agree that it demeans the term, especially if you've struggled for a long time to come out. Then Kris says: 'Yeah, but England really are gay aren't they?'

The second half follows a similar pattern, with England first the givers, then the takers. 'Ooo, me nerves!' squeals John as the tension builds. He's run off his feet by the Brighton Tavern's football-crazy beer monsters. 'Look at my face – I'm sweating like a glass-blower's arse!' he says, before summoning help at the pumps from the pub floor.

This is Nobby – close-cropped white hair, resembles an old boxing coach – who tells me he believes in the United Kingdom. 'English, Scotch, black, white, pink – we're stronger together. We've got our individual ways, but when the crunch comes, when we go to war, we're one nation.

'Listen, I shed a little tear this morning when I read in the paper about them poor Scotch Guards killed in Iraq. And guess what was front-page news? The bloody Wags. I cried some more when I saw that.'

After Steven Gerrard restores the lead, the whiteshirts look like they're going to hold out for a win they don't deserve. But Henrik Larsson, ex-Celtic, revered in Scotland, equalises at the death. England needed leadership on the field tonight but once again Beckham was found wanting. A remote figure on the right wing, he was playing so far within himself that he forced his internal organs onto the outside of his body. His liver was slapping off his thighs and his large intestine was threatening to trip him up.

'Did you hear Beckham at that press conference the other day?' asks Alan, possessor on an impressive Freddie Mercury moustache, who supports Crystal Palace. 'He's asked a question, looks puzzled for a moment or two, then with triumph written across his face, says [estuary squeak]: "I really like them. They're small and fit in your pocket. They taste nice and make your breath smell fresh."'

'"No," says the journalist in the front row, "not Tic Tacs – *tactics*."

'Then this other journalist wants to know about Rooney's fitness. Sven says: "He's OK, but he needs a cortisone injection."

'To which Becks says: "Well if he's getting a new car I want one too."'

Alan has got an audience now. 'What's the hardest thing about rollerblading?' he asks. Don't know, I say. 'Telling your father you're gay.'

I feel like I'm in a 1960s TV light-entertainment spectacular when sparkly sets and corny jokes were the norm and a high degree of campery was mandatory. Any minute I expect the ghost of Frankie Howerd to emerge from the Gents and do a turn. And bearing in mind we're on the south coast maybe the skit would be *Up Pompey!*

Instead we get 'Land Of Hope And Glory' – the Hi-NRG version – booming through the pub speakers. John turns DJ and demands a communal singalong. Then he plays some Hazel Dean, who I haven't heard since the 1980s aerobics boom, then the Sylvester classic 'Mighty Real', a frantic floor-filler from the days of disco. Sir John Betjeman – without the frenzied bpm accompaniment – brings the mood down, giving us time to reflect on another underwhelming England performance. Chaz, by now pretty pissed, tries to start up a chant: 'One David Betjeman! There's only one David Betjeman!' And then Sabrina brings the mood right back up again.

It's the Italian singer/actress/whatever's classic, 'Boys', with the irresistible chorus 'Boys, boys, boys', which is about as Betjemanesque as Sabrina ever got. I join in with everyone else and as I'm yelling 'Boys, boys, boys' with all these gay men I try to keep at the forefront of my mind the unequivocally hetero stimulus of Sabrina jiggling around in a swimming pool or almost bursting out of her skimpy blouse on *Top Of The Pops*.

There's going to be a lock-in at the Brighton Tavern and I'm invited to stay but I make my excuses and head back along the seafront to my hotel. For the last time I pass the Brighton Centre. This was where Maggie Thatcher told the Tory Party

Conference: 'The lady's not for turning.' I'm not for turning myself, despite what happened tonight. It's tempting – in fact, it's positively alluring. I'm sure if I did turn I would feel like the real me, the mighty real me. I would stop living a lie. But, no, I can't. I can't stop supporting England just because they've delivered another chronic performance at this World Cup.

That still leaves one problem. How on earth am I going to tell my wife-to-be that I've just spent the night in a gay bar and had the time of my life?

In Praise of Carly Zucker's Midriff

'ENGLAND CRISIS!' screams the *Daily Mirror*'s front page. Oh no, I'm thinking, who's injured now? Then in small print, and in brackets, this: 'Coleen runs out of clothes.'

Coleen McLoughlin is the fiancée of Wayne Rooney, one of the wives and girlfriends who are staying close to the squad in Baden-Baden with the blessing of the FA. The Wags are there to provide support to 'our boys'. Family-oriented down-time is good for morale, says Sven-Goran Eriksson. So are 'nookie passes', apparently, which prompts Marina Hyde in the *Guardian* to dub the Wags 'on-call sexual helpmeets'. They are also likened to *Austin Powers*' Fembots, the mechanical sirens with bullet-firing boobs.

This is not all the Wags do while they are staying in the Black Forest. Actually they don't 'do' very much of anything. But what they don't do, they do brilliantly. Usually in hot pants and high heels.

A key non-activity is the careful maintenance of the body beautiful. The Wags bronze themselves in big sunglasses and tiny bikinis. To aid them in this pursuit, they fly out 'tan therapists' from experts in the field, Fake Bake. The FA think they are helping, too, by erecting a screen round the pool at the £1,000 a night Brenner's Park Hotel to protect the girls from the paparazzi. The girls order it be taken down. After all, McLoughlin submitted herself to pre-tournament training to determine her most flattering reclining position. Such dedication deserves its reward.

When they get bored with sunbathing, they wander down to the shops and buy more bikinis, more sunglasses (even though Victoria Beckham, Queen of the Wags, brought sixty pairs to Germany) and – very important, this – evening wear. You've got to look your best when you're standing on the bar, pear bellini in one hand, karaoke mike in the other, dancing round your £3,000 Chloé bag and belting out 'We Are The Champions' at gone three in the morning.

In your own way, you're representing England too. So there's pressure, which explains McLoughlin's clothing crisis. Some of the Wags attempted to get six pieces of hand luggage onto the plane to Germany and still that wasn't enough.

On a day – 19 June – that will come to define England's presence in Germany far more than anything the players will achieve, six Wags flash their black Amex cards at staff in the zazziest boutiques and rack up a £57,000 bill in just one hour.

For the Sweden game twenty-four hours later, another contingent hires a private jet to fly them to Cologne: cost £14,500. When their flight is delayed by an hour, Posh Spice lets airport staff have it with both nipples: 'You are treating us like dogs!'

Not surprisingly, there's a noticeable upsurge in demand for facials, de-stressing massages and pear bellinis back at Brenner's afterwards. Gucci, Prada and Diane von Furstenberg are hit with renewed, bored, aimless vigour, as is the Wags' favourite watering hole – Garibaldi's, nicknamed Gazza's – where a single bar bill tops £3,000. In two and a half weeks, the total Wag spend is calculated by the *Daily Star* – bringing us the World Cup news that really matters – at £1,034,239. The players merely talk a good game; their other halves are, in their own way, outperforming them.

Of course there is a Wags backlash – a Waglash – from the bitchiest female columnists. It goes something like this: 'Pah, so much for post-feminism!' Then comes the post-post-feminist retort: 'The Wags are fun and we want their lifestyles!' All of this is good copy. Stories of how the girls are *not* going to the opera or book-grouping, but shopping, partying, competitively dieting and Brazilian-ing for England, will be getting back to the players. Former national coach Sir Bobby Robson fears the team could be distracted from their task. 'We're going to war,' he says. 'You can't fight a war worrying about your wives. Kiss them goodbye and tell them you'll see them in a month.' But from where I'm standing, the Wags *are* fun. England's football has been sore on the eyes and I need distracting from my task.

I'm happy to defend the women from some very English sneering about the lower orders having too much cash to splash. In fact, as I learn more about them, I feel it's my duty.

For instance, I know that Coleen McLoughlin nipped home to have her hair extensions replaced. I know that Abigail Clancy was sent home by boyfriend Peter Crouch 'in disgrace' after the publication of tabloid pictures showing her snorting cocaine. I am more familiar with Stewart Downing's beau Michaela Henderson-Thynne than the Middlesbrough winger and his meaningless five-minute turns as a substitute. And I'm pretty sure I could recognise Carly Zucker by her bare midriff alone.

Joe Cole's girlfriend and a personal fitness trainer, Zucker stays out late with the others, sloshing back Moet, vodka and beer, yet still manages to look fantastic on her pre-breakfast jog.

Such dedication deserves its reward. Zucker is now officially No. 9 in my Most Fanciable Englishwomen list.

Really, though, the best thing about the Wags is that they're blowing the players' money. On the team's form to date, it deserves to be boozed and blinged away.

Get in the Hole!

The scene is Beverly Hills, and a metrosexual confab over skinny lattes. This was imagined by your correspondent a full three years before David Beckham and Tom Cruise started stepping out as bestest friends . . .

Beckham: 'Tom, I love all that running you do, I fink it's amazing.'

Cruise: 'Thanks, David. Running is very important to me.'

Beckham: 'I was wondering, though . . . you run in *all* your movies, how do you do it?'

Cruise: 'When you're the world's greatest actor you can make the studios write that stuff into your contract.'

Beckham: 'No, I mean the actual running. How do you *do* the running?'

Apparently in the dressing-room post-mortem following the Sweden match there was sharp criticism of Beckham – from Steven Gerrard, no less – that the captain had hit, and frequently overhit, too many long balls.

Silly boy. Gerrard really should know by now that this is what Beckham does. No matter that the short pass is the best option, Beckham invariably hits long, for show, for glory – for his own version of Hollywood. He rarely runs; not with the ball, anyway.

Gerrard and the other England players have got to realise that they are not participating in football matches, but movies. They are mere extras; Beckham is the name-above-the-titles star, the 'talent'. His contract allows him to aim sixty-yard diagonals at helplessly scurrying small strikers, just like Tom Cruise's contains the clause about running.

There are obvious similarities between Beckham and Cruise: they are the biggest stars in their domains – the brand leaders. Not the finest exponents of their respective arts but no matter: their PR overrides such fripperies and batters you into submission. They don't have carefully managed careers, these two, they have tyrannies.

When running isn't enough for Cruise, he gets in the special-effects boys. When running isn't possible for Beckham, he signs up for commercials which, thanks to CGI, make it look like he's dribbling through the best defences in the world. That way, for the dullard masses, illusion is preserved.

If this England team were a movie, as opposed to a circus, it would be some bloated epic where the 'star system' has been hopelessly abused; where the leading men can demand, and get, walk-on parts for their ingénues (the Wags) because the top box-office draw (Beckham) is in control of the studio (the FA) rather than the other way round. *England: The Movie* also has a starstruck director (Sven-Goran Eriksson) who, first day on set, gets his priorities right and secures Beckham's autograph for his daughter.

If this England team were a carnival movie it would be *The Big Carnival*, the alternative title for *Ace In The Hole*, Billy Wilder's brilliantly nasty tale of a media circus and its star attraction: a man trapped underground in New Mexico. A real funfair grows up round the site, feeding off his suffering. The man could be rescued; Beckham should be dropped. But they're both kept where they are to boost fading reputations (in the film's case, washed-up hack Kirk Douglas), and for commercial greed.

David Beckham: he wants to *be* Tom Cruise. And I want to be Dougray Scott, the Hibs-supporting hunk who is Cruise's Nemesis in *Mission: Impossible II* – for the final shoot-out when he reflects on life inside a Cruise mask and tells the compact screen god: 'That was the hardest part of having to portray you – grinning like an idiot every fifteen minutes.'

The Football War

Tempers on both sides of the border were running high. There was an immigration problem: incomers weren't exactly being welcomed with open arms. Politicians were scoring points off each other and the media weren't helping matters; in fact they were actively stoking up hatred. And in the middle of it all, Honduras and El Salvador had to play a football match.

On 15 June 1969, the second World Cup qualifying game between the Central American neighbours ended in a riot. Shortly afterwards, the 'Football War' broke out. The fighting lasted less than a week but by the end of it 3,000 were dead and 6,000 injured.

The following summer I watched the El Salvador team take their place in the finals in Mexico. Their presence was short-lived, but to my young mind they were easily the most exotic of the competing nations (on account of the fact I'd never heard of their country). I had no idea their journey to the finals had been so hellish; all that concerned me was filling up their page in my 1970 World Cup stickers album. Digging out the album, I'm reminded that I never did get 'J. A. Vasquez' or 'S. C. Mendez'.

So where are we now? Nine World Cups down the line, and the relationship between England and Scotland is fraught. Politicians posturing in an unashamedly populist manner are all too apparent, as is an excitable media. Meanwhile, there's still some football to be played.

Obviously 2006 is not mirroring 1969 exactly, but it is nevertheless possible to pick a random six days – the duration of the

Football War – where things in Britain get extremely silly. The sequence begins shortly after the anniversary of that infamous match, on 19 June; five days later, the headlines on serious newspapers ask: 'Is the Union unravelling?'

Michael Portillo kicks things off with a mean-spirited column in the *Sunday Times* which surely qualifies him for an ASBO – Anti-Scottish Behaviour Order. On account of his posh hair, I always thought Portillo was English; well, half Spanish, half English. We learned all about the Spanish bit in a BBC travelogue beginning his rehabilitation in the media after his Election Night dumping as the most demonised Tory of the party's post-Thatcher years. Turns out, though, he's (non-Maggie meaning) *one of us*.

The full title of Portillo's party is Conservative and *Unionist*. Even so, he suggests the time is now right to uncouple a sponging Scotland from England and let it drift towards a North Sea with – cheers! – greatly reduced stocks of oil and gas. 'The loss of a twelfth of our population in a region that drags down our national performance could not harm us,' argues Portillo.

'The English are tiring of Caledonian Anglophobia. I am half Scottish by blood [fancy that] but I weary of the whingeing which has continued even though Scots now have their own Parliament.' Portillo accuses the T&T-supporting Jack McConnell of an 'undignified chippiness'. 'It offends me despite the fact that football bores me. Perhaps McConnell needs reminding that his population lives as well as it does thanks to subsidies extorted from English taxpayers.'

£10 billion a year. That's the full extent of the English taxpayers' 'subsidising' of Scotland, according to a leader in the *Daily Telegraph* twenty-four hours later, the day of the England-Sweden match. The cynical Scot – and I've met one or two in my time – will be cheered by Scotland squeezing onto the news agenda, albeit in a negative way, on another day of fevered English flag-waving. The leader backs up a front-page story headed: 'Power of Scottish MPs "a threat to the UK".' This is the anomaly know as the 'West Lothian Question': Scottish MPs in the House of Commons have a say over English laws but now that power has been devolved to Holyrood, English MPs have no similar rights over Scottish legislation.

The thorny issue was so named after Tam Dalyell, the then Labour MP for West Lothian, who was the first to draw attention to it in the 1970s. I learned about the West Lothian Question at journalism college. My public administration lecturer considered it remarkable that West Lothian was synonymous with a piece of political history, just like Suez and the Cuban Missile Crisis, when the region could not boast a football team (these days it can: Livingston).

Why does everything have to come back to football? It's not just me. Here's *Herald* columnist Iain MacWhirter: 'I keep writing that football's only a game, but senior politicians seem determined to make it more than that.'

Then there's the leader in the *Sunday Herald* which details how Jack McConnell's throwaway remark about his non-support for the England team has 'kicked off an almost ferocious constitutional debate [striking] at the heart of the union on the eve of its 300th anniversary'.

Portillo is branded a 'Scotophobe', as is Ken Livingstone, the mayor of London. And Tony Blair doesn't do himself any favours in the land of his birth – he's more Scottish than some who've donned the dark blue of Scotland recently when real, indigenous footballing talent has been so scarce.

When Blair says he's 'irritated' that Scots are not cheering for England he not only angers the Tartan Army; he also upsets his party north of the border. For every demand for Scots to fall into line with the south, according to Iain MacWhirter, 'piles on more votes for the SNP'.

Some of the 'Disgusteds, Tunbridge Wells' might be surprised that in Jack McConnell it is a Labour politician who is honorary president of the Anyone But England Supporters Club. Perhaps they would expect Scots Nats to be fighting over the post.

Then they probably don't know the story of Andrew Wilson. As a rising star in the SNP, Wilson urged Scots to cash in their chippiness and support the whiteshirts in the 2002 World Cup. Last heard of, he was working in a bank.

Another leading member of the SNP, Kenny MacAskill, said at the time that Wilson's vision of an all-new magnanimous Scotland was 'a step too far'. Moderate language from a Tartan Army foot soldier who once described England as 'the great Satan'. So what does MacAskill say now? 'I've moved on and hopefully the country is moving on,' he tells me. 'Scots need to chill out about England and start seeing themselves for who they are rather than who they're not.

'There's a small minority of Scots who seem more obsessed with England losing than Scotland winning. Rather than standing in the pub and cheering for England's opponents, if they devoted the same time and energy to helping run kids football we'd have a better national team and a better country.'

Could this be the same Kenny MacAskill who missed the last England-Scotland game in 1999 because he was thrown in a cell after being arrested? Now the SNP's justice spokesman, he says his behaviour on numerous Wembley expeditions was 'nothing to be proud of'. That was then. 'I'm forty-eight, so I'm of the generation of Scots for whom the outlet for the expression of our identity when we would hopefully put one over our greatest rivals was a football match played once a year. Times change.

'After 1999 [for the record and those detained at Her Majesty's pleasure, Scotland won that day] I decided I wasn't going to get embroiled any more. It's funny . . . in the 1970s, Scots invested so much hope in the national team. We were high as kites if we won and down in the depths if we lost. And yet half of the team were guys you wouldn't trust to walk your dog and who were probably in the pub the night before the game! Great players, though.'

New century, new Parliament – it's time for Scotland to grow up. 'When I called England the great Satan, it was a joke,' claims MacAskill. Or a misprint: now he says they're 'the great Stan'. After Matthews, Mortensen and Bowles, presumably.

MacAskill is perhaps fortunate among his contemporaries in being able to move on. He knows some members of the Tartan Army for whom the Saltire is a security blanket, something to help them cope with divorce and other causes/effects of midlife crisis. For them away trips are just an escape; reverse stag weekends in preparation for second childhoods. 'These guys don't care if Scotland lose – I don't understand that,' he says.

So MacAskill now wants England to win in Germany? Oh that the great rivalry was so simple and straightforward. 'The way this has been spun, I'm supporting them. The reality is I'm not not supporting them, if you get me. Scotland can be a confident nation without needing to cheer for England.' So how will he react if the whiteshirts don't make their date with destiny in Berlin? 'Smirk, probably.'

Meanwhile . . . poor Gordon Brown. He's stuck in Cologne, among the Ingerland hordes, another Scot trying to convince as an England supporter. And on the day of the game, this champion of Britain is greatly inconvenienced by a report from his fellow Scottish Labour MPs which concludes that the only solution to the constitutional kerfuffle is to give the Sassenachs a Parliament of their own.

Brown is probably still trying to get his head round this news as an aide struggles to explain Sven-Goran Eriksson's latest tactical masterplan. Another minion is editing the fans' chants repertoire on his behalf, deleting all mention of Winston Churchill, Barnes Wallis, Gracie Fields, Douglas Bader and especially the Baader-Meinhof Gang. Then, to make matters worse, across the main stand Brown spots David Cameron, the Tory leader and his rival for No. 10. 'What's *he* doing here?' growls Brown in his deep-mined Fife accent, tones that can cause discolouring of crystal decanters in the Home Counties. 'He knows *nothing* about football!'

Brown's cred as a fan is, by politician standards, impeccable. No glory-hunter he, Raith Rovers are his team, in the old lino town of Kirkcaldy. Cameron – Eton-educated, posh hair, 'just call me Dave' – once admitted he could name only three players from Aston Villa, 'the team I half-heartedly support', and was 'distinctly ropey on the offside rule'.

Nevertheless Cameron has fixed a Cross of St George to his bicycle and blagged his way into David Beckham's World Cup party. Now here he is at the tournament, at the football, which Brown regards as his turf, leading a cry of 'England, ra ra ra' and looking for hooligans to hug.

There follows what the *Independent* calls 'an unseemly spat between the two men bidding to be our next prime minister'. Cameron's posse and Brown's droogs argue over which of them ate the most prawn sandwiches in hospitality and who caused greater harm to the environment on the journey to Germany (though they probably didn't address the key question: should Beckham be dropped from the England line-up?)

But the blows being struck with constitution-shaking vigour don't stay verbal, or remain in the realm of political briefings. When I leave Brighton the morning after the 2-2 draw, the headline on the front page of the English edition of the *Sun* is 'BRING ON, ER, ECUADOR'. By the time I get home the tartan version is screaming 'SHAME OF SCOTLAND'.

A seven-year-old boy has been attacked in Edinburgh for wearing an England shirt. Hugo Clapshaw was playing football with his father when he was thumped on the head by what the *Sun* calls a 'racist thug' who then roared: 'This is Scotland, not fuckin' England.' I can sympathise with poor Hugo, who incidentally is half Scots, half Kiwi. The incident happened in Inverleith Park where I first tried to reproduce George Best zig-zaggery and Denis Law salmon-leaps and indeed Bobby Charlton thundercracks in my Man U strip. Before acquiring the top, I turned up for football practice in full rugby gear bought by my mother from a hand-me-down emporium called School Exchange. Neither of us knew there was a difference between football and rugby clobber. Inside the shirt, in the colours of a fee-paying academy, was a name-tag confirming that the previous wearer was a 'K. R. J. Wood-Gush'. This was all the evidence my teammates needed to taunt me as an 'English poof'.

The next day brings news of more attacks. A disabled man, Ian Smith, is dragged from his car in Aberdeen and beaten up for the same 'offence' – wearing a red England strip.

The assaults are deemed racially motivated by the police and are criticised in Parliament – Tony Blair calls them 'appalling and totally unjustifiable'. And word travels round the world. Reports in France, America and Australia all begin with the placeline 'Coatbridge, Scotland' after local resident Allan Robinson has his windows smashed for displaying the Cross of St George. When Robinson accuses Jack McConnell of putting English people in Scotland at risk, Coatbridge – itself home to a football team so apologetic their name comprises two suffixes, Albion Rovers – joins West Lothian in becoming officially notorious.

English retaliation comes not with the broadsword but the broadsheet. In the *Sunday Times* Jasper Gerard describes how he watched the T&T game in an Edinburgh pub offering free beers for everyone if England conceded a goal, then joins the queue to biff McConnell: 'He wants to prove Scotland has its own identity but instead he implies it is a chippy little outpost devoid of confidence.'

Nick Cohen in London's *Evening Standard* recounts watching a World Cup match with friends, all of them 'scrupulous liberals', who suddenly announce they will no longer be supporting Scotland in future tournaments. 'The small-mindedness of Scottish political debate and its unwarranted cult of victimhood exasperated them. They had had enough,' he writes.

Nirpal Dhaliwal, also in the *Standard*, revives the 'subsidies' row of a few long days ago. 'It's time for Scotland to grow up, accept what an enfeebled, dependent wreck it's become, and recognise the debt it owes England,' he blasts. 'For while the Scots gorge on deep-fried death food, it's English taxpayers who subsidise the health system that treats their clogged arteries.'

Rod Liddle in the *Spectator* feigns bafflement at our anti-Englishness when surely the relationship between the English and the 'Scotch' is so fair and equable. 'Instead of oppressing them, these days we reach into our wallets and subsidise them,' he sniffs. 'Instead of ruling over them, we let them run most of their own affairs, without complaining at their manifest incompetence.' Why, then, all this aggro? 'Subconsciously, the Scotch yearn to be oppressed by us and wish they were still a subject race. In which case, hell Jimmy – just say the word, we'll be there for you.'

This full and frank exchange of cross-border views, with the English proving themselves the biggest frankers, is not new to Scots. In *This Is My Country*, my father rounded up other gripes about the Scots and Scotland, some dating back more than 400 years:

> 'In all my travels I never met any one Scotchman but what was a man of sense. I believe (© Ye Olde Mars Bar Company Ltd) that everybody of that country that has any, leaves it as fast as they can.' – Thomas Lodge

> 'The tediousness of these people is certainly provoking. I wonder if they ever tire one another!' – Charles Lamb

> 'A land of meanness, sophistry and lust.' – Lord Byron

How have we strayed so far from football? Possibly because the SNP leader Alex Salmond says of Tony Blair: 'He knows nothing about football.' That goes for a lot of politicos.

What do I think? The gut reaction is the same as when I was the age of Hugo Clapshaw, the boy duffed up in Inverleith Park, the same as when I cheered on the Scot on *Double Your Money* or *The Golden Shot* but rarely the Horse Of The Year Show (because Clydesdale carthorses weren't eligible), the same as when I watched the premiere of *Jock*.

When Gordon Brown's aides label David Cameron an 'immature little twerp' and a 'phoney who doesn't even know the name of the England goalie', I cheer. Even though Brown is a 110 per cent fake Englishman.

And when Michael Portillo, complaining about the influence of the Scottish Raj, has a pop at the Home Secretary, John Reid, who 'appears daily on our televisions to hector English civil servants, judges and the public', I boo – then cheer later when the bullet-headed Reid (Tony Blair's 'all-purpose attack dog', who can make Brown come across like the actor Leslie Howard, the voice of gentle, slightly camp but awfully civilised *Englishness*), is required to speak to the populace after the discovery of a massive terrorist plot to bring down twenty planes between Britain and America and does so in a way that must have Southern sensibilities wondering what threats sound like if this is reassurance: 'The *plees*,' he says, meaning the polis, 'are alert to the *situ-ayshun*.'

For me, politics is fast becoming the new football. The game can't supply me with enough of that essential Scottish-English aggro any more. Scots influence on the Premiership is minimal and even Sir Alex Ferguson, bless him, is not the attack dog he once was. If I want to see a Scot winding up the English – and I do – then I have to look to Westminster.

On the sixth day of this Football War, on the eve of England's second-round match with Ecuador, a *Daily Telegraph* survey reveals that two thirds of voters want Scotland to lose its annual £10 billion 'handout' from the Treasury and Scots MPs to be stripped of the right to vote on England-only laws.

We've got a constitutional crisis on our hands, and football, says the *Sunday Herald*, has been the catalyst. 'Everything British, everything English and everything Scottish is on the political dissection table,' declares its leader on the day of the match.

Scotland On Sunday agrees: 'It seems ever more possible that the end result of the current controversy could be a redrawing of the constitutional set-up which would make Scotland a poorer place in more ways than one.

'There is no point hoping that the genie will go back in the bottle at the end of the World Cup. Not only have the English awoken to both the McConnell row and the wider issues, Britain's internal squabbling is now being debated in bars, journals and boardrooms across Europe and America.'

Not for the first time during this World Cup, I wonder what my father would make of the football *situ-ayshun*. He might well have referred me to another quote used in *This Is My Country*, to illustrate that the more things change, the more they stay the same. It's from the writer and historian Philip Guedalla and a useful character definition: 'An Englishman is a man who lives on an island in the North Sea governed by Scotsmen.'

Lucy is getting worried. 'You're becoming more Scottish by the hour,' she says. Well, that's what this Football War does to you. And as kick-off approaches in Stuttgart, we're all glad that the focus will shift, however temporarily, back to the World Cup, because the fallout is exacting a toll.

Amid tourist bosses' fears that anti-English feeling could cost Scotland millions of pounds in lost revenue, sixty chartered surveyors from London cancel a two-day conference in Carnoustie, Angus. At the weddings of Lucy's friends – which now seem to be coming round weekly – I'm meeting lots of surveyors. If there are sixty less of them in Scotland right now, I wouldn't notice.

But the football *situ-ayshun* is directly impacting on me. A key element of my own wedding is under threat. Lucy's younger brother Edward is down to play the bagpipes in the church, but has had to postpone his practice sessions indefinitely. He lives in London and fears that the natives of Islington won't react well to the skirl of a sheep's bladder disturbing *EastEnders* and their new-found sense of nationhood.

Nationhood – and victimhood.

And what of Jack McConnell? He's had an eventful six days, to say the least. With his aides defending his position in supporting Trinidad & Tobago against mounting claims that it provoked all the ill-feeling to begin with – who's the first minister going to root for now?

'You know me, I always back the underdog,' he says. '*Ecuador*.'

'C'mon the Brits!'

After Brighton – where I was unique twice over, the only straight man and the only Scot supporting England – I am trying for something similar in the second round.

The events of the past few days have compelled me to watch the game in my own country, but an afternoon of wall-to-wall Sassenach-baiting seems too predictable, too safe. In a spirit of conciliation, and in the hope of hearing some Scottish support for England, I jump on a train to Glasgow.

Glesca. No Mean City. Murder Capital of Europe. The capital of Scotland in all but name. Fifty miles from Edinburgh but it might as well be 5,000. My father was such a devout Edinburgh man that when BBC cutbacks required him to move offices to Glasgow he refused and was eventually made redundant.

Glasgow is a place of stooshie bars which has flirted with sushi bars and then reverted back to the originals. A place that Gianni Versace, when he was alive, knew was a safe house for his most outré fashion creations – jackets with only one lapel, head-to-toe gold, tassles on everything. A place where everyone talks out of the side of their mouths. Home to Celtic and Rangers, the can't live with them-can't live without them, stegosaurus vs triceratops double act of Scottish football, to whose supremacist supporters the rest of us fire the pipsqueak counterblast: 'In your Glasgow slums!' But Edinburghers, if they're honest, envy Glaswegians. Theirs is a proper city, man-sized. Edinburgh still grunts away on its Charles Atlas correspondence course.

*

'Where yez whantin', bud?' asks the taxi driver at Queen Street Station.

'A Rangers pub,' I tell him, in my Scottish accent that sounds so different from his Scottish accent, that makes me think I've just addressed him as 'my good man', that has me wondering if I really did urge him not to 'spare the horses'.

'Which whan, tho'?'

He says he can list me the top three – 'the most bitter, bitter, bitter whans' – and he's not talking about the beer. In the end he gives me six.

'Yuv goat yer Louden, yer Grapes, yer Glaswegian, yer Bristol, yer Huttons and . . . here, are yooz frae Embra? Right then, I better take you to Annie Miller's.'

It's my hunch that in a Glasgow pub frequented by Rangers fans, I'll be the only representative from Embra and the only person with a semi-legitimate reason to sing English songs, being a sort-of England supporter as opposed to a Scot who winds up other Scots by singing English songs because he believes his club's history requires it of him. So once again: doubly special.

I have another hunch: that I'm being taken to Annie Miller's because it's Bluenose Lite and that's all a boy from Embra can handle. (Note: Rangers supporters are nicknamed Bluenoses if you're being polite; Huns if you're not.)

Funny place, Glasgow. Well, it thinks it is. Edinburgh might be the official capital of Scotland but Glaswegians are quick to tell you that their city is bigger, friendlier and much, much funnier. I'll just about give them all of that, although I tend to agree with the actor Ken Stott, the TV detective Rebus and an Edinburgher, who tells me: 'In Glasgow friendliness is a stick to beat you with. Such as: "What's the matter wi' you? Go on, smile!"'

Is Scotland funny, compared with England? This is the country, indeed Glasgow is the city, of Rab C. Nesbitt, the string-vested street-philosopher who was very funny, but also reinforced the English view that the city – indeed the whole country – was full of drunks. But in comedy, Scotland shoots, and quite often the ball rebounds back off the bar.

Scotland produced *City Lights*, a dull sitcom set in a bank, rather than *City Lights*, the Charlie Chaplin classic. *Duck Patrol* was a tedious sitcom about park attendants starring the Scot Richard Wilson. It could never be mistaken for *Duck Soup*, vintage Marx Brothers. Yes, there have been giants such as Chic Murray and Billy Connolly but for every couple of Big Yins there has been a pair of – good Scottish word – bauchles like Fran 'n' Anna flashing their Frannie Lee thighs at Terry Wogan and encouraging yet more mockery of my country. Reluctantly I have to concede that all my favourite comedies and comedians are English.

It's a Sunday afternoon, bright and warm, T-shirt weather, which in Glasgow means short-sleeved football tops. Two boys – one in Celtic's green and white hoops, his friend in the new second-choice green and black stripes that rip off Coventry City's 1970s away strip – are playing a fairly sophisticated game of passing an empty plastic Irn-Bru bottle into each other's stride using only one touch as they head in the vague direction of the St Enoch Centre, a massive, glass-walled shopping cathedral.

In Glasgow, Irn-Bru is 'ginger'. There are lots of words that don't travel the fifty-five-minute rail journey between Glasgow and Edinburgh. The generic term for fizzy soft drinks in Glasgow is 'skoosh', but this adaptable word is also used to signify something easily achieved. For instance: 'Today's game for England should be a skoosh. Ecuador is a tiny, hard-up place and despite having Christina Aguilera as a luscious, pouting figurehead – unlike Posh she *can* sing – their people eat guinea pigs.' A feature in the *Mail on Sunday* points up the differences between today's opponents. 'Ecuador's star striker sends half his income to the dirt-poor village he came from to help hundreds of children,' the report reads. 'Doesn't it throw the spoilt soccer spendaholics [that's England] into sharp contrast?' The player who carries most of the South Americans' hopes is Agustin Delgado. He had two years in England with Southampton but quit because he was cold and lonely. 'No one spoke to him,' his mother says, while deep-frying a guinea pig for the reporter.

I've bought all the papers today and in each of them the theme is the same: England have got lucky in the World Cup, they've qualified for the knockout stages without playing well – now is the time for the spendaholics to start performing extravagantly, with a style befitting the best-paid team in the tournament.

'Aye,' says the taxi driver dropping me off, after telling me that his sister recently married into Steven Gerrard's family, 'they should just bloody gie England the cup. That way they're spared the inconvenience of actually havin' tae play.'

My hunch about Annie Miller's, and why I've been brought here, seems correct. I know the Louden is provocatively situated in the – good Glasgow euphemism – *lively* East End, close to Celtic Park, the home of Rangers' bitter, bitter, bitter rivals. It announces itself defiantly with a red, white and blue frontage celebrating nine championships in a row and the words of a chant often heard at Rangers' Ibrox Stadium: 'We are the people.' Annie Miller's, though, is the city centre branch of Rangersism, close to civilisation, or less partisan civilisation, if such a thing exists in this football-mad place. A Glasgow institution, Slater's – supplier of suits for business start-ups, funerals and court appearances – is situated across the road.

Outside, a couple of old-timers enact another Glasgow institution: the fly puff. The three-month-old law banning smoking in public places in Scotland has cast them onto the street. After the fags, it'll be the chants.

From season 2007–8, points will be deducted from teams whose fans sing offensive songs. In Scotland, which has had fewer black players than England, racist chants have been a problem historically and there is still the odd outbreak. The real curse on our game, however, is sectarianism.

The two big words in the Glasgow lexicon are 'Pape' and 'Proddy'. The hatred at an Old Firm match can end some hours after the final whistle in murder, but it starts with the songs, the thunderous anthems of religious intolerance. Celtic vs Rangers is one lot of bigots trying to use Republican chants to drown out the other lot singing about being 'up to our knees in Fenian blood'.

A number of the other lot from Ibrox are Loyalist and also Unionist, so they fly the Union Jack in retaliation against the flaunting of the Irish Tricolour. This was how it was in my 1970s youth when, at the height of the Irish Troubles, Hibs and Hearts fans in Edinburgh would ape Glasgow's Big Two and sing about the IRA and the UDA. Back then, though, I never thought of Rangers and Celtic as anything other than Scottish. At Hampden, the national stadium, there was a Rangers end and a Celtic end, and that was fair enough; they were Scotland's biggest clubs.

But they don't seem so Scottish now. Celtic have amassed a worldwide fan base by romanticising their poor Irish roots. At Ibrox, the Rangers players run out to a brass-band medley of the *Battle of Britain* theme, the *Dambusters* theme and other triumphalist hymns of war valour, which must be particularly appreciated by Stefan Klos, their German goalkeeper.

The emphasis in Govan has been on Britishness, but recently Rangers have got more English. Some fans wear England shirts to games. Admittedly they're in the minority but the England supporters I met in Germany were amazed that even one Scot would do this. When Rangers play Hibs in Edinburgh, a big rugby city, their fans sing 'Swing Low, Sweet Chariot', the song so beloved of the Twickers tailgate-picnickers. And in both Frankfurt and Nuremberg, I spotted among the whiteshirts the odd shimmer of Rangers royal blue. Strange country, England. Bloody strange country, Scotland.

Before the World Cup began, to swot up on the burning issues of Ingerlandhood, I went on the 365EnglandFans.com website. There was a debate about 'Ten German Bombers'. One fan, English-based, said it was offensive and advised supporters not to sing it, whereupon Baxo, who sticks a Rangers crest on his mails, interjected: 'Bollox! It's about German planes being shot down during the war. Howzat racist?'

The offended fan said he hoped Baxo wasn't going to the World Cup as he sounded the sort who would give real England supporters a bad name. After this reproach, a fan calling himself TheSash (after the best-known Rangers anthem) was stirred into print: 'To the halfwit what is a real fan then do you go dressed like a twat in a jester's hat and get your face painted like a five-year-old is that one you prick?'

I laughed at this; the first time anything done in Rangers' name has elicited a response in me that could be termed positive. So I hate Rangers, yet I like it when their fans turn on the English? Well, the only time in my life that I've ever cheered for them was in 1992 in the European Champions League – when they beat Leeds Utd. As I say, bloody strange country, Scotland.

Entering the pub, I'm possibly more nervous than I was when encountering England fans. Maybe I'm remembering the first time I was allowed by my father to witness Rangers steaming into my town (long after other boys my age). Or the first time I was allowed to visit Ibrox – Castle Greyskull as it's dubbed by rival fans.

Because of the parental ban, this young, fevered, bored mind went into overdrive. When finally confronted by Rangers supporters, my reaction was: 'Look at their wild hair! The outsized fake sheepskin collars on their plaid jerkins! Their endless supply of Eldorado wine, a mere sip of which would surely make non-believers go blind! They *must* eat babies!'

So if the Old Firm were to get their way and were admitted to the English Premier League I'd be standing on Hadrian's Wall, chucking stones at them and cheering their departure? Not really. I love to hate them. If Rangers were to unshackle themselves from Scotland, the Scottish Premier League would in a sense become devolved. The rest of us would be awarded more penalties and no longer be denied goals from rebounds off the square Ibrox goalposts, but who would we have to blame for all our ills?

Annie Miller's is dead quiet. Two old men with big conks – Jimmy Durante and Karl Malden – sit by the door. This being a Sunday, they've dressed up: best suits, the Red Hand of Ulster prominent in the lapels. A line from the old Hollywood classic *The Treasure Of The Sierra Madre* – 'We don't need your stinkin' badges' – pops into my head. And just as quickly pops out again.

A handful of other regulars are dotted around, each silent and solitary in their favourite spot. The only one in Rangers colours is a small girl – presumably a child of one of the staff – dressed in red, white and blue from her ringlets down to her flashing trainers. Surely she'd rather be pretty in pink like others her age?

There's red, white and blue all over the walls. Sashes, flags, plaques, portraits of Her Majesty and of the Rangers icons John Greig, Davie Cooper, Willie Henderson, Willie Waddell and William of Orange (1650-1702). There's a rigid formality to the display that reminds me of how much Rangers seem to operate along the lines of a slightly bonkers private army, with the 'No beards' rule for players, the sand-dune slog of training sessions and the firmly knotted militaristic tie which must be worn by the manager at all times.

Among the old team pictures there are the English-heavy outfits from the 1980s and 1990s, featuring Terry Butcher, Paul Gascoigne and Trever Steven alongside some lesser lights: Mark Falco, Colin West, Dale Gordon, Mel Sterland and Terry Hurlock, so 'hard' he played for Millwall twice.

Every team in the Scottish Premier League at that time boasted at least a couple of English imports: big shots up from the south to show us how to play the game. Gazza and the other notables strolled through matches by virtue of their skill. But others just strolled. To them the SPL was a holiday camp, the football equivalent of the very English tradition of the end of the pier, with its worn-out smiles and spurious excitements. These players were Charlie Drakes and Norman Colliers and Dickie Hendersons and Freddie 'Parrot-Faced' Davieses and Mike Winterses and, yes, Bernie Winterses too.

On a night that's passed into variety legend, a real Winters brother took to the stage in Glasgow and was greeted by a lukewarm response that contained definite lynching potential. When his sibling – the really unfunny one – appeared from behind the curtain, a despairing voice rang out from the cheap seats: 'Christ, there's *two* of them!'

In football, it took the punters longer to realise that stuffing our leading teams with English lags would stifle the development of young Scottish talent. In fact they didn't spot this until the arrival of a second wave of foreign has-beens and never-weres. It would be easy, as I study the line-ups in Annie Miller's and struggle to remember some of the less than illustrious imports, to blame England for Scotland ending up in the World Cup wilderness. But the fault really lies with our lords and masters, the game's administrators and the club bosses. The English players simply took the money and ran. Well, not *ran* exactly, but you know what I mean.

In Stuttgart today, England begin stodgily and quickly deteriorate. Ecuador (population: 13.5 million; Agustin Delgado's salary: £20,000) seem to be completely overawed by the superstars in their midst. Rio Ferdinand, star of *Rio's World Cup Wind-Ups*, takes time out from his hectic schedule and, under no pressure, hoofs the ball straight out of play. Joe Cole, after that wonder goal against Sweden, is completely anonymous. And David Beckham appears to be saving himself for the final. The one in South Africa in 2010.

Ecuador's coach Luis Suarez is, according to the *Mail on Sunday*, a 'tough disciplinarian who makes his players stay in Spartan military barracks'. The inference is clear: Sven-Goran Eriksson should be adopting a similar hard-line approach towards his massively indulged superstars. But, despite Suarez regularly quoting Napoleon and sending his players into the tournament with the rallying cry 'Gentlemen, we are going to play in a World Cup – it is time to kill your cows', the Ecuadorians take no encouragement from England's dithering. They look petrified, as guinea pigs must be all the time back home in the capital, Quito.

Incredibly, they venture far enough up field to hit the England bar. John Terry succumbs to the general malaise and stumbles during one of the South Americans' rare attacks; Ashley Cole saves the day. Half-time: 0-0.

I study the pub walls some more. I'm sitting below the biggest display, a crude cartoon celebrating 'Helicopter Sunday' – the day Celtic blew the 2004–5 SPL title in the final minute of the final game and the trophy had to be re-routed in mid-flight to Rangers' match.

Maybe that's why the pub is so quiet: club football rools OK ya bass, as they would say in Glasgow. I'm surprised at the lack of interest in the game but perhaps even for Rangers fans, nothing matters more than their team and the England trimmings they adopt as part of their matchwear are just fashion, mere accessorising.

Then an Orange March files in.

Men in dark suits and dark ties, twenty-strong, all with ruddy drinkers' faces, many sporting gold studs in their ears. Women in their finery and a couple of outrageous Ascot hats ('Every duke and earl and *pee-ah* is *hee-ah*'). It's whiskies all round, apart from the granny who perches on a stool to have her silver hair joshed while she slugs her Budweiser straight from the bottle.

Two men approach my table and sit down. Why have they

done that? There are plenty of free tables. Maybe, though, this is *their* table. 'You've not missed much,' I say, tentatively. One of them grunts and sips his malt. A few minutes pass, then the other one snarls: 'Who are you?'

Honesty is the best policy, I decide, and introduce myself. 'I'm Jock and he's Wullie,' says the bigger and scarier of the two. 'We've just been at the Evangelical church services. Nae second names. Nae official quotes.'

Off the record, these Orangemen – the inscription on their ties gives their branch as Clydesdale – confirm they're Rangers fans and, as regards nationality, well, Wullie has a go: 'I'm fae Possil. So if you wiz to ask me who I wiz I'd say: I'm a Possil man. Then a Glaswegian. Then I'm Scottish. Then I'm British.'

So are they supporting England? 'I'm no' impressed by any of the teams,' says Jock. Wullie's answer is equally oblique: 'That Alan Hansen, he's *English*. If he wiz here I'd pit the heid oan him.'

Jock would like to pit the heid on Jack McConnell. The first minister is at the forefront of the drive to rid football of sectarianism and backs the crackdown on offensive chants. Wullie says: 'If we cannae sing rebel songs, Rangers will just become an English club and sing "Rule Britannia" and all the rest and piss a'body off.'

Rangers already piss off a lot of other Scottish football fans, though for some reason in Annie Miller's today, amid the red, white and blueness of the place, and as David Beckham scores for England and a man at the bar raises a heavily tattooed arm and shouts ''C'mon the Brits!', I choose not to mention this.

Says Wullie: '"Billy Boys" is a Sally Army folk song and "The Sash" [both are among the chants under threat] is a hymn.' He tries to give me a lesson in RE. 'Huv ye read yer Bible, huv ye? A'body's Catholic but we're *Protest*-ant Catholics who're against the Church of Rome. I've got friends on both sides of the border. The Irish border I mean.'

After what's happened off the field this week, and the attacks on England fans, watching the next England match in a Scottish pub might have placed me in the eye of the storm. Not Annie Miller's. This is the eye next to the eye of the storm, and it's got a squint. But things become a bit clearer as England play out the game, delivering another performance which Jock and Wullie rate as 'mingin''.

Jock mentions the attacks on England fans. His relatives in Canada and Australia have heard about them. 'McConnell calls us and Celtic bigots but what's all the anti-English stuff if it's no' bigoted?' he asks.

'I think since it got the Parliament, Scotland kens even less about who it is. Surely it should have been more? At least before it could blame England and, boy, England got blamed for a'thing. Blaming England was the national sport, no' football. Now a'body blames the Parliament and while I dinnae like McConnell one little bit I think a'body's being too hard on it.'

Is this not a bit remarkable? A card-carrying Unionist who is sympathetic to the aims of a devolved Scotland. More than that, who comes clean about wanting England to win the World Cup but thinks he would never hear the end of it and this would drive him out of the country and into the spare room of his brother's house in Toronto. Maybe in the great scheme of things, Jock is not a Darwinian discovery. But he's still the last person I expected to meet today.

Then Wullie pipes up again. 'I built that Parliament, ye ken.' Jock looks at him in puzzlement. 'And I could tell you some stories about a' the corner-cuttin' that went on.' Initially costed at £50 million, the Parly finally came in at £431 million – I want to hear about these 'efficiences'.

Jock is equally intrigued, then for him the penny drops. 'Christ Wullie, you built *Hampden*, no' the bloody Parliament!'

Here's something else that's remarkable: these Rangers zealots admit their club's reputation as a force of bad in football is deserved. 'The Old Firm have ruined Scottish football,' says Jock. 'We lowered the drawbridge for the foreign invasion. Then we took good boys from your wee teams and didnae play them.' Slowly but surely, Jock and Wullie are ruining Rangers' dire reputation.

I've lost my fear of this place. Even when the doors suddenly close, though the crowd numbers no more than thirty. Even when the whispers at the next table are broken by mention of 'Drumcree'. A small, grey-haired woman is waiting on her man to finish his nip and his natter. She opens up a hand. 'I found 6p – and this badge. Look, darlin', it's King Billy on his bonnie white charger. This is going to be my lucky day.'

It's certainly England's. The performance against tiny, timid Ecuador has been another stinker, but they've blundered through to the next stage. This prompts Rangers legend Ally McCoist to claim that with Portugal up next, England are the first team in World Cup history to be given a bye into the semi-finals.

Once again Eriksson is caught fiddling. You would not think the knockout stages of the World Cup would be the best time for tampering with team and tactics. Is there a classic slab of prog-rock on my iPod to sum up his state of confusion? Of course there is: 'Cat's foot, iron claw, neurosurgeons scream for more.' It's King Crimson, and '21st Century Schizoid Man'.

One thing Eriksson is absolutely sure about, though, is David Beckham. The more the hacks demand he be dropped, the more he digs in his built-up heels. He's absolutely in awe of the cult of Beckham. The coach might be the last person you want to be snagged up in the man-dresses, hair extensions and hypnotically snakey tattoo symbolism of the crazy world of Posh 'n' Becks, but that is what has happened. Officially, DestinyEngland is now crazier.

Loyalty to your lieutenant on the field of play is one thing; swooning over the blond son you never had is quite another. We know about the 'Play-where-you-like' favouritism and the superior flight seat-and-hotel room status which Beckham enjoys, but in the wake of *Sven: The Coach, The Cash . . . And His*

Lovers, it is impossible to erase the image of 'Eriksson' and 'Beckham' in their towels in the sauna and the manager lovingly combing his captain's hair, twisting his earring to its twinkliest setting and patting his heavily insured thighs with twigs before reciting in songsongy Swedish the mantra for World Cup success that, increasingly, only Eriksson *believes*: 'So David, the magic list: sponsored boots, lucky shirts, special pants . . .'

You can't deny Beckham his sense of timing, his sense of theatre. Just when Eriksson is being urged to adapt the call to arms of Ecuador's Luis Suarez to England's ugent requirements – 'Gentlemen, we are going to a World Cup, *it is time I killed the sacred cow*' – Becks scores his first goal from a free kick since one against the less than awesome football power of Liechtenstein three years previously.

So, Beckham lives to fight another day. For a while, he can bask in the glory of becoming the first Englishman to score in three WC finals, albeit all from dead-ball strikes. After this one ripples the net, he throws up. What a hero! What a goal celebration! And in the desperate circumstances, his barf – here in Glasgow they would call it a Technicolor yawn – seems entirely apt.

These Rangers fans will live to fight another day, too. They will carry on smoking. They will keep supporting their team within the confines, more or less, of increasingly stricter laws. And in a corner of Scotland that the rest of us thinks is pretty screwed up, they will continue to argue that people in glass houses shouldn't throw stones.

Wullie didn't build the Edinburgh Parliament, not with its swish Catalan stylings, but in another sense he did. His views, however warped they might seem, form part of the Scottish debate. And, as we have seen during this Football War, they are not the only warped views doing the rounds.

Fat Rude, Thick

I am not alone. I am not the only undercover Inglander. Mark – not his real name; he doesn't want his antipathy towards the cause getting out – works for the Fan Embassies in Germany. It's his job to present a happy, smiling face as he dispenses travel and accommodation advice to the England hordes who, if you read some reports, have been moving around the host nation displaying happy, smiling faces of their own. But Mark's countrymen are embarrassing him.

I met Mark in Nuremberg but he could not speak to me there as he was on duty. He gets in touch by email after 200 arrests in Stuttgart, prompting the *Independent on Sunday* to remark: 'After weeks of apparent pan-European harmony, the World Cup as we know it has got under way.'

'I say I'm undercover because I'm pretending to be one of them,' he explains. 'It just makes my job easier. I meet idiots daily. Guys who think there's something heroic about being fat, pissed, rude, thick and English. I'm saying to myself: "I don't give a stuff about England and I think you're a complete wanker."

'The Germans are putting on a fantastic show and how do we say thanks? By singing offensive songs like "Ten German Bombers". It makes my skin crawl.

'If you meet a racist then you know what you're getting. What we're getting in Germany are guys with good jobs, some of them here with their kids, some who will have friends from ethnic backgrounds, who think they're doing no wrong, who think it's all a bit of a laugh.'

Mark isn't the first fan I've met to be worried about England's reinvigorated sense of nationhood. 'I've heard this great gathering of the English being likened to the fetes and festivals of olden times which brought the people together according to the seasons,' he says. 'And I've heard it called a reaction to the fact the team is the only one at the World Cup not representing a nation state.

'I think what we're seeing on the streets of Germany is almost the inversion of Englishness, similar to the way black people reclaimed the term "nigger". A few years ago it was shameful to admit you were English. Now there's pride. But in what?'

Insisting he's not anti-English, Mark adds: 'Our humour, self-deprecation, ability to laugh in the face of adversity, and the willingness, on an individual basis at least, to endear ourselves to others are all fine qualities. But we can behave differently in a mob, in a foreign land, with a few bevies inside us, when we half remember something from school about the empire and how we used to rule the world.'

Mark, who's in his early thirties, is yet another northerner who says he grew up feeling remote from his national team. He took this job so he could watch great football, travel through Germany – and as a geography graduate with an interest in world affairs, view cultural (non-)integration at close quarters.

'I feel even less of a bond with the current generation of England players and I'm sure most supporters are the same,' he adds. 'But I also don't feel any bond with the England fans. Sure, they've spent a lot of money getting here and they obviously believe and that's great. But the behaviour of some of them sickens me. So how can I be an England "fan"? I'm just not.'

Even the German Jailers are Nice

I get another email, this one from Bill Butler, who's still being his own kind of cultural guerrilla in Germany. He 'loved' Cologne. 'No mass culture, every caff was different, very olde worlde, the closest I've seen to London as I like to remember it, but also quite quirky and cutting edge,' he writes.

Bill has been meeting more Germans and now has even greater admiration for their country. 'To be honest I don't mind our war songs, the proper ones like "White Cliffs Of Dover", because they remind us of our finest hour. But maybe we shouldn't be singing them here. You've got to respect Germany for dealing with its war shame and also how the country's developed. I look at us and I look at them and I just think England's fucked.

'The sad thing is, Germans still think of us as a great power. I was telling these lads I met in Cologne that we're now just a dumping ground and we're squabbling with the slippery Jocks so we're hardly "Great Britain" any more.

'These guys wanted to know why they don't hear about strikes in the UK now when in Germany they still happen all the time. The reason is we've given up the ghost. Our attitude is: "Give us as much shit as you like. Give the police as many powers as you want. We'll rack up enormous debt on plasma screens and fat watches and phones that turn into cars and just not care any more." Thatcherism did that. I tell you, Aidan, us old hooligans are the last anarchists.'

There's a PS on Bill's mail about how he enjoyed a full and

frank exchange of views with a Belgian in a bar in Cologne. 'I thought to myself: "Belgium aren't in the World Cup – what's he doing here?" But I guess he was a tourist hooligan. This idiot came to Cologne to challenge himself against the kings of trouble, the English.'

Bob spent the night in a police cell but once again is full of praise for German hospitality: 'We got sandwiches every two hours and regular updates on the football.' (He wasn't charged, however, and was released without a stain on his character, free to be an Ingerlander Abroad.)

Then comes his PPS: 'And you still haven't told me why you hate us . . .'

He's Coming Home, He's Coming Home . . .

It's the same colour, the same yukky yellow-brown. The door in the imposing Georgian block – which leads to the entrance to the first-floor flat, which leads through the hall past the kitchen and underneath the grand staircase to the lounge where my father greeted England's World Cup triumph with such revulsion – doesn't look like it's had a lick of paint in forty years.

But almost everything else about my Edinburgh seems to have changed.

You can't recreate Denis Law goals and sleeve-tugging goal celebrations in the New Town any more. There are too many cars – school-run tanks with spray-on mud – piloted by too many parents worried about stranger-danger. Turn right at the end of my old street, Great King Street, and St Stephen's Parish Church is still there, a four-turreted fixture of the cityscape, but it's no longer a place of worship.

Every Guy Fawkes Night, we middle-class children thrilled to the prospect of a huge bonfire engulfing the church. The pyrotechnics were the work of the kids in Cumberland Street, of whom we lived in fear. This was my first appreciation of cultural difference.

The Cumbie lot probably didn't read *Look And Learn* or save their pocket money in junior bank accounts or say their prayers every night. Their membership of the Tufty Club may well have lapsed. Possibly they crossed the street without singing the road safety song urging respect for 'the Queen's Highway'. It's very likely that they watched ITV.

But their infamy in our house – a lawless street's next generation of hoodlums, even more cold-eyed and heartless than their predecessors – was entirely created and sustained by my father. Four decades on, the Cumbie kids have gone. Now their old stamping ground is as desirable as any in the New Town. And as English. In today's quarter-final against Portugal, at least thirty per cent of my EH4 postal district should, by birth alone, be cheering on DestinyEngland, Circus England, Boring, Boring England or whichever bunch will turn up this time.

The relocated English and the rat-race refugee English love life in the New Town, the classical crescents and squares which sweep down from Princes Street. Two and a half centuries after work began on Robert Adam's grand design, a new avenue has been added behind Cumberland Street to help satisfy the incredible demand for elegant town houses and flats.

The church used to have to hunker up to an ungodly neighbour – Tiffany's nightclub, where I heard the punk poet John Cooper Clarke reiterate what my father had taught me about the *Daily Express*: that it was a paper 'where William Hickey meets Michael Caine, again and again and again and again'. (But the *Express* sustained my Susan George pix fix so I could not wholly share Dad's distrust of it.) Now the bop has gone, too – demolished to make way for yet more housing.

Across the street there used to be a Polish cobbler – the scariest man I knew in 1966 on account of his fiercely impenetrable accent. Today there are 10,000 Poles in Edinburgh. Of course, they don't constitute the city's biggest ethnic group. That would be the English.

In the sedate bars of the New Town the English should be able to gather on one of Ray Davies' sunny afternoons ('I love to live so pleasantly') and cheer on their team, free from persecution. I could have taken a trip down to the Borders village of West Linton to watch this game; a new survey confirms it to be the most English part of Scotland. But Edinburgh gives me that crucial 'outsider twice over' status I've sought since Brighton. If

I choose the right pub today, I could be the only Scot supporting England – and the only person present born and bred in the New Town.

Sven-Goran Eriksson, musical director of *The Sven-Goran Eriksson Classical Collection* (RRP £14.99), has got a big choice to make today. He can continue placing his faith in his team playing rubbish football and somehow blundering through, or he can persuade them that it's high time they started living up to their advance billing. A heavy load rests on his narrow shoulders.

The lobotomising long-ball fest that was the Ecuador match has been condemned on the back pages. James Lawton of the *Independent*, leading the charge as usual, calls it the worst game of a competition which has been lit up by exuberant football from so many other teams.

'Reflect for a moment on Eriksson's journey so far,' he writes. 'A wretched performance against Paraguay, a grotesque effort against Trinidad and Tobago that was redeemed only by a goal from Peter Crouch based on a sly but effective foul; a near meltdown against Sweden and now this – a one-shot victory over a tiny country which woke up, jarringly, to the discovery that they were just three games away from a World Cup Final and sharing a pitch with some of the most lionised performers in the history of the game.'

In the *Guardian*, under the headline 'England have world stage and how the world laughs', Richard Williams says that in 360 minutes of play, England have not produced a single moment suggesting they have the right to be in the same tournament as Argentina, Germany, Brazil and the rest.

Towards the end of the Ecuador match, clinging on, wasting time, they did not want to play football at all. Williams adds: 'This is so far out of keeping with the overall tone of the competition as to be thoroughly embarrassing to the coach, the players and the FA.'

And the rest of the world *is* laughing.

'Worsening with each match' (*Folha de Sao Paulo*, Brazil) . . . 'Boring . . . England wins without enchanting' (*La Gazetta dello Sport*, Italy) . . . 'Weak and embarrassing' (*Der Spiegel*, Germany) . . . 'Absurd' (*El Pais*, Spain) . . . '*Imbeciles!*' (*Die Presse*, Austria). Just some of the unrave reviews, and there's even official censure. Under the heading 'England are spoiling World Cup', the *Guardian* report Fifa president Sepp Blatter's dissatisfaction with the one team in the latter stages who are playing negatively.

The criticism is getting to the players. Frank Lampard was first to crack. Too used to being invited to nominate his favourite Coldplay song, or to share the secret of how he gets such perfect facial skin tone, especially away to Bolton Wanderers in January, he was narked by some off-message television punditry. Lampard doesn't get the role of a free press. Stamford Bridge's zillionaire Russian owner Roman Abramovich has confused the lad by showing him old copies of *Pravda* and its 'Leaders And Their Glorious Lifestyles' page, where negative comment was non-existent. He doesn't understand why all media can't be like Chelsea TV.

Now *The Times* reports that Wayne Rooney, John Terry, Paul Robinson and others have been 'positively outraged . . . when it has been put to them that they have not been on top of their game'. And Rio Ferdinand, star of *Rio's World Cup Wind-Ups*, takes time out from his hectic schedule to whinge: 'Everyone keeps talking about performances, performances, performances. Results win tournaments, not performances.'

Eriksson admits it is 'strange' that England have left a bad smell wherever they've gone in this World Cup. But in Gelsenkirchen, the former coal-mining capital of Germany in the Ruhr where 100,000 England fans are expected, he's confident that his boys can banish the fug and come up smelling of roses. Meanwhile, Italy's *Corriera della Sera* claims he's already done enough to merit top spot in 'the world's league of men paid the most for doing nothing'.

How many flowers do-oo-oo grow in this English country garden? Not many. By even the most generous assessment, none of their players would get into the Team Of The Tournament. By mine, there would be places for four Argentineans and three Germans. And despite his winning goal against Ecuador, David Beckham's role in the England line-up is still being questioned. Here's James Lawton again: 'Another dismal demonstration of his lack of relevance to a team on the move . . . in football you do not have the luxury of a specialist kicker; it is not gridiron.'

But Eriksson is still not going to drop Beckham. The palace revolution to depose the prince is a non-starter. 'I am not married to David,' insists the coach when his unswerving loyalty to the captain is challenged. 'I am not even engaged to him.' So cracks are papered over. Everyone is encouraged to get behind the team. Let's have a 'feel-good story': every week that England stay in the World Cup, an extra £124 million is spent on food and drink. So set 'em up, barman, and let's get on with the show.

Which pub? I'm with my brother Sean and we're walking through the New Town and weighing up our viewing/drinking options. The Wally Dug is first to present itself. We're right in the heart of what Sean calls 'Pashmina Central'. Toppling tower of hair, aforementioned goat's fleece shawl at least in wintertime, denim mini, boxing-champ belt, flip-flops or Ugg boots, depending on the season, eighty-three silver bangles on the left wrist – this is the type of girl who lives here, and most probably Daddy bought the flat as an investment while she studies for her 2:1, occasionally stepping out for some gourmet munchies or the most expensive pint of milk in Scotland.

But all the splay-footed Sophies and Sachas are back home in Surrey or they're roughing it in the Maldives so the Wally Dug – a small basement bar pretentiously lined with books which are placed too high on the wall to be pulled down and perused – can't match that unforgettable night when a lacrosse team dropped in post-match, still in their gear, all muddy and heroic. And so twittish.

We continue on our way, past a hunting, shooting and fishing shop that in our youth sold Zooms, Space Dust, Flying Saucers and other moon-mission era confectionery. Back then, India Street was a virtual slum. Now it houses Kay's, a pub so refined it could well be showing Wimbledon instead of the World Cup.

Andy Murray, the newest great hope in whites, is doing well at Wimbers. Murray is Scottish, and it niggles some of his countrymen that the teenage tennis ace is labelled 'British'. Maybe this won't be the case for much longer, though. After Murray revealed he's supporting 'ABE' at the World Cup, his website was bombarded with insults – one of them making a sick reference to the massacre of sixteen schoolchildren in Murray's home town of Dunblane.

We walk straight past the Standard. This is the kind of bar that thinks sporting its name upside down is 'cool'. Worse, it's the sort that then loses its nerve and flips the sign the right way up. Worse still, it advertises themed entertainment commemorating Scotland's bard, Rabbie Burns, as 'Burn's Night'. If my father were still alive there would be letters of complaint to the local MP, petitions, the lot.

Now we're back where we started, down in Stockbridge, which used to be rough round the edges but is now as desirable as the avenues above it. St Stephen Street was Edinburgh's Haight-Ashbury in the Swinging Sixties, and it still retains a faint counter-culture pong. At its north end is the Bailie, one of the city's finest pubs. This might be the place.

Three balls still hang over the entrance, though the old pawnbroker's shop is long gone. There are few living in Stockbridge these days who need to hock their valuables. Comely Bank, a short walk away, is the most affluent area in all of Scotland.

Exiled Englishmen are welcome here. At times they seem to outnumber the Scots, though they never insist on an English match being shown in preference to Scottish thud and blunder – they're far too polite.

When the sport is rugger, it's difficult to distinguish between the Bailie's England supporters and the Scots: Hamish and Gregor and their well-brought-up chums. There's a small, gnarly band of indigenous Stockbridgers who pre-date gentrification and trust-fund ninnys opening and just as quickly closing hopelessly random shops, but they seem remarkably accepting of this 'progress'. All they ask is that Rupert and Jeremy don't block their view of the TV, or bray too loudly if the Sassenachs triumph, as usually happens. There's banter in the Bailie but never bovver. Bouncers on the door are definitely not required.

Sean and I dive inside and are hit by a wall of warm air. As usual the pub is mobbed but there's no sign of any whiteshirts. This is unprecedented and, we must presume, a consequence of the 'racist incidents'.

The English in Edinburgh seem to have retreated to their high-ceilinged, ornately corniced, stripped-floored, bay-windowed drawing rooms. They won't be alone. Everywhere, Englishmen must be stopping in their castles, otherwise how do we explain 50,000 World Cup-shaped glasses sold by Tesco? In advance of today's 4 p.m. kick-off, Sainsbury's shifted four million cans and bottles of beer. A nation intends to get very drunk, no matter the outcome.

In the Bailie, handbills have been laid out on the bar. 'Ma arse' they say on one side, mocking Mars' sponsorship, and on the other there's some stuff in Portuguese: '*Inglaterra vai para casa.*' Sean, a keen student of languages, has a go at translating. 'I think it means: "England go home." And this bit, I wonder if it's "Rooney is an ass."' Judging by the laughter this creates among the people round about us, the Bailie is not going to be standing foursquare behind Wazza and England. This despite Eriksson promising before kick-off: 'We will stay in Germany until the last day.'

The players vow they'll get it right this time. 'Rooney is ready to finish off Portugal' predicts *The Times*. England may never have gone to war with Portugal but there is now a fairly intense football rivalry. It's behind England's rivalries with Germany and Argentina; nevertheless Scotland are further downgraded as a result. Some Jock-mockers in the media have suggested the Faroes are more our match now – them or even nearer neighbours Rockall. Ha bloody ha.

The edge in England-Portugal matches is provided by the coaches. This is Eriksson vs 'Big Phil' Scolari for the third major tournament in a row, a contest dubbed Mr Burns (*The Simpsons*' nuclear-plant manager) vs Gene Hackman. Adding extra spice this time is Scolari's rejection of the England job. There were twenty reporters camped outside his front door before he'd put pen to paper as Eriksson's replacement. If this is English sport, he decided, you can keep it.

England are now just two games away from the final, 270 minutes from standing on the sponsors' podium and bouncing under a white/red paper shower while David Beckham mimics Serene Bobby and holds aloft the glittering prize, the boy with the (dyed) golden hair. Could they actually fluke a World Cup? Could they really gob one and turn out to be DestinyEngland after all? Anything is possible. Brilliant Argentina, the early favourites, are already out.

If this was strip poker, Eriksson would be down to his elevated shoes, his socks and of course his Threadgold Thoroughgrip Garterettes. But he produces a wacky 4-1-4-1 formation and England start well. There's even a bit of menace about the team although they quickly revert to type: long balls, mishit balls, but no sign of any Goldenballs.

The game is really tense. It takes forty-one minutes for the first corner kick to arrive. If there are England fans in the Bailie, they're not showing themselves. But Giles Pattison is relaxed, happy to declare himself an Englishman, and equally happy to admit he doesn't care if they win or not.

'I hate the way England are playing,' says Giles. 'It's been ugly, ugly football from the first minute of the first game. These are the best-paid players at the World Cup. They are the most hyped. And what have they brought to the tournament? The most defensive football, the fewest passes, the most long balls. I'm embarrassed.'

Just then the half-time whistle sounds. In Gelsenkirchen, the city of a thousand fires, England have been eleven damp squibs. The twisted little firestarters of Cumbie Street would laugh.

'David Beckham, Rio Ferdinand, Ashley Cole – they're media creations, aren't they?' continues Giles. 'Football these days is all about marketing, and making the players into commodities to sell new boots and panties. The phrase "golden generation" is tossed around like an advertising slogan. I'm trying to think of when these players have lived up to their inflated reputations and I'm struggling.'

Short and shambling, fortysomething Giles supports Leeds United. He likes to tell the story of how the great Duncan McKenzie, the Englishman who should have been Scottish, could throw a golf ball from one end of Elland Road to the other. 'And he could jump over a Mini – he did that on *It's A Knockout*.' Giles lives in Surrey with his wife and two children and works as an archaeologist, specialising in the Neolithic period. He's in Edinburgh with his family to visit his mother-in-law.

He has no problem with Scots not supporting England, or with Scots running his country. 'I like Gordon Brown and don't feel like he's stealth-taxed me to death,' he says. 'I'm actually a big fan of tax; tax is good. The Rolling Stones earned £140 million last year and only paid one and a half per cent income tax – they should be booted out of the country.'

Giles also wants to make clear he does not apologise for being English. 'There are lots of good things about England, the country.' Such as? (Long pause.) 'Ha ha, I was discussing this with a friend the other day and I'm sure we came up with something. That's it – queuing! And fair play!

'In England I think there's still a general tolerance. OK, so you've got the *Daily Mail* constituency but there are also the bleedin' heart liberals. I take the piss out of them but I'm probably one.

'I think we're a jack-of-all-trades-type country. Everything we do is done better somewhere else in the world, but nowhere will you find a country which muddles along quite so gamely. The NHS is falling apart but it's still an NHS. The welfare state is under severe strain but at least we've got one.'

I suggest to Giles that by this methodology, his country must be greater than the sum of its parts. It's a *team*, even if the nation's best footballers don't add up to the same thing. 'Maybe,' he says, 'but I've definitely had a patriotism short circuit.'

With Gary Lineker and his BBC pundits still picking at the gristle of the first half (in)action, we nip outside to get some air along with all the smokers and Giles attempts to explain his reluctance to fall in with the whiteshirts.

He says: 'I had a near-death experience with the army. My dad was a soldier and maybe if I'd have followed in his footsteps I'd be more patriotic. But as the man I've become, I would have hated that existence. It never happened because he buggered off when I was three.

'Football can impact on you in a completely arbitrary way. I was only one when England won the World Cup. We didn't have a car but every Sunday an uncle who did took me for a drive and gave me the club badges he got free with Esso. For a while the *Tiger Book Of Football 1971* was my window on the game, and the world.

'We lived in Norfolk and if my dad had stuck around maybe we'd have supported Norwich City together. But I had no one to take me to football. My mum's aerial pointed towards Yorkshire and I grew up watching Leeds United on TV – in black and white. We were the last people I knew to get a colour set. And a little man called Giles [the great Johnny] ensured I would become a fan.'

If you associate 'Queen and country' with your absent father, if your formative football years coincide with England's 1970s sabbatical from the World Cup, if you find a club all by yourself and cherish it, and if they are the incorrigible Leeds United, then maybe a certain contrariness towards the national team is inevitable.

But Giles seems very English when he says that winning is overrated. 'As a Leeds fan I've come to appreciate this.' He also thinks the Premiership is overrated. 'It's supposed to be a mark of status that talented foreigners struggle to adapt because games are too fast. Why is that viewed as a good thing?' Chelsea, whom he hates more than Leeds' sworn enemies Manchester United, recently 'spunked' £120 million on loss-making transfer deals – the amount of debt which almost sent his club under.

He admits to being a contrary bugger. 'If there's a consensus about something, I'll always be the one going, "Yes, but what if . . .?"' He loves 'snarky' non-conformist pop groups such as Half Man Half Biscuit who, like him, don't travel very much ('Half a dozen gigs per year, max. The last time they played London was because the drummer wanted to visit the Imperial War Museum.')

Much like he lifted up a stone and discovered Leeds United, the young Giles investigated music by himself. Saving his pocket money and purchasing a couple of seven-inch singles every week was, he says, an 'act of faith'. I get the impression that as an archaeologist, Giles doesn't trust internet culture or the super-abundance of choice that's supposed to exist now. He certainly hates being told what to like.

'It's not *Team England,*' he says, 'it's the other way round: *the England team*. English football is so corporate and horrible now and I blame Nick Hornby for that. Much as I loved *Fever Pitch*, he's encouraged so many people to "like" football and they're just so undiscerning.'

Just then, the smokers charge back indoors. Giles is gazing wistfully at the trees, the river walkway.

'Let's do a runner!' he says.

'No,' I say, 'your country needs you.'

We've missed the re-start and now a drama of Wagnerian proportions is unfolding. David Beckham is being substituted. DEREK BECKHAM IS BEING SUBSTITUTED! This *never* happens! He appears to be limping. 'Nuthin' wrang wi' him,' mutters one of the Bailie's regulars. This has been Beckham's poorest performance to date. For lack of movement, he's been on a par with his waxwork dummy at Madame Tussaud's, just before the moment in 2004 when a mild-mannered law lecturer, on a mission from Northampton, jumped the barrier and smashed up the Nativity scene featuring Posh and Becks as Mary and Joseph. ('He ripped Victoria's head off' a court was told later.)

Beckham slumps onto the bench, some distance from Eriksson. He removes his blue boots and stares at them ruefully. It's a look I remember from Euro 2004 when he blamed the pesky turf for his penalty miss. He sobs, and Giles scoffs. Becks is to blame, he says, for the celebrity culture that's 'infected' England.

Now strapped inside his anti-contamination tent, the highly contagious captain has been replaced by Aaron Lennon, a little box of tricks from Spurs, and England are playing with more zip. Then . . . disaster. Rooney gets sent off for stamping on Ricardo Carvalho's testicles. 'How very England,' says Giles, reckoning that their chance has now gone. But what's even more England is that, reduced to ten men, they start playing their best football of the tournament.

The defending is heroic. Pink Floyd's 'Time' plays in my head: 'Hanging on in quiet desperation is the English way'. But Portugal can't score. England have forgotten how, and a familiar conclusion looms.

The ninety minutes are up – stalemate. The cameras pan across the undiscerning hordes – the largest every gathering of whiteshirts – who unlike Giles want England to deliver at any cost. 'I'm suspicious of all of this new-found patriotism,' he says, reviving an ongoing theme of my Ingerland quest. 'It's like after the death of Princess Diana when you were considered abnormal if you weren't standing in a mile-long queue in the Mall to sign a book in memory of a woman you'd never met and who you had fuck all in common with. I was scared of being English then, and I'm scared now.'

Extra time, and Eriksson is out on the pitch – cue Pink Floyd again, and 'Brain Damage': 'The lunatic is on the grass'. This could be his very last team-talk. Will it be DestinyEngland right enough – and a £1 million win bonus for the coach? Is he, as one of the selections on *The Sven-Goran Eriksson Classical Collection* suggests, 'God In Disguise'?

Or does the man want to borrow something from my World Cup playlist that better sums up his state of mind, maybe King Crimson and 'Epitaph'?

> Confusion will be my epitaph . . .
> Yes I fear tomorrow I'll be crying

I know, I know . . . King Crimson, like most of my England selection, are bombastic. And in the context of this team, your point is exactly . . . ?

All over Essex-by-the-Ruhr, all over England, and here in Scotland's capital, memories must be turning back to 1966 and Sir Alf Ramsey's psychological masterstroke, before extra time in that final, of alerting his heroes-in-the-making to the West Germans' knackered state. So we are studying this group, examining their body language, to see who truly *believes* (© Mars Inc.)

Today in Gelsenkirchen Frank Lampard is caressing his neck with the middle finger of his right hand. Is the fact his finger is pointing upwards a sign? Or is upwards where his next big blooter of a shot is bound? Is he merely checking whether David Beckham has been borrowing his razors again (the captain justifying this by the fact he endorses the Gillette

Fusion Power)? Who will be the saviour? If there's any justice, it will be Owen Hargreaves, unfairly dubbed the Carlton Palmer of this era.

Then, at the crucial moment, with extra time about to start, Giles announces he's going to watch the blockbuster ending with his mother-in-law. I can only admire his 'snarkiness'. Spiritually, he's gone back to the Neolithic age of football, where the game was always in black and white, save for the pictures in his *Tiger Book Of Football 1971*.

I'm tempted to join him but duty calls. I know I've been following the whiteshirts for *far too long* – a thorough knowledge of Frank Lampard's exfoliation routine confirms that – but I can't stop now. My brother Sean gives up, too. 'I've seen this movie before,' he says, 'and I need to finish off my tax-return form.' So I'm on my own for what could be my last act of football commitment before marriage, and my final one as an honorary Ingerlander.

I run down to Bert's, the pub at the bottom of my street. This is well within The Great Peter Lorimer's range, were I able to call on him for shooting demonstrations, and I'm almost home. Just one more obligation to fulfil: the inevitable penalty-kick tragedy.

Bert's is packed, too, and dripping with dread-sweat. But there's also – still, just – a vague whiff of hope. I stand next to James Rigby, a bank worker and Everton fan exiled in Edinburgh. 'This is the first time I've left the house to watch a game,' says James. 'I've been too scared before.' I tell my small, bespectacled acquaintance this is the first time I've felt like a stranger at my own road end.

Is this football rivalry? The English in Scotland's supposedly civilised capital feeling like prisoners in their own homes? But this is a corner of Edinburgh where the chaps in plum-coloured plus fours are just as likely to be Scottish. In this corner, forty years ago, I knew of a family who, one after the other, had *eight* au pairs – ours.

As England mount a desperate attack, a chant starts up in Bert's. 'Ingerland, Ingerland, Ingerland . . .' I look at James and can see he wants to join in. So I encourage him. Now we're both singing, even though we know it's useless; that the end is nigh.

This England team has many obsessions. David Beckham has an obsession with neat lines and insists on the juice cans in his fridge having their labels turned to the front. Steven Gerrard has a fervour for hand-washing and Wayne Rooney can't get to sleep without the drone of a vacuum cleaner. What a pity that none of them has a fascination for penalties. You'd think they would have got the hang of them by now. But, like so many England sides before them, they are haunted, absolutely haunted, by that white spot twelve yards from goal.

Lampard misses. Gerrard misses. Jamie Carragher scores but has to take his again. And, as sure as the price of *The Sven-Goran Eriksson Classical Collection* will be slashed to £4.99 immediately after this tournament, he misses.

Cristiano Ronaldo, the Manchester United winger, nets the winning penalty for Portugal and the cameras flash back to the halfway line. John Terry is crying, David Beckham, who cried when he was substituted, cries some more. Rio Ferdinand, star of *Rio's World Cup Wind-Ups*, takes time out from his hectic schedule to join the blubfest. I think of Gregory Burke, the playwright, who so wanted to see 'millionaires greetin''.

The pub empties like it's on fire. The sunlight dazzles the eyes; it's too lovely a day for Britain to be convulsing. Everyone seems keen to reclaim the summer, return to normality, maybe take a holiday – stop thinking about football, anyway. I say goodbye to James, indeed goodbye to Ingerland.

'Bad luck.'

'I'm English, I'm used to it,' he says, turning away with a solemn wave.

Bert's is about 300 yards from my front door, not the yukky

yellow-brown one against which I used to batter a 1966 World Cup Willie football, but not far from it.

Next week, my three oldest friends will be guests at my wedding. They have long since moved away from Edinburgh and got married and had kids while I have remained in our old school catchment area (primary and secondary) and, to some extent, in the past.

Old music. Old television programmes. And above all old football matches and the oldest football rivalry of them all. If these things haven't quite dominated my life then they've formed a tough-tackling midfield. I've kept the faith for long enough. Now it's time to move on. Not move away (perish the thought), but definitely, as a man, move up a division.

England are out of the World Cup.

Don't you hate it in football when winners patronise losers? When, in the post-match interview, the victorious player yanks at his ear and says 'to be fair' and then utters something very fair. *And completely insincere?* But bad luck Toilet Duck, bad luck Derek Beckham, bad luck Cashley Hole, bad luck the rest of Circus England. Wayne Rooney, the hero in disgrace, will make one last charge at the trucks, this time to right them. Then the wagons must be packed up and you must drive them home. And all that will be left in Germany of your 'strictly limited three-week engagement' at the eighteenth World Cup will be a huge pile of elephant crap. This is how you will be remembered.

I stop at my garden gate. Some litter has been stuffed into my hedge. Cursing the lout, I remove a chip bag. How Scottish. And there's something else, a black-and-red wrapper discarded from a *Believe* bar. How English. And how very United Kingdom to find them together.

Some People are on the Pitch! They think it's all over! (Not quite yet . . .)

One last spin of the iPod. It's Procol Harum and 'Broken Barricades': 'Your prayers are answered, your idols absurd'. The day after England's exit, Jack McConnell says he has 'no regrets' about cheering on each of their opponents in turn. But Sven-Goran Eriksson says 'sorry' nine times. 'Goodbye tosser' is the *Sun*'s headline in whomping 120-point type, with the paper noting that none of the apologies relates to 'Sven-Grovel Eriksson' trousering £25 million for five years of unfulfilled promise. 'Sven-Conman Eriksson' rants the *Sunday Times.*

'The most disgracefully unprepared team in England's World Cup history,' seethes the *Daily Mail*'s Jeff Powell, 'was managed by a money-grabbing charlatan and captained by a narcissist so obsessed with himself that when the inevitable humiliation came he cried for himself, not his country.'

There is no apology from Wayne Rooney for getting sent off, or even an admission of guilt. 'He's not that sort of person,' says Eriksson.

Some headlines from a day of quiet reflection: 'Wayne: I'll split him in two' . . . 'Give Ronaldo one in the eye'. Cristiano Ronaldo, in the current style, brandished an imaginary red card at the referee and apparently it was this snide act that got Rooney dismissed. Nothing to do with Rooney's attempted castration of an opponent or anything.

Ingerland need someone to blame and rather than Rooney or

David Beckham or Frank Lampard – twenty-six shots at goal, more than any other player in the World Cup, and twenty-six failures – or even the Wags, a winking Ronaldo will do nicely. And so the *Sun* slap the 'nancy boy's' face on a dartboard.

After the holidays (beach reading: take your pick from the books by the platinum ponces), August brings a new start, a new coach and new hope. The man in charge is Steve McClaren, Eriksson's No. 2, his Andrew Ridgeley, his Debbie McGee, his Muttley, so not really that new. But right away he bears his newish teeth (they were buffed up for TV) and drops Beckham.

'Becks dumped on cutting-room floor' . . . 'Film studio sacks Becks, accusing him of creative suicide' . . . 'Becks: *The End*'. It's quite a story and . . . hang on, I'm getting Beckham mixed up with Tom Cruise, given a kiss-off by Paramount Pictures just a month after Beckham is booted by England. This is enough to raise suspicions in some people – OK, in Beckham alone – that they could be one and the same.

'I spoke to Tom Cruise when I was axed – he helped me' runs the *Daily Mirror*'s front page for its Beckham exclusive. What I wouldn't give to be able to evesdrop at the Caesar salad power lunch where these two offer each other mutual support and ponder their next moves . . .

Beckham: 'You're such a good friend, Tom. After you was that cold-hearted hit man in *Collateral*, I decided to copy you for our game wiv Northern Ireland.'

Cruise: 'You mean you dyed your hair grey and walked out onto a Belfast field armed with a Ruger Mk II and a Heckler & Koch USP?'

Beckham: 'No, I wanted to trip up the public . . .'

Cruise: 'With one of your special tackles, David?'

Beckham: 'No, I wanted to surprise them, make them fink differently about me. I told Sven to play me at sweeper. We lost.'

Cruise: 'That's too bad. But listen, David: you're still the World's

Second Biggest Male Celebrity and you shouldn't take being rejected by your entire country lying down. If I were you I'd launch my own scent . . .'

Beckham: 'Fanks, I just might. [Long pause.] Tom, if I'm the World's *Second* Biggest Male Celebrity, who's the Fir—'

Cruise: 'David, it's just a number. Scientology would teach you not to get hung up on stuff like that. Listen, I'm having some friends over to the house, Sunday. It is and it isn't a church thing. I'll tell security to expect you.'

McClaren, the promoted bib-and-cone man, replaces Beckham with Max Clifford. The PR veteran used to play for the other lot, not Anyone But England but their near neighbours, Let's All Laugh At England, Ha Ha Ha Ha. He brokered the Faria Alam kiss 'n' tell that so embarrassed Eriksson and the FA. Clifford has been hired to make McClaren look good. Which, when you think about it, was all Beckham was doing for Eriksson in the last few years of their 'arrangement'.

The real new skipper is John Terry. After Beckham, surely a sound choice meeting the approval of all? This is the headline in the *Daily Mail*: 'Gambler, womaniser, drinker and brawler. So *that's* why Terry has been made captain.'

Let's recap: the same old tabloid outrage, the same old spin, the same old madness. And in October, at the start of the qualifying campaign for the 2008 European Championships, the same old rotten results. A dismal 0-0 draw at home to Macedonia is followed by a 2-0 defeat away to Croatia featuring possibly the most embarrassing goal ever conceded by an England team after a fresh-air attempt at a clearance by goalkeeper Paul Robinson. 'You're not fit to wear the shirt,' sing the loyal brigade who travel to Zagreb. Rooney flicks them a V-sign. Already McClaren's position is under threat. And there's more: the same old Eriksson payouts. The former coach is still earning £13,000 a day from the FA, under a settlement due to continue until the following summer.

There's always the Wags. It's announced that they'll be celebrated by Liverpool's Year of Culture, particularly the 'Scouserati' of Coleen McLoughlin, Abigail Clancy and Steven Gerrard's fiancée, Alex Curran (hurray!) Ah, but McClaren has confirmed he'll ban them from all future tournaments (boo!) Well then, there's always the Premiership, *The Best League In The World*. Except that two months in, Liverpool and Arsenal give up the ghost. Manchester United and Chelsea are the only contenders – it's a two-horse race, just like in Scotland.

What of us? Jack McConnell vows to eradicate the 'Scottish cringe'. (His critics claim his ABE stance has perpetuated it.) McConnell wants future generations to grow up with confidence. To encourage them, he points to a group of entrepreneurs who've made successes of their lives – by getting the hell out of Scotland.

The day after England's completely predictable exit – penalty shoot-out, quarter-finals – Scotland receives some not entirely unexpected news. Despite ten years of healthy eating campaigns, its diet is worse than ever. OIS – Only In Scotland, I fear, would the captain of the national football team, so surely the country's leading sports role model, go to war with his club manager over his right to scoff Monster Munch.

And what's more Barry Ferguson wins, forcing Paul Le Guen to quit Rangers.

Racism in Scotland is on the increase. The end-of-year incident toll is no surprise after the World Cup, but the Commission for Racial Equality warns some of the main troublemakers – the politicians – that ill-feeling between Scotland and England may provoke 'uncomfortable and unhealthy views' which could curb the ambitions of those seeking the highest office.

Doubtless anticipating as much, David Cameron tells Scotland: 'I'm sorry.' For the Highland Clearances, Glaswegian drunks on *The Bill*, Scots sportsmen being labelled 'British' when they win and 'Scottish' when they lose, and jellied-eel vendors and cream-tea matrons squinting suspiciously at Scottish banknotes. And he even says sorry for the poll tax. The hugger of hoodies and hooligans adds Scots to his clammy embrace when he admits the English are 'ignorant' about Scotland.

What a crazy, mixed-up world. A Tory apologising for the poll tax. A Scot, Gordon Brown, desperately trying to save the Union. What a year in Anglo-Scottish (non-)relations! And what of Tony Blair? The *Scotsman* asks him whether he feels Scottish or English. The prime minister, Edinburgh-born, avoids answering. It's a very Scottish question to ask; but it's also very Tony Blair to offer a response which Ian Bell in the *Herald* interprets as 'Scottish, kind of, but only if you insist'.

Does this matter? Maybe not. According to an opinion poll a few days later, there's now a majority on both sides of the border in favour of breaking up the UK. Most Scots want independence, says the survey, but the *Sunday Telegraph* also reports that an 'astonishing' fifty-nine per cent of English voters would rather Scotland went it alone.

The *Sun*'s front-page follow-up – 'Union crack' comes with a headline of world-ends-tomorrow dimensions while Tim Spanton, the reporter I met in Frankfurt who walked all the way to the World Cup, fantasises about how a Balkanised Britain would shake down . . .

It's 2012, the year of the London Olympics, which are officially opened by the queen, just back from her annual holiday at Butlins in Bognor Regis (no more Balmoral for her). 'Edinburgh-born Tony Blair is no longer PM and Gordon Brown, who was not allowed to succeed him, is now Emperor of Scotland,' imagines Spanton. 'Income tax has been cut by 5p since we no longer have to subsidise the Scots . . . and there was more joy earlier this year when the English Parliament got round to banning bagpipes.'

The future is already here. The expat Scots of the Norfolk Caledonian Society have staged a Hogmanay ball since 1934, but residents in Norwich say enough is enough. The ceilidh is banned for being too noisy.

Christmas is coming. Can bookshops shift any more copies of Rio Ferdinand's *My Story* and Ashley Cole's *My Defence*? Unlikely: these are by far the worst sellers among the World Cup titles, the latter being written in the mockney equivalent of gangsta-speak (wanksta?) Caspar Llewellyn Smith in the *Observer* writes of the Cole tome: 'In a sense it's the pick of the bunch because all the stupidity and venality that infects the English game is laid bare here.' Sales to date: a paltry 4,669.

Ferdinand's kick 'n' tell is bombing too and Frank Lampard, recipient of a £500,000 advance, fails to deliver at Waterstone's, just like in Germany. It's true that a sussed football public already knows a lot about life away from the pitch – the dogging and drugging, the gang bangs and bungs – and demands more from players' biogs. But that doesn't let the platinum ponces off the hook. Llewellyn Smith's *Observer* colleague Kevin Mitchell says that as a result of their books stiffing, the age of the footballer memoir may be nearing the end. Cashley Hole: you're a word-killer!

And so it goes, on and on. Ferdinand, whose schedule is made less hectic by the cancellation of book engagements, lands a new TV show blinging up footballers' pads (because as a rule they're so spartan, right?) Lampard endorses a new skin-cream range – acknowledging the kind of goals he scores but also his attitude to criticism, it's *Déflexion* by Yves St Laurent – but away from the snug certainties of Stamford Bridge, the chant directed at him is: 'Where were you in Ger-man-ee?' Then, after Beckham is touted for, but fails to get, a knighthood, he chooses the only route open to a spurned, static, image-obsessed fading football idol and scuttles off to America where his place-kicker skills will be properly appreciated.

At a rate of £128 million over five years – that's 80p a second.

I love all this. In the summer, unable to cheer for England's rivals, there were times when I felt like Beckham's – sorry, Tom Cruise's – wife Katie Holmes in a maternity ward run under Scientology rules ('STRICTLY NO SCREAMING'). Now I can laugh at the team, and I do.

I can laugh when they promote new strips and no one, not their image consultants, not the FA, not the little voice of reason you hope still functions inside their own heads, tells them it would be a good idea if they didn't strike the same moody, dry-ice-shrouded – cue the Bonzos' Vivian Stanshall one more time – 'Look at me I'm wonderful' poses as before because, post-Germany, the fans might find that a bit insulting.

But something about my reaction has changed . . .

The laughter is still instinctive and innate. It's the same as when Poland's Wlodzimierz Lubanski danced past Bobby Moore as if the Serene One was made of stone to help keep England at home for the 1974 World Cup . . . or when Italy's Roberto Bettega flicked his greying bouffant at the ball to give them their 'Access No Areas' passes to Argentina four years later.

Or . . . when my father impersonated Malcolm Muggeridge or Bernard Levin or David Niven playing Bonnie Prince Charlie in the 1948 movie, complete with a 'terribly, terribly' accent.

Or . . . when he mimicked the English public schoolboy trying to be awfully brave about the horrors of boarding only to weaken when signing off his letter home: 'PEth, thend more fudge! PPEth, I love you Mummy. PPPEth, I'm thircling my tearth ath they fall on the page . . .'

Or . . . when he sent up another familiar (to him) English-type – the bonkers squire – with an angry letter to the *Telegraph* in one hand and a blunderbuss in the other, the sort of chap who would describe the 2006 World Cup as a 'fur-lined, ocean-going balls-up'.

But once the chortling subsides there is sympathy for the fans.

The scariest ones I met were the friendliest. The oldest were the least cynical. The most cynical were the funniest. And the most youthful and apple-cheeked-and-mythic-wooden-rattle optimistic stopped well short of looking like they would swap their white strips for white robes and sign up for a self-sacrifice cult at the click of Sven-Goran Eriksson's boosted heels. In short, none of them was as one-dimensional as the team.

I didn't meet a Palmer-Tomkinson or a Peregrine-Worsthorne or a Poncet-Wilberforce or a – cue Monty Python – Tarquin Fintimlinbin-Whimbimlimbusstop-F'tang-F'tang-Ole-Biscuitbarrel or a Lord Cedric Furnival Crabthorn Percy Constance Charles Plunk who, like the fine upstanding chap of that name in the Molesworth books, insists: 'Just call me Pongo.' All of the intelligence, all the crucial signifiers passed on by my father for spotting the English and fraternising with them, proved completely useless in the field. Funny, that. And to think that if Dad had stuck with his original choice of name for his eldest son, I'd have been a Tarquin, too.

Posh does not always mean English. Posh does not always mean bad. A double-barrelled name does not always mean ownership of a double-barrelled shotgun. English does not always mean – cue Dad – men who 'strut this earth like medieval popes'. And English – strange but true, come on, face it – *does not always mean bad.* These are some of the things I learned from hanging out with the boys from the Mersey and the Main and the Clyde. Should I have learned them before? Of course . . .

Very little about nationality is an exact science. But the Scot who has 'issues' with England would argue that the chemical formula hubble-bubbling inside him comes pretty close. It's like the whisky-making process, and the label on the bottle cannot be disputed, particularly if it confirms the classic forty-year-old blend. That means we are talking about a perspective on England that has been (im)maturing since – it's that year again – 1966. Chippiness may be an ingredient – in this case, my father perched on a wobbly gangplank above the still and stirred it in with a giant spoon – but at least it is vintage chippiness.

From a distance, and based on their chants, some of the

English fans I encountered in Germany seemed to *believe* (© Mars Inc.) they still ruled football and/or the world and were winners in perpetuity of the Noël Coward memorial prize for being spiffing gents and scintillating wits. But up close, in conversation over beer and sausages, none of them exhibited a superiority complex. There is such a gulf between player swank and supporter still-mustn't-grumbleness that you cannot believe they are the same nationality.

Some of the English I met could be classed as glory-hunters. Then there's the opposite kind: those who revel in the national team's clattering ordinariness. Scotland, it should be said, has plenty of both. Some of the English were football snobs who believe you're no one if you weren't around in the 1970s, standing on crumbling terraces in pre-Sven platforms, dodging bricks and bottles and watching the sport when it was tough, hairy, mud-caked, glam-rock-soundtracked and *real.* Well, I'm with those guys. Some of the English were ignorant about Scotland, but I'm no authority on England. And get this: not one of them mentioned 1966. (True to form, though, I dropped 1967 into the discussion a couple of times, despite the fact this game means nothing to me. I even scrawled the 3-2 'unofficial champs of the world' scoreline on the giant St George's Cross carried round Germany to collect 'Good luck' messages for the whiteshirts.)

We're not that different, and maybe that partly explains why we Scots are so preoccupied with the English. Anything that marks us down as separate and distinct should be preserved, cherished and buffed to a sheen, just like you would the toecap of a fourteen-eyelet Dr Martens boot.

More important on this odyssey/idiocy have been the differences between one part of England and another. They are non-negotiable, something which should be borne in mind by all those in thrall to the New Patriotism, who would have us believe that the whiteshirts are followed by one big, joyful, inclusive, multicultural band.

Geordies and Mackems have no affinity with Londoners and neither do Scousers ('We're not English, we're Scouse' is a popular banner around Anfield). Cockneys like Bill Butler say: 'I have nowt in common with people from Swindon.' Meanwhile my Swindon correspondent Leigh Nugent travels the world excusing himself for being English and for that he should surely be granted full ambassadorial privileges.

But they all have at least one thing in common. These fans deserve a better football team, one that isn't so obsessed with image and celebrity. A team that isn't – before a ball has even been kicked – visualising the victory parade, the mass adulation, the national holiday, the knighthoods, the sponsorship of every waking moment (including 'to be fair' and every fart), the new Wembley stand dedications, the street namings, the statue unveilings, the free drinks for life, the national-grid-powering glow sparked by the merest mention of '2006' and the effortless conferment of 'hero' status at a time when young men are sent to die in unjust wars.

Paul Wilson in the *Observer* judges Eriksson a 'complete failure' but says the players must share the blame. They were at the heart of what he identifies as 'the English problem'. Not so long ago, the English problem was 'the English disease' and hooliganism was the rest of the world's ready reference. Now it's the players' spectacular self-delusion.

For Scots, England's 2006 has echoes of 1978, when there was a strong feeling we would come back from Argentina with the World Cup. Spectacularly, we didn't. The national mood took a battering; for a while we thought Scotland, the whole country, was rubbish. But twenty-eight years ago no one cried (for us, Argentina) – not Joe Jordan or Archie Gemmill or any of the players.

These are different times. 'People want glamour and tears, the grand performance . . . I'm not very good at that,' admits Helen Mirren playing HRH in the film *The Queen*. In such an exhibitionist age, everyone greets, especially millionaires. And in such a grasping age, instead of humility from England there is hubris. Both Eriksson and Lampard maintain to the end – the sullen, paranoiac, utterly deluded end – that England *should have won.*

(Nine months on from Gelsenkirchen, the situation hardly improves. Before a Euro qualifier away to Israel, six players are targeted by McClaren for delivering less than stellar performances. They are, post-Beckham, the big knobs: Terry, the captain, and the five literary lions among the Three Lions, namely Rooney, Lampard, Gerrard, Ferdinand and Ashley Cole. But this dressing-down doesn't have the desired effect and the team fail to win or even score in Tel Aviv, confirming for McClaren the worst start of any England manager. Then for the next game, against Andorra, the poorest side in Europe, McClaren drops Lampard. A bold move, but the coach doesn't have the guts to go public. Not fancying the subs' bench, Lampard tries to book himself onto the next flight home. Once again England are undone by the fatal combination of weakness and arrogance. They fail to qualify for the 2008 championships and McClaren's fate is sealed when he's caught watching a match under his FA brolly rather than braving the downpour.)

The England midfield four may have flopped in Germany but that was nothing compared with the quartet of Tony Blair, Gordon Brown, David Cameron and Jack McConnell – what a shocking World Cup they had.

The politicians used football. They saw all those supporters and thought: 'Voters!' More precisely: 'Thick, easily manipulated voters!' So they donned box-fresh fan-wear and jumped on the bandwagon, the one lagging behind the last supporters' bus, and made dismal attempts to capture and exploit the national mood.

Scots have a phrase for the most ruthless of opportunists: to achieve the desired aim, they're the kind who would *sell their grannies.* Cameron, as incisive on the subject of football as a Diana Ross penalty kick, did just that. So did Brown, who went from flogging match programmes at Raith Rovers to trading in his nationality. (As Prime Minister, he would prove that unlike McClaren he wasn't afraid of rain. But despite the strong start during the 2007 floods, the good ship Broon would then spring a leak.)

Blair, Brown's fellow Scot-in-denial, may have struck a chord with his speech about Princess Diana being 'the people's princess', but he showed he knew diddley about the people's game, first by trying to persuade Scots to support England and then being so exasperated when we didn't all fall in behind the Cross of St George.

The prime minister didn't understand that rivalry in football is as important as the grass on which it's played. Perhaps if he had not resigned he would have pushed through legislation to have it removed from the game completely. It would have been the biggest victory to date for the finger-wagging frumps of the nanny state. Protective goggles for conkers were obviously the slippery slope. And by the way, slippery slopes are now banned as well.

As for McConnell, I knew what he was trying to say, in principle I agreed, and at other times I might have backed him to the hilt, but the big problem with his 'ABE' stance was that it was presented with a complete lack of wit and class. He needed some jokes. He needed to demonstrate that for his people, the England football team represented, *pace* Jimmy, the insurmountable Hill. That while nothing perpetrated by pundits down the years in that team's name constituted Greaves bodily harm, it still rankled. That, despite the advent of the Parliament, the Scottish populace were still victims of a tyranny – a Clive Tyranny – of commentary-box jingoism and smirking. But McConnell also needed to show that while football is important, it is at the same time unimportant. All of this called for a deftness of touch, like the penetrating pass that lands like a feather, totally beyond Scotland's *heid bummer*.

It Is Now

When I get back to the office, where the little plastic crosses atop the computers of exiled Ingerlanders are already defaced and drooping, Bill Butler emails me a World Cup sign-off from his beloved East End.

'We got fed up with pubs,' he says, 'especially after the Ecuador game. I went down the Wellington for that one but it was full of poshies. [Crikey, Bob, are you still banging on about class? You'd never catch me doing that.] These twits in front of me wouldn't stop yapping. I'm like "Lampard, for fuck's sake!" and they're still yapping. It was "Toby-this-and-Tristan-that". Eventually I had to have a word . . .

'So for the Portugal match me and the lads went to this hospital in Dagenham, Essex which has a function hall and a big screen. What a let-down. And what a pathetic end to a World Cup we were supposed to win.

'Did I say it was a mental hospital? All of us have been in and out of loony bins. After the last penalty we were all crowded round the reception desk asking if they had any spare beds!

'Anyway, you must be delighted. Maybe this will be our last correspondence so you'll have to tell me – just why is it that you Scotch gits hate us?'

It's not hate. But it can never, ever be love, at least not for the England football team. We *are* different. My father's friend, the screenwriter Alan Sharp – who used to wear a Stetson to matches, at the time as embarrassing to me as much as Dad's snuff addiction – summed up in *This Is My Country* why for a Scot, or a Scotch git, supporting Scotland is the only option:

> Football is the process which takes all those diverse elements of Scottishness which, in their real form, involve psychology and history and sociology, and it nutshells them, so when you see a Scottish football team, they play exactly like Scotsmen. They've not just got blue jerseys on, they've got all that complex inferiority/superiority thing, they play in a certain kind of very fragile, arrogant, aesthetic way, and you realise that you're looking at your own image when you see a Scottish football team playing with all its defects and its enormous richness as well. To that extent it is very easy to identify, to commit, and there's a constant reminder, in a way a very pungent reminder, of your origins.

Nowadays, of course, I'm very proud of having watched football with Alan Sharp while he sported a ten-gallon hat, and my father while he snorted Samuel Gawith's finest, even if neither predilection reminds me of my origins.

The question of 'hate' seems to belong to a different age, another me. I can't remember the last time I impersonated an English accent, or rather impersonated my father impersonating one, and I can't remember the last time I asked Lucy, my wife-to-be, for an update on the Auchter-*ah-dah* music scene, where all those pop combos made up of perfectly rounded vowels hang out.

Because our wedding is in France, we evade any bagpipe crackdown. I banish all thoughts of Carly Zucker and Susan George and have eyes only for Lucy. I dance Scottish reels badly, but if you can't make an idiot of yourself at your own wedding, when can you do it? I wear the kilt, and it doesn't matter that my brother Sean doesn't wear it. 'You don't need the kilt to prove you're Scottish,' he says. He's right. At one point I imagined this wedding as being like the re-enactment of some ancient battle. Guess what? It's just a wedding.

On his last trip to Wembley for the old Home Internationals, my friend John Fraser witnessed the Scotland and England supporters undergo extreme makeovers: the Tartan Army became a slicker outfit, more like a brand; and the English reclaimed their stadium and some pride. An end and a beginning, John called it. I must effect a similar transformation in myself.

In his best-man's speech, Sean describes me as being stuck in the past. A past dominated by football, by one fixture and by one almighty grievance. Jimmy Hill, David Narey, *toepoke*: that's what I remember. Until, in an idle moment, I go back to the tape. This is what Jimmy actually said: 'If you wanted to be rude you could call it a *toepoke*. If you wanted to be kind you could call it *exhilarating Brazilian skill*, but what matters is it went in.'

All of this is in the past. Cue Scotland's dreich national anthem: 'And in the past it must remain.' In the 299th year of the Union between Scotland and England, I have married a girl who . . . well, she might be English and maybe before now her nationality would have required confirmation, one way or the other, and . . . *bloody hell*, who do I think I am? The heir to the throne, a particularly berkish prince, fretting over a phone call to the royal gynaecologist, re the condition of his bride-to-be's *hyphen*?

Aidan Gordon Smith, without the hymen, has married a girl who is not one hundred per cent Scots. Big deal. The kilt, as my father noted in *Jock*, is a 'corruption' – the patterns weren't part of the original. So what is the one thing uniquely Scottish we can hold dear to our hearts? Our continuing World Cup failure?

Or is it that we're *thrawn*? The first time I heard the word was in *Jock*. It means contrary, *perverse*, but even if you didn't know that, you might have been able to guess.

'Damned thrawn . . . loyal to the point of lunacy . . . lousy lovers . . . clumsy . . . suicidally arrogant . . . socially graceless,' wrote Dad, summing up the Scottish character. 'Our greatest compliment is: "It's no' bad." Tell us about some magnificent human achievement and we'll say: "Him? Christ, I kent his faither!"'

About halfway through the play, Jock is stung by a complaint from a visitor to his military museum. It accuses him of having 'too subjective a view of history' and, it follows, Scotland's attitude towards the English.

Jock is severely narked by this. 'What do they want? *Real* blood?' he roars. Then he picks up a side drum and compounds the felony. 'This load of rubbish was captured by Highland soldiers in the American War of Independence, the Crimean War or some bloody campaign or other . . .'

Like Jock, then, I've skimmed over the story and missed out important bits in the rush to get to the next joke. When I started this book I was the same age – forty-eight – as my father's damned thrawn soldier. Now, as I end it, I'm worried that, like Jock, I've been too subjective, both about the four decades since the day I was first exposed to frighteningly exciting, full-on *swearing* ('Bloody bastardin' shite!'), and Dad himself.

Was Jock his alter ego, or have I misrepresented him? Did he really hate the English? Obviously, I wish I'd asked him these questions before he died. I kent my faither but maybe not as well as I thought.

Did he mean it at the time (1966 leading to the turbulent 1970s) only to soften his stance in old age? He was terrible for picking something up and putting it down, for weekend pastimes that held his attention for just the one weekend. He was an angler. He was a sailor. He collected blue glass. He burned holes in polystyrene slabs, spray-painted them and called it art. He was a restaurateur, dishing up quality pies. He drove Lotuses and Rileys and – remarkably, considering he was nineteen feet tall – MG Midgets. He exercised with a Bullworker. He grew Kerr's Pink potatoes. He played the zither. Then there were the safari-suit years (or months, or days . . .) Maybe he was Anglophobic in the same way.

Or . . . maybe he was joking. Like he was about the sword wound. Like he was about the toenail clippings in the marmalade. Like he was about the existence of *The Marvellous Mice On The Moon*, one of his books for children. So much of his fatherly wisdom was bunk. Glorious bunk, but bunk all the same.

And maybe the man who wrote at the start of *This Is My Country* 'I don't remember realising that I was Scottish', but who made sure his eldest son was in absolutely no doubt about what *his* country was, and who its next-door neighbours were, and how they should be greeted over the garden fence (sent up with extreme prejudice) . . . maybe, if he could see me now, he would gasp in disbelief: 'My god, I've created a monster!'

This is what I'm thinking when Scotland beat France, the people's world champions, in a Euro 2008 qualifier to wipe the crusty gunk from their eyes and be born anew as a football nation.

This is what I'm thinking when it's revealed that the construction crew working on the new Wembley include a healthy number of Scots, all of whom have buried Lions Rampant, Saltires, tartan scarves and dark blue shirts under the pitch in a daft, brave and completely ingenious attempt to curse the place.

And this is still what I'm thinking right up until 13 December when I pick up that day's papers and read how Steve McClaren wants to bring back the Home International Championship. What a turnaround!

England – DestinyEngland – began the year believing they were to be crowned champions of the world, while Scotland remained a football irrelevance for much of 2006. Scots have a relevance to other aspects of English life, not least in running England, but increasingly this is viewed by the English as an irritation. Some of them almost regard it as illegal. They want shot of Scotland. And if we're not going to support the whiteshirts, then they're going to blast us into deep space. An eight-year-old boy's most urgent enquiry – 'Daddy, why are places so far apart?' – will become utterly redundant.

Re Faither, though, I can say this: he would love the irony. England don't win the World Cup (oh, how they don't win it). Their manager looks around for other teams to play, to thrash. In desperation, and not for the first time, England turns to Scotland. I check the date again. 13 December would have been my father's birthday. And if I half shut my eyes, I can just about see him. He's in his armchair and the Paraguayan occasional table is loaded with missiles. From the pocket of his safari-suit jacket, he pulls out the snuffbox and spoons up a hillock. He's glowering at the TV and the newsreader, seeming to sense Dad's presence, shuffles his papers ('You're on!') and starts to dry up ('*You're bloody on!*') because he knows that the only Scottish item in his bulletin today is gratuitous and haggis-related.

Saved by the football. Only now the commentator is going to get it. This man is doomed and right from kick-off I'm willing him to muck up, to describe the pitch in 'green and pleasant' terms, to urge the medieval popes to greater strutting, or when a jammy goal is scored, to drop in the fatal 'we'.

Go on, Dad!

Acknowledgements

No hip hop-style acknowledgments that go on for ever – I'm Scottish, don't forget – but thanks are due to my editor, Tristan Jones, and the staff at Random House, and to Mark 'Stan' Stanton, my agent. Friends and family supported me, supporting England, and Irvine Welsh and Glenn Gibbons, chief football writer of *The Scotsman*, both ghosted in, Martin Peters-like, with invaluable help at crucial times. I am grateful to Les Snowdon and Tom Little, my editor and deputy editor at *Scotland on Sunday*, for the leave of absence. This book was written in the Reference Room of Edinburgh's Central Library and the dedication shown by its gentlemen of leisure towards their specialist subjects (moths, magic, paddle steamers) drove me on. Finally, thanks to the England fans: your team were rubbish but you played a blinder.